Laura T Reynolds

Sugar and Modern Slavery

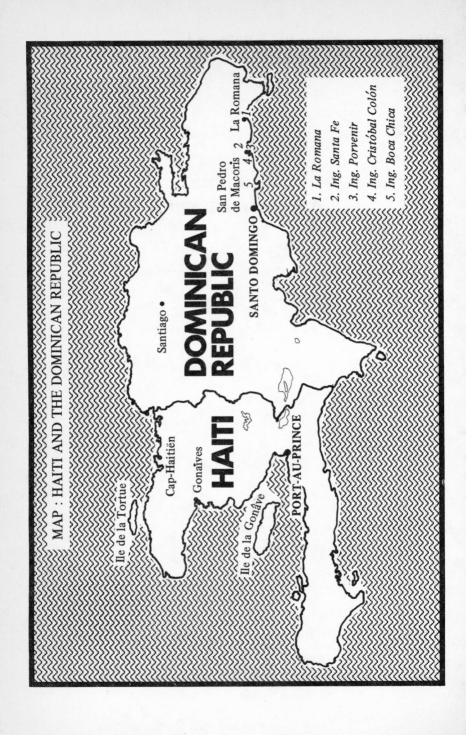

MAP : HAITI AND THE DOMINICAN REPUBLIC

1. La Romana
2. Ing. Santa Fe
3. Ing. Porvenir
4. Ing. Cristóbal Colón
5. Ing. Boca Chica

Ile de la Tortue

Cap-Haïtièn

Santiago •

DOMINICAN
REPUBLIC

San Pedro
de Macorís   La Romana
              2
SANTO DOMINGO   4 3   1
                5

Gonaïves

HAITI

Ile de la Gonâve

PORT-AU-PRINCE

Sugar and Modern Slavery

A Tale of Two Countries

Roger Plant

Zed Books Ltd.
London and New Jersey

Sugar and Modern Slavery was first published by Zed Books Ltd., 57 Caledonian Road, London N1 9BU, UK, and 171 First Avenue, Atlantic Highlands, New Jersey 07716, USA, in 1987.

Copyright © Roger Plant, 1987.

Cover designed by Andrew Corbett.
Printed and bound in the United Kingdom at The Bath Press, Avon.

British Library Cataloguing in Publication Data

Plant, Roger
  Sugar and modern slavery : a tale of two countries.
  1. Sugar workers—Dominican Republic
  2. Sugarcane industry—Dominican Republic
  3. Alien labor, Haitian—Dominican Republic
  I. Title
  331.6′2′729407293   HD8039.S8606

  ISBN 0-86232-572-2
  ISBN 0-86232-573-0 Pbk

Library of Congress Cataloging-in-Publication Data

Plant, Roger
  Sugar and modern slavery.

  Bibliography: p.
  1. Sugar workers—Dominican Republic. 2. Sugarcane industry—Dominican Republic. 3. Alien labor, Haitian—Dominican Republic. 4. Haitians—Employment—Dominican Republic. 5. Forced labor—Dominican Republic.
  I. Title.
  HD8039.S852D657 1987   331.7′6361′097293   87-13315
  ISBN 0-86232-572-2
  ISBN 0-86232-573-0 (pbk.)

Contents

Acknowledgements

This book could not have been written without the support of very many individuals in the Dominican Republic and Haiti. My principal thanks are to those persons who — often at considerable risk to themselves — guided me around the Dominican sugar plantations and surrounding districts, and around those remote parts of rural Haiti from where the Haitian cane-cutters originated. Most of these people would probably prefer to remain anonymous, but particular thanks are due to two individuals who did much to facilitate my own research, and who have never avoided publicity in their attempts to seek improved conditions for Dominican and Haitian sugar workers. These are Julio de Peña Valdez, leader of the CGT in the Dominican Republic; and Ramón Antonio Veras, the Dominican lawyer and writer who has done more than anyone else to expose the contemporary conditions of Haitian migrant workers in his country. I am also grateful to the trade union groups and social research organisations which provided much assistance in the Dominican Republic, including: CGT, FENAZUCAR, UGTD, CEPAE, CEDAIL and CEDEE, among others. A number of Dominican government officials (from CEA, ONAPLAN, the Labour Ministry and the Agriculture Secretariat) also gave their time generously to discuss the issues covered in this book, providing much useful documentation.

My thanks also to the Anti Slavery Society, which sponsored the fieldwork for this book, and submitted its findings to United Nations bodies. A number of people have read earlier drafts of this book, making helpful comments and suggestions. Particular thanks go to Christopher Abel, Philip Alston, Solon Barraclough, James Dunkerley, Enrique Marín, Robert Molteno, Klaus Samson and Alan Whitaker. I am also grateful to Pat Noble for invaluable bibliographical assistance, and to colleagues from Zed Books for their encouragement and editorial advice. And finally, my thanks to Tracy and Teresa for constant support, and for putting up with the further lengthy absences from home required by an investigation of this kind.

Roger Plant
1987

Glossary

Glossary of Spanish and French Terms

Acuerdo: Agreement (as in the inter-state agreement between the Dominican and Haitian governments).

Affranchis: Liberated.

Altiplano: High plateau, uplands.

Ambafil: Literally "below the wire". The term used for those Haitian workers who cross the frontier illegally.

Anticipo: Advance payment.

Baldío: Uncultivated land.

Batey: Living quarters (on the sugar plantations).

Batey central: Central complex, on the sugar plantations.

Bracero: Hired hand, day labourer (generally used in the Dominican Republic to refer to cane cutters).

Capataz: Foreman.

Cargador: Loader (of sugar cane).

Carreau: Haitian unit of measurement = 1.29 hectares.

Carretero: Carter, driver of carts.

Casernes: Barracks.

Cassava: Manioc.

Cédula: Identity document.

Cocolo: Term used for the migrant workers from the neighbouring Caribbean countries, mainly from the British West Indian islands, who cut cane on the Dominican plantations in the early 20th century.

Code Noir: Haitian code for the treatment of slaves during the French colonial period.

Code Rural: Haitian legal code for the conduct of rural land and labour relations in the early 19th century.

Colono: An outgrower, supplying sugar cane to one or other of the *ingenios* (also used to refer to squatters and tenant farmers, though in the Dominican Republic generally referring to the sugar outgrowers).

Contratista: Labour contractor.

Conuco: Small plot of land.

Convenio: Agreement, convention.

Corvée: Forced labour on roads levied by law.

Cuadrilla: Gang or team of workers.

Cuadrillero: Member of a *cuadrilla*.

Fermage: Literally "rent", a tied labour system in post-independence Haiti.

Fiche: Payment slip.

Fogonero: Stoker.

Gourde: Haitian unit of currency.

Guandule: Dominican root crop.

Habilitador: Recruiter or purveyor of labour.

Hacienda: Ranch or estate.

Hectare: Unit of land measurement = 2.47 acres.

Ingenio: Sugar mill. In the Dominican Republic the term *ingenio* is generally used to refer to the entire land complex of the 16 sugar mills, including the surrounding cane fields.

Jefe de cuadrilla: Team leader, or person in charge of the teams of cane cutters.

Kongo: Popular term used for the Haitian cane cutters brought in to the Dominican Republic from Haiti under the bilateral contract.

Latifundio: Large landed estate.

Machete: Long knife used for cane cutting and other agricultural work.

Microfundio: Exceptionally small farm (generally taken to be too small to provide for a family's subsistence needs).

Minifundio: Small farm.

Pacto colectivo: Collective agreement (between management and workers of an enterprise).

Pesador: Weigher.

Picador: Cane picker.

Quintal: Unit of measurement of weight = 101.4 pounds.

Regalía: Bonus payment.

Sacada: Term used in the Philippines, of Spanish origin, for seasonal migrant labour in the sugar cane harvest.

Sindicato: Trade union.

Tarea: Literally meaning "task", the amount of land that can be worked by one person in one day. In the Dominican Republic, one hectare is equal to 15.9 tareas.

Temporero: Temporary worker.

Terrenos comuneros: Communally owned lands.

Tickero: Ticketer.

Tienda: Shop, store or company store.

Tiendero: Store-keeper.

Tonton Macoute: Literally meaning "Uncle Knapsack", the name by which the Duvalierist political agents, officially termed the "Volontiers de Securité Nationale", were popularly known.

Trapiche: Small and traditional sugar mill.

Vale: Promissory note or voucher.

Viejo: Literally "old", the name given to the Haitian residents, legal or illegal, in the Dominican Republic.

Zafra: Sugar harvest.

Abbreviations

Abbreviations

ACP:	African, Caribbean and Pacific (as in ACP countries covered by the Lomé Convention)
AIFLD:	American Institute for Free Labour Development
CAP:	Common Agricultural Policy
CASC:	Confederación Autónoma de Sindicatos Cristianos
CATH:	Confédération Autonome des Travailleurs Haïtiens
CBI:	Caribbean Basin Initiative
CEA:	Consejo Estatal de Azúcar
CESITRADO:	Confederación Sindical de Trabajadores Dominicanos
CGT:	Central General de Trabajadores
CGT–M:	Central General de Trabajadores–Mayoritaria (a group that split off from the CGT in 1983)
CIIR:	Catholic Institute for International Relations
CNG:	Conseil National de Gouvernement
COMECON:	Council for Mutual Economic Assistance (Warsaw Pact Countries)
CSA:	Commonwealth Sugar Agreement
CTD:	Central de Trabajadores Dominicanos
CUT:	Central Unitaria de Trabajadores
EEC:	European Economic Community
FEDOCA:	Federación Dominicana de Colonos Azucareros
FENAZUCAR:	Federación CGT de Trabajadores Azucareros
FENSA:	Federación Nacional de Sindicatos Azucareros
FOUPSA:	Frente Obrero Unido pro Sindicatos Autónomos
HASCO:	Haitian American Sugar Company
HFCS:	High Fructose Corn Syrup
IAD:	Instituto Agrario Dominicano
IDSS:	Instituto Dominicano de Seguridad Social
IFAD:	International Fund for Agricultural Development
ILO:	International Labour Organisation
IMF:	International Monetary Fund
INESPRE:	Instituto para la Estabilisación de Precios
INVI:	Instituto Nacional de Vivienda

ISA:	International Sugar Agreement
ISO:	International Sugar Organisation
MPD:	Movimiento Popular Dominicano
ONAPLAN:	Oficina Nacional de Planificación
PL–480:	Public Law 480 (US governmental food aid programme)
PLD:	Partido de Liberación Dominicano
PRD:	Partido Revolucionario Dominicano
PREALC:	Programa Regional de Empleo para América Latina y el Caribe (ILO's regional employment programme for the Latin American and Caribbean region)
SHADA:	Société Haïtienne–Americaine de Développement Agricole
TCRI:	The Central Romana Incorporated
UGTD:	Unión General de Trabajadores Dominicanos
UNCTAD:	United Nations Conference on Trade and Development
USAID:	United States Agency for International Development
VAT:	Value Added Tax
WISFC:	West Indies Sugar Finance Corporation
WILPF:	Women's International League for Peace and Freedom

Chronology

Chronology

1492: Christopher Columbus lands in Haiti, at the Mole St Nicholas.

1505: Sugar is introduced to Hispaniola, from the Canary Islands.

1521: First recorded consignment of sugar exported from Santo Domingo to Spain.

1520s: African slaves are first transported to Hispaniola.

1659: France gains control of Tortuga Island, off the mainland of the western part of Hispaniola.

1685: Publication of the *Code Noir*.

1697: Treaty of Ryswick, by which Spain recognises French rule over the western part of Hispaniola.

1740 onwards: Revival of the colonial sugar industry in Santo Domingo.

1791: First slave uprising in the French colony of Saint-Domingue.

1793: Liberation of slaves decreed in Saint-Domingue.

1804: Jean-Jacques Dessalines declares liberation of Haiti in Gonaives.

1822–44: Haitian occupation of Santo Domingo.

1825: Haitian independence recognised by France.

1826: Haitian *Code Rural* adopted.

1844: Dominican independence declared for the first time, and slavery abolished in the eastern part of the island.

1856: First recorded sugar exports from the independent Dominican Republic.

1865: Dominican independence declared for the second time.

1868: Outbreak of civil war in Cuba affects sugar production there, providing the impetus for growth in Dominican cane sugar production.

1874: First steam mill in the Dominican Republic.

1875–82: 35 steam mills built in the Dominican Republic.

1879: First recorded migrant labour from the Antilles to the Dominican Republic.

1884: First recorded strike by Dominican sugar workers.

1893: *Ingenio* built by the Bass family in the town of La Romana.

1911: New Dominican legislation facilitates the alienation and division of the *Terrenos comuneros*.

1912: New Dominican law enacted to restrict coloured immigration.

1915–34: US occupation of Haiti.

1916–24: US occupation of the Dominican Republic.

1930: General Trujillo assumes power in the Dominican Republic.

1937: Trujillo orders massacre of Haitian population in the Dominican Republic.

1942: Government of Haiti enacts laws to stem clandestine traffic of Haitians to Dominican Republic.

1948: Trujillo constructs his first sugar mill, Ingenio Catarey near Villa Altagracia.

1951: First Dominican Labour Code. Commonwealth Sugar Agreement drawn up.

1952: First bilateral agreement drawn up between the Dominican and Haitian governments, for the import of Haitian *braceros*. Ingenio Haina, built by Trujillo and claimed by him to be the world's largest sugar mill, comes into production.

1953: Dominican Republic joins the International Sugar Organisation.

1956: United Nations adopts its Supplementary Convention on the Abolition of Slavery, the Slave Trade, and Institutions and Practices similar to Slavery.

1957: ILO adopts Convention on the Abolition of Forced Labour. François "Papa Doc" Duvalier attains power in Haiti.

1958: Haiti and the Dominican Republic register ratification of the ILO's Forced Labour Convention.

1959: Haiti and Dominican Republic renew bilateral agreement concerning Haitian *braceros* in the Dominican Republic.

1961: Assassination of Trujillo, and nationalisation of his 12 sugar mills.

1962: First Dominican land reform law, aiming to settle 70,000 families.

1963: Dominican President Juan Bosch overthrown in military coup. Decree of October 1963 outlaws all Communist-inspired activities, and paves the way for repression of the trade union movement.

1965: April, US invasion of the Dominican Republic.

1966: Joaquín Balaguer elected President of the Dominican Republic. CEA created to administer the nationalised Trujillo sugar mills. New bilateral agreement for importation of Haitian *braceros*.

1967: Destruction of trade union on the Central Romana, and disappearance of union leader Guido Gil.

1971: Death of "Papa Doc" Duvalier. His son Jean-Claude Duvalier named president of Haiti for life.

1974: Repeal of the US Sugar Act, and temporary end of the US quota system for sugar imports. World sugar price reaches peak of almost 65 cents per pound.

1978: PRD wins Dominican elections. Antonio Guzmán replaces Dr Joaquín Balaguer as president.

1979: Anti Slavery Society denounces slavery-like treatment of Haitians before United Nations.

1978–79: Increase in Haitian exodus draws new international attention to plight of the Haitian boat people.

1982: US reintroduces country quotas for sugar imports. Salvador Jorge Blanco of PRD wins Dominican elections, and appeals personally to President Reagan for more favourable treatment.

1983: January, ILO Mission of Enquiry visits Haiti and Dominican Republic to investigate allegations of Haitian forced labour, publishes critical report in June.

1984: April "food riots" in Dominican Republic lead to over 100 deaths. Gulf and Western sells La Romana and other Dominican assets.

1985: Dominican quota for the US sugar market reduced by over 40 per cent.
1986: February, Jean-Claude Duvalier flees Haiti. Mass opposition in Haiti prevents the recruitment of *braceros* from taking place. Renewed widespread Haitian forced labour in the Dominican Republic. May, Dr Joaquín Balaguer elected to a fourth term as President of the Dominican Republic.

Introduction

In 1982 I was asked by the Anti Slavery Society, the oldest of the international human rights organisations, to investigate the situation of Haitian migrant workers in the Dominican Republic. Three years earlier the Anti Slavery Society had received reports which suggested that the plight of Haitian cane cutters in the Dominican sugar industry was akin to slavery. According to these reports, over 10,000 Haitian workers were sold every year by Jean-Claude Duvalier, then Life President of Haiti, to the Dominican government for temporary work on the twelve nationalised sugar plantations in the Dominican Republic. There, they were not free to leave the plantations during the six months of the harvest season, were padlocked in barracks at night, and reportedly had only a few dollars of savings to take back to Haiti at the end of the harvest. And there were further reports that Haitians illegally resident in the Dominican Republic were being kidnapped by army officers and troops and sold for profit to state-owned or privately owned sugar enterprises. On the basis of these reports, Colonel Patrick Montgomery of the Anti Slavery Society denounced the Haitians' conditions before the United Nations Working Group on Slavery, in Geneva. For the first time the issue of Haitian "slavery" was out in the open.

The Dominican government was furious. In 1978 a new government, formed by the social democratic Revolutionary Dominican Party (PRD), had taken power. It argued that the conditions denounced before the UN in fact dated from the previous regime, and that there had been widespread improvement in the situation of human rights — including labour rights — since that time. And so the Anti Slavery Society asked me to investigate. Between April and June 1982, in the first of several visits since that time, I travelled widely around the Dominican Republic and Haiti. On the Dominican side of this large Caribbean island, I visited the majority of the plantations, talked with hundreds of Haitian and Dominican cane cutters, accompanied trade unionists, and interviewed countless government officials. On the Haitian side, I spent most of the time assessing conditions in the deprived rural areas from which the migrant workers tended to come.

At the end of the 1982 investigations, there were few improvements to report. For Dominican workers, there was apparently some freedom to organise, except where strikes for better pay and conditions in the sugar industry were concerned. For the hundreds of thousands of Haitian workers, things were as bad as ever. Under the new government, an even larger contingent of Haitian workers had been purchased from the Duvalier regime. The Dominican government had published the details of an official-sounding Bilateral Contract for the Importation of Haitian Workers (see Appendix), the social provisions of which were generous enough on paper, but this appeared to be only a public relations exercise. The contract spelled out in detail the rights of the imported Haitian cane cutters (to housing, health care, social security, rest periods, adequate wages and so on), but the Haitian workers themselves did not even get a copy of it. The contract had nothing to do with the abysmal reality of the Haitians' conditions, which will be described in detail in later chapters of this book. Furthermore, as I found, there had been widespread raids and kidnappings over the past few years, carried out by the Dominican army against the large, illegal Haitian community resident in the Dominican Republic. These Haitian enclaves, though technically illegal, were tolerated as long as the able-bodied males signed up for the sugar harvest every year, for virtually no Dominican cuts cane in his own country. But if the Haitians did not register for the cane harvest, they were rounded up by military force, and dragooned on to the plantations. Furthermore, in isolated rural districts near the Haitian border, I came across reliable and mutually corroborative accounts of traffic in Haitian labour. Under this system, it was said, the army captured Haitian males in the locality and sold them to their superiors, who in turn sold them for a higher price to the recruiting agents of the state and private sugar mills.

In August 1982 my own report to the United Nations Working Group on Slavery provoked the same kind of denial from the Dominican government. The Army Chief of Staff termed the allegations slanderous, on the grounds that they impugned the image of the Dominican Armed Forces, and the President promised an investigation.

The following year, in January 1983, there was a thorough investigation by an international body concerning the allegations of Haitian forced labour in the Dominican sugar industry. Acting at the behest of member unions, the International Labour Organisation despatched a Commission of Enquiry, whose report was published in June 1986. It upheld the forced labour allegations, and likewise found that the Dominican army played an active part in arresting illegal entrants and supplying them to the Dominican sugar plantations. It had heavy criticism for the notorious bilateral contract, noting that the financial provisions were secret (with the implication that Duvalier exported the cane cutters for personal profit), and that the social provisions were obviously not implemented. The ILO's report contained a series of practical recommendations for ending the forced labour practices.

I returned to Haiti and the Dominican Republic in June 1986. By that time Duvalier had fled from Haiti, driven out by a swelling protest movement in the Haitian capital and provincial towns. One of the demonstrators' major grievances had been the plight of the Haitian cane cutters in the Dominican Republic, and the widespread corruption that went along with the bilateral contract. In January 1986, just a fortnight before Duvalier's overthrow, thousands of young Haitian protesters marched on the market-place of the small town of Leogane, one of the two major recruitment centres for the contract, and prevented the recruiting operations from going ahead. Speaking out passionately against this system of "slavery", many

Haitians told me then that the contract would never be repeated. On the Dominican side of the frontier, the absence of the contracted Haitian workers provoked the government to desperate measures. First, there were attempts to rope in civil servants for the harvest. Then the army was brought in to cut cane. But the raids, kidnappings and exactions of forced labour from the resident Haitian community reached their highest ever pitch. In the capital of Santo Domingo, and in small farms in isolated regions of the country, the army forcibly moved all Haitians they could find on to the sugar plantations.

Is this slavery? There are formal definitions and less formal connotations. In 1956 the United Nations adopted a Supplementary Convention on the Abolition of Slavery, the Slave Trade, and Institutions and Practices similar to Slavery. It outlaws traffic in persons, the "capture, acquisition or disposal of a person with intent to reduce him to slavery", and "all acts of disposal by sale or exchange of a person with a view to being sold or exchanged". Readers of this book can judge for themselves whether the conditions described in later chapters should be considered as slavery under the terms of the UN's Conventions.

But everywhere I went in Haiti and the Dominican Republic, persons of all persuasions tended to equate the Haitians' conditions with those of slavery. Many Dominicans give as one of the reasons why they do not cut cane that this task is the "work of a slave". Even Joaquín Balaguer himself, the newly elected President of the Dominican Republic, used similar language in a recent book on the Haitian question, referring to this "new form of denigrating slavery that is practised today on the Dominican sugar mills".

The conditions of recruitment, life and labour are grotesque, and must be denounced. One purpose of this book is to denounce these conditions. But it is also important to understand their causes, and why it has proved so difficult for successive governments in the Dominican Republic to eradicate practices which not only constitute severe human rights violations but also lead to gross inefficiency. The Dominican Republic, for all its exploitative labour practices, is a relatively high-cost sugar producer because of its low productivity levels. Furthermore, it has spent millions of dollars a year importing migrant labour from a neighbouring country, when its sugar industry is bankrupt and when unemployment among its own nationals has reached dangerously high levels. It puts more and more land under export-crop cultivation when it has a severe deficit of staple crops for domestic consumption, and consequently has to import food at higher and higher cost as the prices of its traditional exports collapse on the world market. In 1984 the Dominican Republic, under pressure from the International Monetary Fund, imposed sharp increases in the price of imported foods — staples such as bread and cooking oil — triggering off "food riots" which resulted in over a hundred deaths. Why can the Dominican Republic not grow more food? What are the factors within the Dominican development model which have led to growing reliance on imported migrant labour when half the Dominican peasantry is unemployed or under-employed?

When criticised by the Anti Slavery Society and the International Labour Organisation (ILO) in 1983, the Dominican government of the time responded as follows: "One of the worst forms of slavery today is practised by the developed countries when they keep down the prices of basic products by subsidising and dumping products competing with those that are vital for the countries of the Third World." Is there truth in such statements, and is there nothing that the Dominican Republic can do to improve the desperate conditions in its sugar industry in the light of such adverse international factors?

These are all questions to which this book is seeking some answer, through a case study of two countries in the Caribbean. To answer the questions, one needs to examine the growth and evolution of the sugar industry from the beginning, and the development model to which it has given rise in both countries. We begin with the colonial period, and the classical days of slavery.

1 Sugar and Slavery: The Colonial Legacy

For Europeans the "discovery of America" is dated in the year 1492, when Christopher Colombus and a small group of Spanish explorers landed on the north-western coast of the Caribbean island of Hispaniola — in that part of the island which is now Haiti. The western part of the island was quickly abandoned, when no gold was discovered there. Early Spanish settlement concentrated in the western regions of Hispaniola, today's Dominican Republic, where gold was found in sufficient quantities to attract a steady flow of colonists from the Spanish mainland.

The first sugar planters soon followed upon Columbus's tracks. The cane plant was introduced from the Canary Islands in 1505, and ten years later the early sugar industry was well under way. Jeronimo priests, who arrived in 1516 and took over the administration of the new colony for a while, were said to be enthusiastic sugar planters. But labour, as everywhere in the Spanish colonies, was in short supply. At the time of conquest Hispaniola had a sizeable native population of Taino Arawak peoples, who may have numbered more than half a million. But the Spaniards grumbled at their attitude to forced labour and had little use for them. The work of one imported negro was equal to that of "four or eight Indians" in the Antilles, said contemporary sources in the 16th century.[1] The Taino Arawaks suffered like their fellow Indians throughout the Americas after the Spanish conquest: they were captured, enslaved, killed, fell prey to infectious diseases and soon died in their hundreds of thousands. Exactly how many there were at the time of conquest can only be guessed. Bishop Bartolomé de las Casas, a man believed to exaggerate, claimed there were three million. By 1508, official Spanish census figures could count only 60,000 survivors. By the 1550s that number had been halved, and in 1570 contemporary documents gave a figure of approximately 500. A veritable genocide had taken place.

Jeronimo priests and other local planters appealed for the right to import negro slaves, and the Spanish Crown readily concurred. By 1518 the first slaves had reached Hispaniola, and four years later the first slave uprisings were recorded in a sugar mill called Diego Colón. But in the 16th century the numbers were never large, if compared with the later periods of negro slavery in the Caribbean. In 1546, a contemporary writer mentions 20 water-run *ingenios* (sugar mills) and four *trapiches* (smaller animal traction plants) in the whole of the island.[2] It took some 20 slaves to run a small mill, 50 a medium-sized one, and no more than 100 for the largest *ingenios*. Slaves were utilised for other kinds of work — for construction, agriculture and domestic service. But capital was scarce, and imported slaves were never considered cheap. By 1606 there were said to be less than 10,000 slaves on the entire island of Hispaniola.

By that time the early sugar industry had undergone a dramatic decline. Seeking the reasons, present-day Dominican analysts have claimed that it was for sheer lack of markets for the product. Spain's rigid protectionism towards its colonies, preventing them from trading except through the *Casa de Contratación* in Seville, had left its poorer colonies in a state of ruin when the metropolis itself was in decline. During the colonial period, the small Spanish colony of Santo Domingo never recovered. Almost two centuries later there had been no revival of the sugar industry, though the slave-run economies of other Caribbean colonies were by then thriving. By the late 18th century, the Spanish part of Hispaniola had approximately 20 *ingenios* and *trapiches* in all, and between 10,000 and 12,000 registered slaves. The majority of slaves, however, were not to be found on the sugar plantations. They were scattered around the countryside, often working as managers of isolated cattle ranches.[3] In the colonial era, white masters evidently mixed freely with black slave women. In racial terms the Dominican Republic was already on the way to becoming what it is today: a small percentage of whites at the top of the social strata, an even smaller percentage of pure blacks, and then a predominantly mulatto population.

In the western part of the island, the colonial legacy could not have been more different. The French, who were eventually to rule there, arrived comparatively late in the colonial period. Their stepping-off point was the small island of Tortuga or Tortue off Haiti's northern coastline, which had been something of an international buccaneering ground throughout the 16th and early 17th centuries, competed for by English, Dutch and French pirates. The French finally gained control of Tortuga in 1659, and moved on to the Haitian mainland. They began a 130-year period of colonial domination which was to bring vast profits to their sugar planters and untold misery to hundreds of thousands of black slaves, and was finally to erupt in a revolution which left Haiti in the hands of liberated slaves as the first independent republic in Latin America and the Caribbean.

The French planters had what their Spanish counterparts lacked: a ready market in a flourishing part of Europe. Saint-Domingue (as western Hispaniola was now called) soon became the most prized of French overseas possessions. A few statistics give a picture of the situation by the end of French rule. In 1780, there were a mere nine *ingenios* and eleven *trapiches* in the Spanish part; in 1773, no less than 723 *ingenios* in Saint-Domingue. In 1783 some 600 slaves worked on the sugar plantations of the east; in 1791, the total slave population of Saint-Domingue was estimated at over half a million and may have been more. One Haitian historian argues that the inclusion of slaves not shown on the tax rolls brought the actual slave population to over 700,000.[4]

The Spanish Crown had formally ceded Saint-Domingue to the French in 1697, some 40 years after *de facto* possession took place. But in little more than a century of colonialism, France turned it into the largest of slave colonies. The numbers jumped rapidly. The May 1681 census gave 2,000 slaves; by 1700 there were over

10,000. By 1764, 10,000 slaves were arriving per year; by 1786 this had more than doubled, and in 1787 a further 40,000 were imported.[5] Slave trading was an expensive but lucrative business. By the mid-18th century Saint-Domingue's sugar planters had driven the British from Europe's markets, and they soon outstripped the production of all islands in the British West Indies. By the time of the revolution, Saint-Domingue was accounting for over a third of all France's foreign trade.[6]

What of the slaves' conditions? On paper, there was protection. France had a *Code Noir*, and Spain a succession of *Codigos Negros*, legalistic manuals on the proper treatment of slaves. Both provided for Sundays and feast days off (Spanish planters once groused at a Catholic legacy of 93 annual holidays).[7] A Spanish ruling of 1768 stipulated that all slaves over 16 years of age were to receive 3 lbs of meat and 6 lbs of cassava or plantain per week, as well as medical treatment and other benefits (a few years later the planters got together, and drafted a new code to replace the meat ration with wheat).[8] The French version provided for a mere ounce of meat per day. But sufficient food there probably was. One historian paints a somewhat rosy picture of the daily life of the negro slaves in the French West Indies:

> In general, the Code [Noir] was accepted as a satisfactory set of rules governing the relationship of owners and slaves. Perhaps the clauses best observed were those pertaining to food, clothing and shelter, although frequently owners were charged with niggardly treatment of their slaves. There was ample land for gardens and owners commonly allowed a satisfactory portion for each slave family. There the slaves grew manioc or cassava, a tuber of which they were fond and which constituted their main food.[9]

The Code may have looked good enough. But, as another historian writes, "The planters were not Angels." He cites the secretary of the slave leader Henry Christophe, who gives an altogether different picture of the treatment meted out by French masters to their black slaves:

> Have they not hung up men with heads downward, drowned them in sacks, crucified them on planks, buried them alive, crushed them in mortars? Have they not forced them to eat shit? And after having flayed them alive with the lash, have they not cast them alive to be devoured by worms, or on to anthills, or lashed them to stakes in the swamp to be devoured by mosquitoes? Have they not thrown them into cauldrons of cane-syrup?[10]

The Haitian slave revolution broke out in full force in 1791, two years after a better-known cataclysm in France. It was infinitely more bloodthirsty, with widespread atrocities on both sides reducing Saint-Domingue to anarchy and chaos before the new Republic of Haiti was officially born in 1804. It was also a complex struggle, with more than oppressed black slaves and imperious white masters as antagonists and interest groups. The catalyst to the revolution was actually the demands of the free mulatto population of Saint-Domingue, seeking the rights which accrued to them from the revolutionary proclamations in far-off Paris. But as violence grew, their demands served to fan the flames of a slave rebellion which ended white supremacy once and for all.

According to the *Code Noir*, the free mulattos, otherwise known as the *affranchis*, were technically to be regarded as full French citizens. Property rights they undoubtedly had. By 1791, they apparently owned between one-fifth and one-fourth of all land and slaves in the colony.[11] But whatever the law said, they suffered active discrimination in all other walks of life. They could not eat or sit with whites, hold public office in the "respectable" professions, or hold seats in the colonial assembly. And so, anticipating their Creole counterparts in Central and South America by a decade, they took up arms against the metropolitan élite in the name of freedom, equality and fraternity. But nowhere else in the western hemisphere did the local and foreign élite have such a mass of downtrodden slaves under them. The slaves joined the revolution, their leaders made moves to take it over. Inevitably, civil war ensued.

In the midst of all this, Napoleon took over France and decided to recover Saint-Domingue. By 1802 word arrived that his commander in Guadeloupe, General Richepanse, had restored slavery on the small Caribbean sugar colony.[12] It angered Napoleon's new commander in Saint-Domingue, Captain-General Victor Emmanuel Leclerc, who now saw black resistance double, and wrote suggesting the following desperate strategy to the Emperor, if Saint-Domingue was to be held:

> You will have to exterminate all the blacks in the mountains, women as well as men, except for children under twelve. Wipe out half the population in the lowlands, and do not leave in the colony a single black who has worn an epaulet.[13]

In the end the reverse occurred. All white men and women were massacred by the victorious rebels, and the new Republic of Haiti was born in 1804. Not only French supremacy but also the sugar economy came to an abrupt end. In 1781 the colony had exported 930,000 *quintales* of raw sugar; 20 years later, in the midst of rebellion, the amount was down to 185,000 *quintales*; by 1818, over a decade into independence, exports were a paltry 55,000 *quintales*.[14] In fact, Haiti's first independent leaders strove hard to keep the colonial agricultural structure intact. Slavery was abolished, but Toussaint L'Ouverture tried to replace it with something little different. His policy was to rebuild and maintain the colonial sugar plantations and work them through a compulsory labour system known as *fermage*, whereby all those ex-slaves who did not enlist in the army were attached to plantations which they could leave only on explicit permission from the authorities. Toussaint's successor, the ex-slave Dessalines, continued with much the same policy until his murder in 1806. His successors, Pétion and Henry Christophe, bowed to the ex-slave demands and began to distribute the plantation lands. Finally, the next President, Jean-Pierre Boyer, reintroduced forced labour in the *corvée* system and made the last attempt to restore the plantation economy. He failed. By the mid-19th century none of the old colonial plantations was left intact. Haiti became an independent nation of small farmers.

Developments in western Hispaniola soon had their effects on the eastern region, and the history of both parts of the island now became closely enmeshed. The slave rebellion in Saint-Domingue had broken out when the metropolitan powers of France and Spain were themselves at war, and the Spanish colony of Santo Domingo was to feel the effects of both. In the second half of the 18th century there had been a belated revival in Santo Domingo's sugar production, leading to new demands for the importation of African slaves. Between 1740 and 1783 eleven new *ingenios* were constructed, and labour was once again in scarce supply. In 1785 a priest named Sánchez Valverde complained that the sugar factories, mills and *trapiches* were producing little for want of negroes, providing enough sugar only for the domestic market, a few exports to Puerto Rico and very sporadic exports to Spain. He noted that whereas in the French colony of Saint-Domingue there was an average of 600 slaves for a medium-sized mill, this was the entire number of negroes working in the 22 factories in the Spanish colony. Pressed by Santo Domingo's sugar planters, in 1786 the King of Spain gave the green light for the unlimited import of black slaves.[15] Thus the slave liberation movement in Saint-Domingue spilled over to the Spanish side. In October 1796, rebellion broke out on the largest *ingenio* in the east. The owner fled, his cane fields and property were burned down, and the revolt was ultimately put down with the loss of a large number of slave lives.[16]

Soon after that, the Spaniards lost control of their colony. First, with the war going badly in Europe, Santo Domingo was ceded to France. Then, in 1801, Toussaint L'Ouverture launched the first of three Haitian invasions from the western side, and briefly unified Hispaniola under the control of the new Haitian Republic. The French returned, but were soon defeated by a second Haitian invasion. Then the Spaniards reconquered, but suffered new outbreaks of rebellion at the hands of slaves who had once been manumitted and now found themselves in bondage again.

The third Haitian invasion — and the one to have the most lasting effects in Santo Domingo — was led by Jean-Pierre Boyer in 1822, and lasted for over two decades until 1844. One of Boyer's first acts in 1822 was to abolish negro slavery in the eastern part of the island. He then promised to grant land parcels to all freed men, to enable them to escape from the control of their former masters and live as free farmers.[17] But the freedom was to be relative. Boyer sent circulars to the Haitian military commanders governing each of the eastern communities, instructing them that

> it is necessary in the interest of the State as well as our brothers who have just received their liberty that they be obliged to work, cultivating the land on which their survival depends, and receiving a part of the income fixed for them by the regulations.[18]

While expropriating vast church domains, and distributing them to freed slaves as well as to his military supporters, Boyer also attempted to protect the few large private plantations that then existed in Santo Domingo, to find the necessary labour for them, and to force large and small farmers alike to cultivate such marketable export crops as cocoa, sugar cane and cotton. In 1824 Boyer's stringent *Code Rural* (see Chapter 4 on Haitian history) was enacted, being applicable in both parts of the island during the years of the Haitian occupation of Santo Domingo. Under this Code, farmers could not leave the plots on which they lived — or to which they had been assigned — without prior authorisation from military and civil authorities. Once employed by a plantation owner, a worker was obliged to serve him for a minimum three-year period, and could not leave without incurring penalties of fines, imprisonment or forced labour. Plantation labour was to be supervised by soldiers, themselves fed by the plantation owners.

Boyer's *Code Rural* had been adapted to conditions in the western part of Hispaniola, where Haiti's new rulers made unavailing attempts to retain the plantation system of the French colonial era. In Santo Domingo — where there had been few plantations apart from the church estates and a handful of sugar *ingenios*, and where most of the land was owned communally — it proved virtually unenforceable. As Dominican historian Frank Moya Pons has written,

> In theory, the French system that Boyer wished to impose seems more just and more modern, in so far as it guaranteed (in theory) a title to each proprietor and a property to each person. Under the Spanish system of communal lands, however, the population of Santo Domingo was not pressed by necessity to have legal titles to land, for the system allowed the population to occupy, exploit and enjoy the usufruct of all the land they needed without causing hardship to any of the actual proprietors. This was what Boyer and Haitian bureaucrats never came to understand and what helped to keep alive the germs of opposition in the eastern part of the island.[19]

The harsh Boyer dictatorship left a legacy of deep Dominican loathing and distrust of their Haitian neighbours, after the Haitians were thrown out in 1844. But slavery at least had been abolished. When Dominican independence was declared for the first time in that year, its Constitution proclaimed that slavery was "abolished for ever". But there were to be many more years of turbulence before the Dominican Republic was firmly established as an independent nation. There was a fourth and final Haitian invasion in 1849, then a period of civil wars among rival Dominican factions, a further annexation by Spain in 1861, and a prolonged War of Restoration until Dominican national independence was declared for the third and final time in 1865. Slavery still existed elsewhere in the Caribbean, for example in Cuba until the early 1880s. But the Dominican Republic was firmly against the colonial legacy of slavery, offering asylum to those who could escape from the neighbouring slave societies. As the Constitution of 1877 proclaimed, "All slaves who enter Dominican soil are free men."

Notes

1. R. Mellafe, *Negro Slavery in Latin America* (University of California Press, Berkeley, 1975), p. 16.
2. Juan Bosch, *Composición Social Dominicana* (Ediciones Alfa y Omega, Santo Domingo, 1981), p. 28.
3. Ibid., p. 105.
4. Cited in R.D. Heinl and N.G. Heinl, *Written in Blood: The Story of the Haitian People* (Houghton Mifflin Company, Boston, 1978), p. 25.
5. Ibid., p. 25.
6. Ibid., p. 32.

7. Carlos Larrazabal Blanco, *Los Negros y la Esclavitud en Santo Domingo* (Colección Pensamiento Dominicano, Santo Domingo, 1975), p. 117.

8. Ibid., p. 125.

9. S.T. McCloy, *The Negro in the French West Indies* (University of Kentucky Press, 1966), p. 20.

10. Heinl and Heinl, op. cit., pp. 26–7.

11. Mats Lundahl, *Peasants and Poverty: A Study of Haiti* (Croom Helm, London, 1979), pp. 321–2.

12. McCloy, op. cit., p. 106.

13. Quoted in Heinl and Heinl, op. cit., p. 113.

14. Bosch, op. cit., p. 120.

15. Larrazabal Blanco, op. cit., p. 56.

16. Frank Moya Pons, *Manual de Historia Dominicana* (Universidad Católica Madre y Maestra, Santiago, Dominican Republic, 1981), p. 183.

17. Frank Moya Pons, "The Land Question in Haiti and Santo Domingo", in Manuel Moreno Fraginals and others, *Between Slavery and Free Labour: the Spanish-Speaking Caribbean in the Nineteenth Century* (Johns Hopkins University Press, Baltimore and London, 1985), p. 186.

18. Ibid.

19. Ibid., p. 197.

2 A Sugar Republic: Growth of the Dominican Sugar Industry (1865–1961)

Towards the Modern *Ingenio:* 19th–Century Developments

On gaining their hard-fought independence, Dominican leaders found a new nation-state with a small population, a backward economy, limited natural resources and an unclear place in the modern world. For the next few decades there was a spate of civil wars, with the leaders of some political factions apparently determined to sacrifice this independence altogether. Only five years after the independence declaration of 1865, President Buenaventura Báez had negotiated a treaty of annexation to the United States. He was thwarted only by a United States Senate which, unaccustomed at least then to colonisation in its backyard, voted against ratification of the treaty. Otherwise, the Dominican Republic might well have gone the way of its sugar-producing Caribbean neighbour, Puerto Rico, which was annexed by the United States after the Spanish–American wars at the turn of the century.

During the Haitian occupation, the economy had more or less collapsed. Despite Boyer's attempts to boost agricultural production for export, the sugar industry had foundered after its brief late 18th-century revival. The last of the old Dominican sugar mills, wrote a contemporary observer, perished in the year 1822.[1] The reasons for the collapse were much the same as on the Haitian side — the liberation of black slaves, the disruption of the economy during the wars and the ensuing loss of markets. A subsistence peasant economy now took root alongside the large traditional cattle ranches.

By the end of the Haitian occupation in 1844, the church lands had been broken up, but the private plantations survived. Apart from this, the predominant system of land tenure was of *terrenos comuneros* (communal lands) in which ownership was generally shared by two or more individuals who had communal usufruct of the land. Title was not valued, and for the most part there were no written titles. Gradually, farmers built up production of export crops, mainly cocoa, coffee and tobacco. The latter two crops were grown on relatively small farm plots and required little surplus labour. Both coffee and tobacco were being exported by the late 1860s. The most successful ventures were in tobacco, for which a market was found in Germany. Ninety per cent of exports went to Hamburg, where Dominican tobacco was apparently favoured because it was cheaper than the superior brands from nearby Cuba.

Small-scale sugar production was also revived by the mid-19th century. The first exports were recorded in 1856, the sugar coming from 200 or 300 traditional *trapiches* around the southern towns of Azua and Cristóbal. But they were small amounts, with total production for local consumption and export being in the region of 50,000 *quintales* (or 5,000 tonnes). The Dominican Republic was far behind its Caribbean neighbours. At this time Cuba had over 1,000 large *ingenios*, and Puerto Rico over 400, with slavery still well entrenched in both countries.

It was the outbreak of civil war in Cuba, in 1868, that provided the major impetus for the growth of the Dominican sugar industry. The Cuban planters moved south to the Dominican Republic when slave revolts at home threatened their survival there. Some 3,000 Cubans reached the Dominican Republic within a few years, bringing new technology, money and the well-known Cuban entrepreneurial sense. Conflicts elsewhere in the world also provided benefits for the new Dominican industry. The war between France and Germany in 1870 severely affected European beet production, and the civil war in the United States took a similar toll on the cane fields of Louisiana.[2] Taking full advantage of the opportunities, Dominican governments now enacted a series of measures to stimulate capital investment in sugar and other large-scale agricultural production, with tariff exemptions for machinery and tools, limited exemption from export taxes, and government land concessions.[3]

Technology was brought up to date. The Dominican Republic's first steam mill was constructed in 1874 by a Cuban named Joaquín Delgado. Several of his compatriots followed suit, and European and American investors in turn arrived to seek their fortunes. Between 1875 and 1882 a further 35 steam mills were established, and production rocketed. Eleven of the new mills were completely mechanised, and a further 19 were semi-mechanised with steam engines and horizontal rollers. With the technological improvements, the *ingenios* were able to increase productivity, reach higher levels of crystallisation, and become serious competitors on the world market. By 1877, production was over two million pounds of raw sugar; three years later it was six times that amount; by 1882 it had doubled again; and by 1893 it was up to 77 million pounds.[4]

The new *ingenio* owners were generally foreigners, or at least of overseas origin. They had English and US names like Hardy, Hatton, Bass and Smith: or Italian ones like Zanetti and Vicini. There were many Cubans, but few Dominicans. The smaller outgrowers, though, who cultivated the sugar crop on small land parcels for sale to the mechanised *ingenios*, were Dominican nationals. The early *ingenios* often cultivated little land of their own. Sometimes they bought up the adjoining land, and leased it to *colonos* (outgrowers) who exchanged the raw cane for processed sugar. Alternatively, the *colonos* might own their own lands, and enter into contractual arrangements with the *ingenios*.

At first, with labour in desperately short supply, competitive wages were paid by the foreign capitalists. Dominicans were apparently attracted by the high salaries of the time, and many of them were willing to part with their small *conucos* (subsistence plots) and join the emerging proleteriat. As one contemporary observer wrote in 1880: "foreign capitalists come and establish four or five sugar plantations on fertile lands, at almost giveaway prices on the sea shore or by navigable rivers . . . the masters are surrounded by a population which used to be the owners of the land and are now its labourers."[5]

But the high salaries were short-lived, and reportedly did not compensate for the decline in living standards. As another historian observed, one notable effect of the sugar industry within a few years of its early development was the absence of fruit and vegetables in Santo Domingo itself (the capital city) now that all the surrounding lands had been turned over to sugar cane cultivation, and the few subsistence plots and small farms had disappeared.[6]

In the 1880s the writer Eugene María Hostos was already complaining of the monopoly over land and labour exercised by the new sugar magnates.[7] The industry was just emerging from one of the first of its many crises. Following a crash in world sugar prices in the early 1880s, many of the first entrepreneurs had gone bankrupt. From over 30 *ingenios* in 1882, there were only 20 left in 1893. Moreover, the capitalists who rode the financial storm now emerged as the owners of several *ingenios* at once.

The most successful of all was the Italian Juan P. Vicini. In the 1870s he had but one *ingenio* to his name. By 1893 he had added to his empire the mills of Ocóa, Italia, Encarnación and Constancia, all in the vicinity of Santo Domingo. He had also moved into the new sugar-producing area of San Pedro Macoris in the east of the country, purchasing the Ingenio Angelina from one of the early Cuban entrepreneurs.[8] Vicini was doubtless helped by his status as close friend and chief private moneylender of the dictator of the period, President Ulises Heureaux (1887–99). But he was also well connected in US financial circles.

By the end of the century, United States investors were turning their eyes more seriously to the Dominican Republic. In 1893 the Bass family — already the proprietors of Ingenio Consuelo in San Pedro Macoris — built its large new mill in the town of La Romana some 20 miles further to the east. The mill was called the Central Romana. It grew rapidly after that, accumulated an unprecedented amount of land, until it became the vast property of the Gulf and Western Corporation in the 1960s. By 1920 the land area of the Central Romana was registered at 855,891 *tareas*, a size which was to quadruple over the next half century.

If the monopoly of land and labour was already evident in the 1880s, it was to develop substantially over the next few decades. In 1893 there were but 218,000 *tareas* controlled by the sugar mills and outgrowers. In 1925, a year after the end of the first US military occupation, there were no less than 2,826,980 *tareas*. By that time, almost all of the lands were in the hands of vast United States conglomerates. The Central Romana passed into the hands of The Central Romana Incorporated (TCRI), a subsidiary of the US-owned South Puerto Rico Sugar Corporation. The second major investor was the West India Sugar Finance Company (WISFC), incorporated in Connecticut. WISFC at first concentrated on the indirect financing of sugar operations, and then turned to direct purchase in the Dominican Republic. By 1925, of the 21 *ingenios* then operating, eleven belonged to the larger foreign corporations,[9] and 98 per cent of sugar exports went to the USA.[10]

So by the end of the US occupation in 1924, the Dominican landscape was well on the way to adopting today's patterns. In the eastern provinces of San Pedro Macoris and La Romana, there were vast plantations reaching as far as the eye could see. As many observers lamented, no fruit, vegetables or other crops were to be found. Cattle ranches there were in plenty, but largely for the production of the oxen used for pulling the sugar carts from the cane fields to the *ingenios*. Railways were constructed on the largest *ingenios*, but animal traction was still needed to bring the sugar from the ever-expanding cane fields to the modernised loading operations. There was little or no land available for subsistence needs. The seven large *ingenios* of San Pedro Macoris occupied 67 per cent of all land under cultivation in the province.[11] The Central Romana was soon to exceed that amount. Nor were sugar operations limited to the east. In the south-western town of Barahona, the US-owned Barahona Sugar Company rapidly accumulated vast areas of over 300,000 *tareas*.

Salaries had also been depressed by a large influx of foreign migrant labour. The Dominican peasant would no longer part so willingly with his land. So how was the land accumulated, and what effect did this new massive expansion of the sugar industry have on the traditional agrarian structure? The first lands to be affected were the largely unoccupied *terrenos estatales* (or state lands). New immigration laws passed in the 1870s granted tax exemption to foreign settlers who brought such land under commercial cultivation. But there was pressure from the new capitalists to break up altogether the system of communal landholding which dated back to the colonial era and was the predominant model of land tenure in subsistence farming areas. In 1911 the government enacted a law on the division of communal lands, repealing earlier legislation which had prohibited their sale or alienation. In the following year a new law of property inscription gave all *comuneros* just one year in which to register their land titles. The familiar history of the Latin American peasantry set in. As in the Central American republics of El Salvador and Guatemala (where the expansion of commercial coffee farming in the same era had led to massive land concentration in a few hands, the abolition of communal structures, and similar laws on compulsory land titling), the peasants were the losers. Illiterate farmers, with no knowledge of or access to the law, had little idea of what was going on. The sugar companies with their skilled lawyers were quick on the uptake.

North Americans had interests other than sugar in the Dominican Republic. The rise of the sugar industry had brought major private and public expenditure in infrastructural projects, communications, railroads, port facilities and the other components of agro–industrial modernisation. Until 1892 the country's main foreign creditor had been the Westendorp Corporation, based in Amsterdam, Holland. In that year Westendorp went bankrupt, and its Dominican interests were bought up by a group of US entrepreneurs who formed the San Domingo Improvement Company.[12] The company created subsidiaries, the San Domingo Finance Company and the San Domingo Railways Company, and was soon extracting lucrative commissions from the growing Dominican debt. When the San Domingo Company took over responsibility for the administration of all national customs revenues, as security for its loans, the arrangements led to strong protests from rival European financiers, and then to closer control by the government of the United States. It was a new era, far different from the 1870s when the US Senate had rejected direct annexation. In 1905 an agreement drawn up between the US and Dominican governments reflected the degree of Washington's control. Until the

Dominican debt to the United States concerns was completely paid off, there could be no tariff reforms without the specific agreement of the President of the United States; and there could be no reduction of port and customs duties without his consent.[13] In the following year, Dominican President Ramón Cáceres enacted a law exempting the sugar companies from all production and export taxes. It was a blatant concession to the foreign capitalists. At the same time, new taxes were slapped on Dominican farmers to service the burgeoning debt. Armed factionalism returned to the country, and civil war broke out in 1912. Some four years later, in May 1916, US marines landed in Santo Domingo for the first time. The pretext was the restoration of order in the midst of anarchy, and the need for stern measures to safeguard the collection of customs revenues. But Haiti had already been invaded in the previous year, and there were a further 2,500 marines in Cuba between 1917 and 1923.

While Europe was occupied with a war of its own, the US government was determined to consolidate its control over what had now become its *mare nostrum*. US sugar companies evidently took full advantage of the next eight years. In 1922 an angry Dominican writer named Elías Gambiaso published an impassioned pamphlet against the occupation, *The Four Monsters of the Annexation*. He described the strategy of the Barahona Sugar Company: two US citizens had been granted usufruct over a limited amount of land, but proceeded to fence off most of the Barahona province. The peasantry were enticed to Barahona market to sell their produce, and arrived back home to find the same US citizens denying them access to their own lands. Authorities were bribed, and there was no lack of violence. The account may be exaggerated, but most probably is not. How else did the Barahona Sugar Company manage to accumulate over 300,000 *tareas* in a few brief years?

Barahona was the fastest grower, but other *ingenios* were not too far behind. Consuelo was up from 174,860 *tareas* in 1915 to 318,412 in 1925; Santa Fe from 202,438 to 393,548; Cristóbal Colón from 46,000 to 143,064. La Romana outstripped the rest, from 17,486 in 1912 to no less than 931,729 *tareas* in 1925.[14] Behind this frenzied increase lay the chance of immense profits. The First World War destroyed the European sugar beet industries, and created world-wide shortages of the commodity. In particular, 1920 was known as the "year of sugar". From $3 per *quintal*, the price rose as high as $18.[15] The Dominican Republic was now a major world producer.

The First *Braceros:* Origins of Migrant Labour

In 1884 — according to contemporary observer Eugene María Hostos — there were 6,000 workers on the Dominican sugar plantations. Of these 5,500 were Dominican nationals, and 500 were unspecified foreigners. They were most probably blacks from the British West Indies, the first of the so-called *Cocolos* who were to provide the bulk of migrant labour over the next 30 years. By 1879, workers were already being imported from the neighbouring Antilles to meet the sugar planters' labour requirements.[16]

The year 1884 was turbulent, with the first recorded strike of Dominican sugar workers against the low rates of pay for their piece-work. Sugar planters had reduced real wages in an effort to cut down their costs, and the labour force in San Pedro Macoris walked out in protest. "The peons don't want to accept the salaries offered to them," wrote the San Pedro newspaper *Eco de la Opinión*, "because although they are higher than before, they don't meet the current cost of daily subsistence items."[17] Dominican sociologist José del Castillo has compared sugar workers' wages to the cost of living at that time. He found that nominal wages were on the increase between 1880 and 1883, up by 80 per cent in Santo Domingo and 20 per cent in other regions. But food prices were also soaring. This was partly because many food items were by now being imported and were affected by tariffs; partly because the *bodegas* on the plantations had a monopoly on food items; and partly because locally produced food items suffered from the effects of the movement of the labour force towards the sugar mills. He also found that the cost of rice went up by 172 per cent between 1879 and 1884, that a bottle of milk rose from 5 centavos to 30 centavos between 1885 and 1894, that the price of beef tripled in the 15 years after 1879, and that the cost of plantains was up by 900 per cent during the same period.[18]

In the meantime salaries on the sugar *ingenios* remained fairly stagnant, and the work continued to lose its appeal for the Dominican peasantry. At this time the peasants still had a ready alternative for, although the cane industry had changed the land face in the immediate environs of Santo Domingo and the eastern region of San Pedro Macoris, there was abundant land elsewhere in the country. Moreover, Dominican workers remained on their *conucos* for much of the year, only moving to the cane fields when the rates were competitive. In the 1892–93 harvest, as the Santo Domingo newspaper *Listín Diario* observed, there was a marked labour shortage for the *zafra*, although all the *ingenios* were actively milling, because the Dominicans preferred other work. They could earn 4 pesos for a day's work clearing scrub in the mountains, while for a tonne of harvested cane the rate fluctuated between 2 and 3 pesos.[19]

So the planters began to look in earnest for an alternative labour supply. In 1893 a group of North American entrepreneurs despatched a boat to Puerto Rico, paying the return fare of the recruits. Then another group of planters got together, agreeing to finance a contingent of cane cutters from Cuba, Puerto Rico and the Canary Islands. Manuals were published on the characteristics of the ideal cane cutter. He would be a non-politicised and industrious worker from the French, British or Danish colonies (the planters were wary of the Cuban and Puerto Rican blacks, reputed to be trouble-makers at home as they were imbued with a militant character after the slave wars on their own sugar plantations).

Eventually, the planters settled on the *Cocolos*, black workers from the British sugar islands in the eastern Caribbean, the Virgin Islands, Jamaica, and the Turks and Caicos. By the early 20th century they were arriving in sizeable numbers. Just under 3,000 were brought over for the 1902–3 sugar harvest. They were supposed to return home at the end of the *zafra*, but many of them remained. Their descendants can still be found throughout the Dominican *ingenios* today, speaking a broken English that distinguishes them from the rest of the labour force.

The *Cocolo* immigration served the purposes of the planters and sugar companies by depressing wages to levels far below those acceptable to Dominican nationals. In

1900 a San Pedro Macoris newspaper, noting that over 1,500 *Cocolos* had arrived for the current harvest, complained that they were given wages as low as 25 cents per day and were "ruining the labour market".[20] In 1907 *Listín Diario* complained about the *Cocolo* immigrants for different reasons, describing them as disease-bearing beggars and vagrants in what sounds like a contemporary diatribe against Haitian immigrants. The following year, as an agricultural inspector from San Pedro Macoris reported, there were *ingenios* like Consuelo in which not a single Dominican could be found.[21] A racial enclave society was already developing.

In Dominican society at large, there was growing antipathy to the *Cocolos* on racial grounds. In 1912, to the apparent disgust of the sugar planters, a new law was enacted restricting coloured immigration. The British Consul of the day described it succinctly as a measure "designed to improve the race through the enticement of white immigrants and Spaniards from the Antilles, and the restriction of native immigrants from the European colonies in the Antilles".[22]

There were anti-*Cocolo* labour demonstrations on several *ingenios* at this time, and pamphlets were distributed which threatened to burn the cane fields if further foreign labourers were employed. In 1915, a new society was formed with the express purpose of opposing the importation of black cane cutters. As historian Patrick Bryan narrates,

> Just before the harvest in 1915, a society was founded in the Dominican Republic to agitate on behalf of Dominican labour. The first contingent of workers from Anguilla was greeted with a riot. The efforts of the society to encourage the use of Dominican labour led to widespread disturbances in the country districts and "gave rise to disorders and attempts to strike".[23]

The importance of *Cocolos* continued until the 1920s. Though many stayed behind in the Dominican Republic, the majority appear to have returned home. As José del Castillo writes,

> The immigration of cocolos as *braceros* was handled legally. They were brought in through the ports of Santo Domingo, San Pedro Macoris and Puerto Plata. The traffic was organised by the captains of small ships that covered the routes between the small islands and Dominican destinations. In the majority of cases the captains worked under previous agreement with the mills. Most of the workers returned to the country of their origin at the end of the harvest, taking with them a part of their earnings in the form of savings. These savings, according to English sources, were considered to justify the continuation of the migratory movements.[24]

The First Haitian *Braceros*

Between 1916 and 1924, as we have seen, the Dominican Republic was occupied by the United States. And between 1916 and 1934, Haiti was similarly occupied. During the years of the occupation, as we saw earlier, there was a huge increase in the Dominican land area under sugar cane cultivation. And as labour demands increased correspondingly, a cheaper supply was to be found next door in Haiti. Officially, the US administration professed to control negro immigration. In 1919,

Governor Snowdon enacted Executive Order No. 372 which prohibited the immigration of *braceros* "of any race except the Caucasian, their immediate families and other dependants, except through the designated ports and frontier posts".[25] Evidently, there were few Caucasian takers. On the US-owned plantations, notably on the Central Romana, the Haitian presence increased rapidly, and was soon to outstrip the Dominican labour force. In 1920, when over 22,000 *braceros* were given special permission to remain in the country, slightly over 10,000 of them were of Haitian origin. From then on, the organised recruitment of labour from the other Caribbean countries was to disappear gradually, and clandestine and technically illegal Haitian labour was to take over.

At first, the Dominicans wanted anyone rather than their black neighbours to cut cane. Memories of the long occupation under Jean-Pierre Boyer, and the sporadic Haitian invasions since then, were still too fresh in people's minds. Alarm bells were sounded as early as 1885, when it was found that Haitians were employed on some of the *ingenios*.[26] By the turn of the century *Listín Diario* was already warning of the dangers of the "clandestine Haitian invasion". But as labour shortages remained acute, and declining world prices cut into profits from the early 1920s onwards, Haitian recruitment turned out to be a viable option and eventually the only one. By 1920 the Dominican census listed 28,258 Haitians in the country. By 1935 the official census figures gave a total of 52,657, but the true number was certainly far greater.

On the Haitian side, population pressures were reaching a critical point. For a while, there was a ready outlet for migrant labour in Cuba. In 1912, the US-owned United Fruit Company secured permission to import the first 1,400 Haitian labourers for its Cuban properties. Over the next decade they arrived in droves, some 27,000 in the five-year period from 1914 to 1919.[27] Anything up to 300,000 may have made the trip to Cuba between the years 1915 and 1930.[28] After that year the Cuban outlet was effectively closed. The depression brought an end to the organised traffic, and in 1937 the Cuban army strongman Fulgencio Batista expelled every Haitian who fell into the clutches of his military patrols. In the same year, the mushrooming Haitian population in the border regions of the Dominican Republic was massacred. But from then on, as will be seen later, cheap Haitian labour became an increasingly accepted fact of life in the Dominican sugar industry.

The Era of Trujillo, 1930–61

In 1930 all of the Dominican *ingenios* bar those of the now naturalised Vicini family were in foreign hands. Three decades later the situation had changed drastically. The Central Romana, now bigger than ever, was still owned by a United States consortium. The Vicini group still held on to its three medium-sized properties. But of the 16 *ingenios*, 12 were now the personal domain of one man, General Rafael Leonidas Trujillo. Some of the older *ingenios* had been purchased from the foreign companies, other new ones had been built with the help of forced labour and extorted public funds. The ultimate extravaganza, the huge Ingenio Haina on the outskirts of Santo Domingo, outstripped even the Central Romana and was boasted by Trujillo to be the world's largest sugar mill.

Trujillo, who rose from humble origins through the ranks of the National Police and subsequently through the US-created National Guard, was to become a notorious Caribbean dictator. The many books written about him are sick chronicles of endless political murders and assassinations for personal vengeance, avarice and unbridled corruption.[29] During the 31 years that he ruled, either directly or through a string of puppet presidents, he accumulated a personal fortune estimated at anything between $1 billion and $1.5 billion. He monopolised in turn the country's salt, rice, wood, oil and tobacco industries, and even managed to turn the new social security system into a personal profit-making enterprise. In the late 1940s he moved into his latest venture, the sugar industry.

It took him just over a decade to accumulate three-quarters of the country's *ingenios*, buying and forcing most of his North American competitors out of the business. It is worth asking why Trujillo, who relied on US diplomatic and military support to retain power, was able to move so strongly against US private investments. If the *ingenios* were a source of such immense profits, then why was he permitted to take them over, and create a Somoza-style agro–industrial empire? In many respects Trujillo was similar to Nicaragua's first Anastasio Somoza. Originally seen as the US strongman, a bastion against leftist nationalism and Communism in the early cold-war period, he was a typical client dictator of the era. But whereas Somoza accumulated huge personal wealth at the expense of the national peasantry and bourgeoisie, he never clashed with international capital. There had never been significant US private investment in Nicaraguan agriculture. But Trujillo, while enjoying US support, skilfully exploited nationalist sentiments against foreign control of the Dominican economy. How was he able to do it?

A number of explanations have been put forward. Some authors have claimed that the foreign investors willingly sold out, at a time of rising world sugar production, declining demand and usually low world sugar prices. Others have seen Trujillo as a bizarre manifestation of the national and nationalistic will, in which the laws were changed and state coercion was used in order to force foreign investors to capitulate.[30] Another view is that Trujillo played along with the more powerful of the foreign companies who had the full support of the US government, while sweeping aside those minor foreign capitalists who were an easier prey. Thus the Central Romana survived in foreign hands, while the smaller *ingenios* did not. The third version is probably closest to the truth, though the sugar ventures were hardly Trujillo's greatest success story. Robert Crassweller, his US biographer, terms the Trujillo enterprise "not a business but a romance" and claims that "on a cash-flow basis the entire operation lost money".[31] To see why this was the case one must look at the changing nature of US sugar production, the changing sugar markets, the new protectionist policies devised by the major sugar-importing countries, and the constant instability of the world pricing system.

While US investors poured money into the Dominican sugar industry in the early 20th century, the country was still secondary to the major prize, the large island of Cuba to the north. Cuba had been wrested from Spanish control at the turn of the century, at the same time as Spain's other major sugar-producing colonies, Puerto

Rico and the Philippines. Unlike the other two, Cuba was never annexed by the United States, but it was subject to regular occupation by the US marines — from 1898 to 1902, from 1906 to 1909 and again from 1917 to 1923. Furthermore the Platt Amendment of 1901 gave the United States a permanent right to intervene in Cuba's domestic affairs to protect its own interests, and to establish military bases there.[32] Cuba soon became the foremost sugar producer for the United States market, with the bulk of the industry falling swiftly into the hands of US corporations. On the eve of the First World War, US investments in Cuban sugar were already estimated at over $200 million. By 1919 some 40 to 50 per cent of Cuban *ingenios* were in US hands.[33] Throughout that period, Cuba's sugar exports soared. Production was up from two million tons in 1913, to three million in 1916, nearly four million by 1920, and five million by 1925.

But by the 1920s the Cuban "dance of the millions" was effectively over, and a struggle commenced to obtain new markets in the face of stagnant US demand and increasing competition from alternative suppliers for the coveted US market. In 1920 the United States took 95 per cent of Cuba's sugar crop, ten years later less than 50 per cent.[34] After the shortages of the early post-war years, there was now a glut in world sugar production. From a high point of 22 US cents per pound in May 1920, the price had plummeted to under 2 cents by 1929. As early as 1921, the US had placed a tariff on imported Cuban sugar, whereas the produce of the North American sugar-producing colonies (Hawaii, the Philippines and Puerto Rico) enjoyed duty-free entry. The process continued after the slump of the 1930s. By 1933 Cuba's share of the US market had dropped to 25.3 per cent from 49.4 per cent in 1930,[35] losing out to the new sugar colonies and the jealous domestic producers within the United States. In these circumstances, US corporations began to withdraw from direct ownership of Cuban *ingenios*. The vast Cuba Cane Corporation, which had jumped on the sugar bandwagon during the feverish years of the First World War, sold its Cuban assets, and North American banks also began to withdraw from a now less profitable business.[36] The sugar industry fell on hard times until its fortunes were changed in the 1940s by the world war.

In the Dominican Republic, it was a similar tale on a smaller scale. After the boom years of the early 1920s, the bad times led to a new concentration of *ingenios* in the hands of foreign corporations with the capital to weather the storm. The Cuba Dominican Sugar Corporation, largely controlled by the National City Bank of New York, was formed in 1924 and had taken over five *ingenios* by the following year.[37] By 1931, when the world sugar price had reached a rock bottom of under 1 cent per pound in the wake of the great depression, Cuba Dominican sold out to the West Indies Sugar Corporation. Even more than the Cubans, the Dominican-based concerns found that they were increasingly denied access to the US market. The percentage of sugar exports to the United States fell by 66 per cent between 1920 and 1925, and by 1930 only 1.7 per cent of exported produce found its way to the US market. New markets were found elsewhere, and some 95 per cent now went to England, Canada and France.[38]

It was a shaky business, and for a long time Trujillo wanted nothing to do with it. He invested where secure profits were to be found. The salt mines of Neyba were an adequate example. He took over the salt company when the going price was half a cent per pound, then fixed a monopoly price six times higher. As the state came under his personal control, a get-rich-quick strategy was best geared to the slowly reviving domestic market. As late as 1941, the world sugar price was still at its low level of the depression era, under 1 cent per pound, but the new European war brought revival. By 1947 it had risen to 5 cents, and in the following year Trujillo plunged in. He began on a small scale, with the construction of the modest new Ingenio Catarey on the road to Santiago, but soon followed this with plans for the huge Ingenio Haina complex. When Haina came into production in 1952, its theoretical capacity was already larger than that of the Central Romana; the problem now was acquiring sufficient sugar-cane lands to keep the new plant at full milling capacity. According to Crassweller, the dilemma was solved through a typical Trujillo stratagem. He ordered the assassination of the largest landowner of the region, then struck a bargain by which the landowner kept his life and a job in the operational end of the new sugar empire, while Trujillo kept the coveted land.[39]

Other purchases then followed in quick succession. In 1952, Ingenio Montellano, near the north coastal town of Puerto Plata, was bought apparently on a compulsory basis for less than half of its actual value. In the following year the *ingenios* of Ozama near the capital, Amistad in the north, and Porvenir in San Pedro Macoris were bought from their respective Canadian, Puerto Rican and US owners. In this year Trujillo took the ingenious step of selling for cash to the Agricultural Bank all hitherto acquired sugar properties, only to buy them back on generous credit terms when the world sugar price had risen a few years later. He also distributed some half a million adjoining lands to Dominican outgrowers — a good propaganda measure against the foreign corporations who farmed the bulk of the land themselves — only to reclaim most of them later on the grounds that the beneficiaries had failed in their contractual obligations.[40]

With the smaller foreign *ingenios* in his pocket, Trujillo then turned to bigger game, using the banner of economic nationalism. His strategy involved an interesting use of new labour legislation. In 1951, the dictator's carefully controlled Congress had enacted the Dominican Republic's first Labour Code. Like similar codes enacted throughout Latin America around this time, it fell within the corporatist model of society, laying down in meticulous detail the obligations of employers towards their workers and vice versa, but placing heavy restrictions on the workers' capacity to fight for the enforcement of these rights. Strikes were illegal unless declared to be otherwise. Trade unions preaching the class struggle were explicitly banned. As militant labour activists languished in Trujillo's gaols when lucky enough to escape assassination, the document was generally of little use to workers. But its provisions were useful when the interests of government and workers coincided.

While abysmal conditions in his own properties were conveniently overlooked, Trujillo campaigned for a vigorous application of the new labour laws on the five *ingenios* that remained in foreign hands (Barahona, Boca Chica, Consuelo and Quisqueya of the West Indies Sugar Company; and the Central Romana of the South Porto Rico Sugar Corporation).[41] Almost all the *bateyes* of Ingenio Barahona were declared a "public danger" by the Department of Health. The Central Romana was taken to court for violations of numerous articles of the Labour Code.

The official Trujillo-controlled union, the Confederación de Trabajadores Dominicanos (CTD) launched a series of strikes which for once were not stamped down by the authorities. The complaints were as legitimate then as they would be today: excessive work hours, discriminatory payment for foreign workers, the use of the *vale* credit system through which workers were paid in vouchers that kept them in a state akin to debt-bondage, and appalling living conditions in the *bateyes*. Pressure was put directly on the foreign magnates. Edwin Kilbourne, general manager of the West Indies Sugar Company, was once put under house arrest with a heavily armed guard controlling his movements. Eventually, towards the end of 1956, the West Indies Sugar Company capitulated and sold to Trujillo for US$35,830,000. Robert Crassweller gives a graphic description of the final stages:

> The management and stockholders of the West Indies Sugar Company recognised that the government was not above wielding considerable leverage against the company. There were innumerable possibilities for harassment, and none of them contravened any law. They might, indeed, masquerade as devotion to the principle of active enforcement. The company's private plane, essential for transportation between widely scattered properties, could be grounded on various technicalities. The supply of labour could be restricted easily and patriotically by the enactment of special regulations with idealistic preambles and malicious working clauses. It appeared to be harmless, and only neighbourly, for the government to request from time to time the loan of tractors and other heavy equipment. If the requests happened to be made during the critical harvest periods, and the government agents forgot to return the tractors for three or four months, how could one complain? The stockholders read the signs. They decided to sell, provided a favourable figure could be negotiated.[42]

Rumour has it that Trujillo also had his eyes on the Central Romana but never realised this ultimate ambition. Since then the Central Romana has had living and working conditions considerably better than those in the 15 other *ingenios*.

Trujillo's sugar interests eventually changed his attitude to the Haitian question. In the early years his main interests had been to tighten and formalise the arbitrary borders between the two countries, to colonise the sparsely settled frontier regions with subsidised Dominican settlements, and eventually perhaps to exercise definitive control over internal events in Haiti itself. To these ends, he was determined to evict the growing numbers of Haitian peasants who crossed the valleys separating the countries, spreading their own subsistence plots, markets and noticeably Haitian cultural norms. For as long as the US occupation of Haiti lasted, until 1934, Trujillo's overtures were tactfully limited to diplomacy and propaganda. Meetings were held with Haiti's President Vincent, the last of them in 1933, and agreement was reached on the new frontier lines. Trujillo requested repatriation of Haitian peasants infiltrating to the Dominican side of the border, and sporadic border conflicts ensued.

Trujillo then became more belligerent. Perhaps inspired by the Cuban dictator Fulgencio Batista's mass expulsion of Haitian immigrants in 1937, Trujillo decided to rid his own country of the growing Haitian presence. But whereas Batista had only to ship the victims out to sea, Trujillo resorted to far more brutal measures. An appalling massacre took place in October 1937. In just two or three days, a number of

Haitians variously estimated at between 10,000 and 20,000 were rounded up by military guards, and executed on the spot. It was a rapid, calculated and vicious act of genocide. All blacks — men, women and children — whose accent betrayed Haitian origins were killed with deliberate savagery. As many contemporary observers reported, the foreign sugar enclaves were the only safe places of refuge. Trujillo wanted the massacre kept secret as far as possible, and was careful not to arouse the protests of the influential foreign corporations.

It took a long time for news of the atrocities to reach the outside world. Over a fortnight later, the *New York Times* reported a border clash in which "several Haitians had been shot".[43] It was thanks to a brave investigative journalist from the small *Collier's* magazine that the truth began to leak out. He found scenes of carnage and brutality unprecedented in the Caribbean since the days of Haiti's bloody wars of independence. In first aid stations across the Haitian border, he encountered thousands of survivors of the episode, battered peasants dying in their primitive surroundings.[44] The deliberate cruelty unleashed against those left behind in the Dominican Republic has been described by the American writers Robert and Nancy Heinl:

> In Santiago, some 1900 poor souls were herded into a barracks or compound. Here — on express orders to use clubs, machetes or primitive weapons, not firearms — killer squads hacked and flailed indiscriminately at women, children, men, until their arms were tired and fresh executioners replaced them. Army trucks, hauling mutilated dead into desolate ravines of the countryside, left trails of stinking, stale blood along streets and roads. At ports and coastal areas, convoys unloaded bodies onto commandeered fishing boats and coasters, which shuttled them offshore to swarming shark and barracuda.[45]

There were calls for an international commission of enquiry. Eventually a makeshift commission was formed, from the diplomatic representatives of Guatemala, Peru and Argentina. But Trujillo got off lightly, paying an indemnity of US$750,000 to the government of Haiti.

The flow of Haitian workers was never stopped. It now became an exceedingly lucrative enterprise for military officers and border guards on both sides of the frontier. In the early 1940s the Haitian government enacted legislation attempting to stem the flow of clandestine traffic, but apparently to little effect. As one Haitian statesman wrote to new Haitian President Dumarsais Estime, after his election in 1946:

> This law [of 1942] is not applied, for innumerable Haitian migrants have entered the Dominican Republic with the complicity of the companies and the authorities. A route has even been created in the chain of Morne des Commissaires to favour these clandestine operations. Last year, for example, the customs administration of Cap Haitien pointed out that, thanks to the political circumstances of the time, 6,000 migrants crossed the frontier in some northern regions; and, according to the testimony of some people I interviewed myself, it is in military lorries that they have been "packed" on foot, in groups of 60, to take them to the sugar mills. All this has resulted in terrible accidents, with wounded and dead.[46]

The author of the above memorandum had more to say about the beneficiaries of the new slave traffic (though perhaps to save his own skin he insinuated that things had changed under recent governments):

> The recruitment of this labour force before 1941 had been organised by high and important officials, large and small members of the bourgeoisie, and even among some of those "escaped from hell", the "viejos" who, in accordance with the legendary formula, have become the sellers of their ill-informed brothers. It is said that huge sums have changed hands among the top brass while the small fry earns a dollar per head.[47]

In 1952 General Trujillo, now at the head of his new sugar empire, decided to formalise the recruitment of Haitian cane cutters, signing the first of the contracts authorising the Dominican government to buy Haitians from the neighbouring country. It was the time of Labour Codes and formal legality, and the new *Acuerdo* (Agreement) was presented to the Dominican Congress for rubber-stamping. The 1952 *Acuerdo* was to provide the basis for the bilateral contracts signed between the two governments almost every year since then. It provided for a substantial payment to the Haitian government, and in theory guaranteed certain rights for the Haitians. They were to have an individual labour contract on the sugar plantations, to have their return transport paid, and to enjoy salaries no different from those of the few remaining Dominican cane cutters. The Agreement was to last for five years, with a possible extension by Congress. In fact, a new *Acuerdo* was drawn up in 1959, lasting until the end of the Trujillo era.

Under the first *Convenio*, 16,500 Haitians were brought over. The number declined after that, and by 1957 was down to 3,500. Perhaps large numbers of Haitians stayed behind. Perhaps the contract was opposed by Trujillo's corrupt military, as it would cut into the profits of the border traders. Perhaps Trujillo himself lost interest, once his legalistic campaign against the foreign corporations had served its purpose. In any event the number of resident Haitians continued to rise sharply. The official figure for Haitian residents in 1960 was 29,350. It is hard to believe this. There were nearly half that number in the Central Romana alone.

Trujillo's life was abruptly terminated on 30 May 1961, in a hail of machine-gun fire outside Santo Domingo (or rather, Ciudad Trujillo, as the capital city had by then been renamed). The Trujillo era ended a few months later, when the dictator's family was finally ushered out of the country. His playboy son Ramfis had returned from Paris on hearing of Trujillo's assassination, took over the command of the army and hoped to perpetuate a Somoza-style dynasty. But before his death Trujillo had become a despised pariah in the Western hemisphere. International pressure, orchestrated by Washington and the rest of the Organisation of American States, ensured his son's swift removal from the scene.

In the previous year Trujillo had organised an unsuccessful attempt on the life of his arch-enemy abroad, the new democratic President Romulo Betancourt of Venezuela. In the backlash to this atrocity, almost every country in the hemisphere — including the United States — had broken diplomatic relations with the Trujillo regime. The usually passive Organisation of American States was shaken into activity, and recommended severe economic sanctions against the Dominican

Republic. By the time Trujillo's death finally came there were many assassination plots in the air, and ample evidence that the US Central Intelligence Agency had lent a helping hand.[48]

A new era had begun. The old-style corrupt dictators of the region, Pérez Jiménez of Venezuela and Fulgencio Batista of Cuba, had fallen in quick succession in 1958 and 1959. The Cuban revolution of January 1959 had changed the political — and subsequently also the economic — face of the Caribbean. United States foreign policy now veered towards governments that opposed Fidel Castro, were sympathetic to US private interests, and initiated sufficient social and political liberalisation to provide a safety net against further Castro-style revolutionary upheavals. Romulo Betancourt of Venezuela, who fulfilled all three conditions, was the ideal president from the new US perspective. Trujillo looked good on the first count, was a big question mark on the second, and failed miserably on the third.

Trujillo's main legacy to the country, apart from an evil legend and a society riddled with corruption at all levels, was his mammoth sugar holdings. They were expropriated and nationalised after his death, and there were considerable hopes for the future. In July 1960 the United States had declared its embargo against Castro's Cuba, and eliminated the world's largest sugar producer from the world's largest consumer market. Among the lesser sugar producers of the region, there was a rush to enjoy the new outlet. Landowners of such client-states as El Salvador, Guatemala and Nicaragua quickly diversified into sugar, and lobbied to get a share of the new US quotas. Until Trujillo's death, the Dominican Republic suffered from US Congressional initiatives limiting sugar imports from countries under dictatorial rule — the measure was aimed primarily at Castro, but Trujillo was included. Though Dominican sugar entered the US, the price was none too favourable. The Eisenhower administration heeded the OAS sanctions, imposing a special tax on Dominican sugar equal to the US premium. In just over a year, the tax had deducted some $22,750,000 from expected Dominican earnings.

Trujillo's monopolisation of the sugar industry may not have been a decisive factor in his downfall but it was probably a contributory one. In his book *The Unfinished Experiment* (the account of his short-lived presidency in 1962–63), former Dominican President Juan Bosch argues that Washington favoured liberalisation of the Dominican government, not only as the solution to a political problem that affected its position in Latin America, "but also to pave the way for dropping the boycott on Dominican sugar, an economic move of great importance to US consumers".[49] But the optimism was not to last. The vast sugar industry, once portrayed as the "white gold" of the country, was eventually to become more of a sweet white elephant.

Notes

1. Juan J. Sánchez, *La Caña en Santo Domingo* (Imprenta de García Hermanos, Santo Domingo, 1893), p. 24.

2. José del Castillo, "The Formation of the Dominican Sugar Industry", in Manuel Moreno Fraginals *et al.* (eds) *Between Slavery and Free Labour: the Spanish-*

Speaking Caribbean in the Nineteenth Century (Johns Hopkins University Press, Baltimore and London, 1985), p. 215.

3. Ibid., p. 216.

4. Guillermo Moreno, "De la Propiedad Comunera a la Propiedad Privada Moderna, 1844–1924", *Estudios Dominicanos*, Vol. IX, No. 51, 1980, p. 79.

5. Jacqueline Boin and José Serulle Ramia, *El Proceso de Desarrollo del Capitalismo en la República Dominicana, 1844–1930* (Ediciones Gramil, Santo Domingo, 1981), Vol. 2, p. 172.

6. Frank Moya Pons, *Manual de Historia Dominicana* (Universidad Católica Madre y Maestra, Santiago, Dominican Republic, 1981), p. 411.

7. Harry Hoetink, *El Pueblo Dominicano, 1850–1900* (Universidad Católica Madre y Maestra, Santiago, 1972), p. 34.

8. Sánchez, op. cit.

9. Franc Báez Evertsz, *Azúcar y Dependencia en la República Dominicana* (Santo Domingo, 1978), p. 43.

10. Juan Bosch, *Composición Social Dominicana* (Ediciones Alfa y Omega, Santo Domingo, 1981), p. 231.

11. José del Castillo, *La Economía Dominicana durante el Primer Cuarto del Siglo XX* (Fundación García Arévalo, Santo Domingo, 1980), p. 25.

12. Moya Pons, op. cit., pp. 419–20.

13. Ibid., p. 439.

14. Báez Evertsz, op. cit., p. 47.

15. Ibid., p. 122.

16. Cited in Patrick E. Bryan, "The Question of Labour in the Sugar Industry of the Dominican Republic in the late Nineteenth and early Twentieth Centuries", in Moreno Fraginals, op. cit., p. 239.

17. José del Castillo, "La Inmigración de Braceros Azucareros en la República Dominicana, 1900–1930", *Cuadernos del CENDIA* (Universidad Autónoma de Santo Domingo), Vol. 162, No. 7, n.d., p. 31.

18. Castillo in Moreno Fraginals, op. cit., pp. 228–31.

19. Ibid., p. 31.

20. Ibid., p. 38.

21. Ibid., p. 40.

22. Ibid., p. 42.

23. Bryan, op. cit., p. 244.

24. Castillo in Moreno Fraginals, op. cit., p. 232.

25. Castillo, op. cit., n.d., p. 48.

26. André Corten and others, *Azúcar y Política en la República Dominicana* was (Biblioteca Taller 71, Santo Domingo, 1973), p. 37.

27. Hugh Thomas, *Cuba or the Pursuit of Freedom* (Eyre & Spottiswoode, London, 1971), p. 1540.

28. Paul Moral, *Le Paysan Haïtien* (Editions Fardin, Port-au-Prince, Haiti, 1978), p. 71.

29. For example see the book by Gerardo Gallegos, *Trujillo: Cara y Cruz de su Dictadura*, date unknown.

30. See Máximo Luis Vidal, "La Industria Azucarera y Su Mercado" (cited in Báez Evertsz, op. cit).

31. Robert Crassweller, *The Life and Times of a Caribbean Dictator* (McMillan, New York, 1966), p. 259.

32. Jenny Pearce, *Under the Eagle* (Latin America Bureau, London, 1981).

33. Thomas, op. cit., p. 541.
34. Ibid., pp. 557, 560.
35. Ibid., p. 562.
36. Ibid., p. 1147.
37. Castillo, 1980, op. cit., pp. 58–9.
38. Báez Evertsz, op. cit., p. 75.
39. Crassweller, op. cit., p. 253.
40. Báez Evertsz, op. cit., p. 97.
41. Ibid., pp. 92, 100.
42. Crassweller, op. cit., p. 255.
43. *New York Times*, 21 October 1937.
44. R.D. Heinl and N.G. Heinl, *Written in Blood: The Story of the Haitian People* (Houghton Mifflin Company, Boston, 1978), pp. 526–7.
45. Ibid., p. 527.
46. Quoted in André Corten and others, op. cit., p. 1·10.
47. Ibid., p. 96.
48. Crassweller, op. cit., pp. 435–6.
49. Juan Bosch, *The Unfinished Experiment: Democracy in the Dominican Republic* (Pall Mall Press, London, 1968), p. 8.

3 Sugar and the Social Structure: The Dominican Republic, 1961-85

The first years after Trujillo's assassination were a time of fervid political activity, culminating in a second United States occupation of the Dominican Republic in April 1965. Predictably, following three decades of virulent dictatorship, a strong nationalist movement emerged in the early 1960s which demanded widespread social and economic reforms, including a curb on the growing US influence over the Dominican economy. Washington, in the meantime, was pressing for moderate social reforms and gradual liberalisation through pro-US politicians and the military establishment who would make no direct moves against North American-owned assets in the country. The protagonists were the university professor and writer Juan Bosch, who spearheaded the populist movement demanding widespread nationalism and significant land redistribution, and Dr Joaquín Balaguer, the last "puppet" president during the Trujillo era, who led the pro-Washington camp. They have remained the country's most prominent political figures in the quarter of a century since then, both of them contesting the most recent presidential elections (won by Balaguer) in May 1986.

After the May 1961 assassination of Trujillo, governments came and fell rapidly. Balaguer retained the formal presidency until he handed power to a civilian triumvirate on 1 January 1962. When new presidential elections were held in December of the same year, Juan Bosch won with mass popular support, but was ousted by the military seven months after his inauguration, in September 1963. A rightist civilian triumvirate was then set up, but in turn was toppled by a further military coup on the eve of presidential elections in April 1965, which Bosch clearly stood a good chance of winning. Bosch's supporters took to arms, a major civil insurrection broke out, and the US marines were despatched to Santo Domingo on 28 April. They were followed by a peace-keeping force of the Organisation of American States. Once again, a provisional government was established: and when new presidential elections were held the following year Dr Balaguer came back to power. He survived consecutive presidential terms, retaining office until August 1978.

The 30 years of the Trujillo era had radically transformed the Dominican economy, making it more than ever dependent on sugar for its foreign exchange earnings. And sugar was no longer a crop in the hands of foreign capitalists within an enclave economy. It was now the mainstay of the national economy, the bulk of it under Dominican ownership and control. After 1961, successive governments had to wrestle with the problems inherited from the Trujillo era. To diversify or not to diversify? How to find new and regular markets, and how to deal with the perennial problem of labour shortages during the harvest season?

Over the past quarter of a century, Dominican governments have regularly pledged to seek a way out of sugar dependency, to redirect the thrust of agrarian policy in order to favour small and medium farmers and to increase the production of staple foods, and to "Dominicanise" the sugar harvest in order to reduce the dependency on imported Haitian labour. Two major agrarian reform laws were enacted, in 1962 and 1972, and there have been countless development programmes and projects aimed at improving national food production. At the end of this 25-year period the results were disastrous. The Dominican Republic is dependent on various forms of Haitian labour for over 90 per cent of its cane cutting, and also for much of the labour in the other export crops that have proliferated during this period. Land concentration has increased rather than decreased, and rural landlessness has increased progressively for Dominican peasants, to proportions similar to those found in the most conflict-ridden Central American countries. The Dominican Republic is as dependent as ever on sugar, even though it has been produced at an annual loss of tens of millions of dollars during the 1980s.

Why? Many Dominicans blame the Haitians, the hundreds of thousands of illegal immigrants who have poured into the country since the early 1960s. They criticise the Dominican peasant, alleging that there are cultural reasons — the historical associations with slavery — for his refusal to cut cane. But in this chapter, a different argument is put forward. There is considerable evidence that, whatever the rhetoric and the letter of the agrarian laws, both state policy and the interests of large commercial farmers favoured the influx of cheap Haitian labour in order to depress rural wages, undercut the militant Dominican peasant and labour organisations which demanded improved living and working conditions, and advance an agrarian strategy that favoured the interests of the larger farmers producing primarily for export, whatever the social costs for Dominican and Haitian rural workers alike. The strategy required the creation of a vast labour reserve of technically illegal immigrants who had no legal recourse against severe exploitation, and could be expelled arbitrarily from the country whenever their labour was no longer required. To understand this, it is important to analyse, first, the agrarian strategies pursued by the government of Dr Joaquín Balaguer in particular; second, the international politics of sugar during this period, and the factors which allowed for continuing dependency on sugar; and third, the role played by imported Haitian labour within this agrarian model.

Agrarian Reforms and Land Use

Throughout the Trujillo era, there had been a steady growth in both absolute rural landlessness, and in *microfundios*, farms too small to provide for the subsistence needs of the peasant family. While natural growth of the rural population had contributed to pressure on the land, the expansion of the sugar estates in the area around Santo Domingo was a further important factor. The fragmentation of rural land was particularly noticeable during the last decade of the Trujillo dictatorship. In the ten years up to 1960, the number of minute farms of less than half an acre more than doubled, to 67,000. While 36 per cent of all rural properties had been less than 5 acres in 1950, in 1960 no less than 70 per cent of just over 450,000 properties were of less than 5 acres.[1] Moreover, an agrarian census taken in 1960 revealed that half of approximately 400,000 smallholders owned no land of their own, that many of the remaining "owners" were without clear titles to the land or sufficient land to produce beyond minimum subsistence needs, and that in addition there were 50,000 landless rural labourers.[2]

In 1962 the Dominican government passed its first "modern" agrarian reform law, with the United States pledging to finance much of the reform programme through its bilateral aid funds. The law provided for the creation of a Dominican Agrarian Institute (IAD), a semi-autonomous body under the Department of Agriculture, with the responsibility of distributing state-owned land to needy peasants and landless rural workers. Initially it had slightly under one million acres at its disposal, including 145,000 acres expropriated from the Trujillo family and close Trujillo supporters. Beneficiaries of the land distribution were not to receive immediate title, and had to purchase it in instalments with the assistance of credit provided by an Agricultural Bank set up to finance the programme. The programme was never ambitious, aiming to settle 25,000 families by 1967, with a final target of 70,000 families to be attained by 1970. The final target was later lowered to 45,000 families only, and some of the state lands involved were turned over to cattle grazing on larger properties. By 1965, according to one author, only 2,700 families had been settled on a total of 33,000 acres.[3]

The extent to which private lands should be liable to expropriation — over and above the expropriated Trujillo estates — was one of the controversial debates in the early 1960s. While President Juan Bosch had urged the expropriation of the larger private estates, and included a provision in his short-lived Constitution paving the way for more radical land redistribution, the government of Dr Balaguer made no moves against private property throughout the 1960s. Until 1971, an average of only 1,000 families per year benefited from effective land distribution. In the meantime, larger and larger land areas were taken up with extensive cattle rearing, as new haciendas sprang up in the areas around the capital city. Between 1960 and 1971 the land area cultivated with basic grains remained static, while the lands under export-crop cultivation increased by approximately one million *tareas*. While more and more *colonos* turned to sugar production for neighbouring *ingenios*, cattle rearing was up by an estimated 50 per cent during this period.[4] Furthermore, as the cultivation of export crops increased, wages were maintained at desperately low levels. According to an experienced agrarian reform consultant who visited the Dominican Republic in 1969, the poorest three-quarters of the farm population was earning only some US$40 per capita per year — figures comparable with estimated peasant incomes in the most backward peasant farming levels of the impoverished Andean countries. And according to an agricultural census made in 1971, 75 per cent of all cultivated lands were now taken up primarily with export crops. First, inevitably, came sugar; then coffee, cocoa, peanuts, coconuts and bananas in that order.[5]

It was perhaps the alarming figures from the 1971 census that prompted the Balaguer government to put more sting into a new series of land reform laws promulgated the following year. One law empowered the IAD to take over all *baldío* (unoccupied) lands and state lands under private occupation for redistribution to the landless peasantry. Another abolished share-cropping and primitive tenurial arrangements on farms cultivated with subsistence crops, handing over the property to all share-croppers working lands under 18.5 hectares, and granting them the option of buying the remaining lands worked by them. Two additional laws empowered the IAD to exact compulsory purchase of all rice lands over 31 hectares, and distribute them to the peasantry. Finally, a fourth law allowed for the expropriation of all *latifundia* on a sliding scale (from 93 to 281 hectares depending on the quality of the land). In the private sector there was mixed reaction to these laws. Many landowners hastily broke up existing contracts with share-croppers to evade application of the law, and this preventive strategy led to some of the bitterest peasant struggles. Some rice farmers quickly moved over to other crops, while others made good with the generous compensation offered to them. Eventually the law on share-cropping was amended, to stipulate that the landowners and the peasant farmers should share the benefits, and application of the law soon petered out altogether. The law on *latifundia* was never really applied, even though the IAD stood to gain up to seven million hectares of land from its meticulous application. Sugar lands, incidentally, were completely untouched by the land reform measures.[6]

The Dominican laws, and their ultimate effects, were perhaps typical of the modernising land reforms "from above" enacted through much of Latin America during this period. Pressure came very much from Washington, which was determined to abolish the inefficient traditional *latifundio*, run on semi-feudal lines, and to replace it with more efficient commercial farming run on strictly capitalist lines. As leftist guerrilla movements increased their activities in a number of countries afflicted by gross social inequality — including the Dominican Republic where several guerrilla movements were active in the late 1960s and early 1970s — Washington governments were also concerned with the counter-insurgency implications of land reform. But the abolition of share-cropping, for example, regularly had the effect of increasing the numbers of the rural proletariat. Where land reforms were enacted from above, with generous compensation for traditional landlords willing to sell, and with exemptions for landowners willing to replace their semi-feudal systems with salaried labour and commercial farming methods, the logical move was to bring more of the land acreage under export-crop production, and simply to displace the squatters who had formerly enjoyed the use of a subsistence plot in exchange for the provision of cheap labour during key agricultural periods. Overall, the effect of these reforms on national food production has been negative. In 1970, for example, Latin America as a region was a net exporter of commercial cereals, and the majority of Latin American countries could claim a measure of self-sufficiency in food production. Now, as overall food production has stagnated throughout the region, food import bills have reached massive proportions. In the Central American and Caribbean region, total food import bills increased from just over $300 million in 1960 to over $3 billion in 1980 (figures given in current US dollars).[7]

For several years after 1972, the pace of land distribution did certainly escalate, most particularly for lands that were to be used exclusively for rice production. Between 1972 and 1977, over 47,000 land parcels were distributed, covering approximately 820,000 acres. Rice-growing lands were organised in co-operatives, which received ample technical assistance from the IAD, and there was a significant 24 per cent increase in rice production between the years 1973 and 1978. But the agrarian strategies of the 1970s succeeded neither in curbing the continued sharp growth in levels of absolute rural landlessness, nor in increasing the production of staple foods other than rice which provide the traditional diet of the Dominican peasant and poorer urban population groups. Between 1970 and 1980 the rural population almost doubled, from 1,688,369 to 2,934,054.[8] The wholly landless rural proletariat was up to 188,000, and three-quarters of all farm plots were still estimated to be under 5 hectares.

In view of this population growth, the statistics on staple food production during the same period are alarming. While Dominicans consume a certain amount of meat — mainly pork — when they can afford it, the subsistence crops within their traditional diet are rice, beans and maize, a certain amount of root crops such as yams, dasheen and sweet potatoes (*yuca, guandule, yautia, batata* and *name* are the Spanish terms for some of the most favoured root crops), together with plantains and other vegetables such as onions, peppers and tomatoes. Given the fertile climate and terrain of the country, the peasant has been accustomed to a substantially varied diet on the basis of these traditional foods. Statistics on the production of these items over the past decade are at times confusing — I have encountered varying estimates from the Department of Agriculture, the National Statistics Office and the Department of Planning[9] — but all three of them point either to an absolute decline in the volume of most of these crops over the past decade, or, at best, to a marginal increase of all crops apart from rice and maize.

A British author has provided the most favourable picture of the production of five basic food items (rice, *yuca*, sweet potatoes, plantains and beans) for the six years between 1973 and 1978. He notes that, except for a marked drop in 1975, there was an overall rise in production during the six years in question. However, he continues, this has to be seen in the perspective of a 15.6 per cent population growth during the same period. The only crops that actually outstripped population growth were rice and beans. He nevertheless concludes that agricultural production is still far below the level required to provide all sections of the population with an adequate diet.[10]

Recent research by several Dominican authors paints a far bleaker picture, arguing a major crisis in the production of traditional root crops. One researcher, using provisional statistics provided by the State Secretariat of Agriculture between 1972 and 1982, draws the following conclusions. In 1980–81 *yuca* production was less than half the average at the beginning of the decade. Maize production was, on average, fractionally lower than ten years previously, with a peak in 1976 and a very substantial decline in the following years. There had been a very sharp drop in the production of potatoes and sweet potatoes, and a smaller but nevertheless significant drop for such traditional items as red beans, *guandule, name* and *yautia*.[11]

There is no doubt that the rice production strategy was a significant success during the same period. It was up from 391 tonnes in 1973, to 465 tonnes by the mid 1970s, and to a peak of 573 tonnes by 1981, according to provisional official statistics. Rice production has indeed been the lynchpin of the Dominican Republic's agrarian reform and rural development strategies during this period, and has now rendered the Republic self-sufficient in this one important item. Even so, perhaps because of the wide availability of this product throughout the Caribbean, it has continued to figure among the import items. As one researcher has written:

> The amount of imports of agricultural produce carried out each year, is an indicator of the magnitude of the crisis which afflicts the rural sector of the Dominican Republic. From 1972 to 1981, the country has imported food products, as much for direct consumption as for industrial use, to the value of 632.8 million Dominican pesos. Between 1972 and 1981 the largest percentage of the imports was in rice, valued at 172.1 million pesos, or 27.3% of the total. The value of soya, cotton and peanut oil was 101.7 million, 100.4 million and 56 million pesos respectively. . . . To meet the needs of the domestic market, the state has had to import up to 66 million pesos worth of corn, representing 10.4% of the total, and 65 million pesos worth of wheat, or 10.3% of the total. Another important import item is beans, of which 30.5 million pesos, or 5% of the total, has been imported. The size of the agricultural imports demonstrates the existence of a crisis affecting likewise the peasant, capitalist and reformed sectors of agriculture . . . the progressive deterioration of our agriculture is felt most keenly by the peasantry, which has simply not been given the wherewithal for full and viable employment.[12]

The same author then cites a recent report by the International Fund for Agricultural Development (IFAD), which points to the severe agricultural crisis that has escalated since the early 1970s, and states that: "The agrarian reform has not acquired sufficient rhythm to neutralise the fragmentation of farms and migration to urban areas, nor did remaining policies prove vigorous enough to alter the situation of the poorest rural sectors."

There is no need to cite further statistics. The general trends should be clear enough from this rudimentary analysis. Agrarian policies involve more than land distribution, and production and productivity levels *per se*. Fiscal policies, agricultural subsidies and marketing arrangements are of equal importance. The Balaguer government essentially gave concessionary treatment to cattle farmers and other commercial farmers who required substantial imports to get their enterprises under way. At the same time, it subsidised food purchases for poor urban consumers, through the state organisation INESPRE. But such subsidies were only viable for as long as the state could afford the cheap food imports for subsequent distribution. In a later chapter we shall see how the sudden elimination of these subsidies, at a time of acute financial crisis in the 1980s, sparked off the food riots in April 1984 which left up to a hundred people dead throughout the country. But such a situation arose in the first place precisely because successive governments over the last two decades had ignored the needs of the subsistence peasantry, the producers of staple food crops and the hedge against food shortages, and put all their financial eggs in the agro–export basket. It is now time to turn to the sugar sector, which is the main — if not the only — obstacle to an agrarian strategy based on the principles of self-sufficiency.

The Politics of Sugar

After Trujillo, no new sugar *ingenios* were constructed. *Ingenios* have changed hands, the most notable transactions being the purchase of the huge Romana complex in the east of the country by the multinational Gulf and Western in 1967, and its recent sale to a Cuban American consortium in 1984. The twelve *ingenios* once owned by Trujillo were expropriated by the state in 1961. Between 1963 and 1966 they were administered by the *Corporación Azucarera Dominicana* (CAD). After 1966 a new state body, the State Sugar Council (CEA) took over CAD's functions, and continues to administer the state-owned *ingenios* to the present day. A massive and notoriously inefficient organisation, it acts virtually as a state within a state, responsible for all recruitment and labour as well as most technical aspects of the Dominican Republic's sugar policies.

Thus the sugar industry today consists of three main sectors, in terms of formal ownership. First come the twelve *ingenios* under CEA administration and control. The largest is the massive Central Río Haina to the north of Santo Domingo, divided into several separate complexes comprising small towns of their own, with a total capacity of over two million tonnes. Then the vast Central Barahona in the south-eastern town of Barahona, near the Haitian border, again covering huge areas with its scattered *bateyes*, and with a total capacity in excess of a million tonnes. On the outskirts of Santo Domingo are the *ingenios* of Boca Chica and Ozama, with a capacity of approximately three-quarters of a million tonnes each. In the eastern regions — the area of the greatest militancy by the sugar worker organisations — lie the large Ingenio Consuelo, and the three smaller mills of Porvenir, Quisqueya and Santa Fe. To the west of Santo Domingo is the Ingenio Catarey. Towards the north of the country are the dilapidated — and currently most threatened — *ingenios* of Montellanos, Amistad and Esperanza. The twelve *ingenios* fall under the general management of the State Sugar Board, composed of leading government officials including the Ministers of Finance and Agriculture, the Governor of the Central Bank and the Executive Director of the Dominican Sugar Institute, as well as representatives of the *colonos* and of worker organisations. In addition, each state plantation has a separate executive committee, including a workers' representative.

In the private sector, there is the vast Romana enterprise with its 126 separate *bateyes* stretching over hundreds of square miles, which forms part of a huge agro–industrial complex including livestock production, the manufacture of by-products derived from sugar cane, and other extensive interests in the tourist industry. Then there are the three *ingenios* (Angelina, Caei and Cristóbal Colón) owned by the Vicini group of Dominican nationality. Moreover, there are the several thousand *colonos* who grow approximately one-quarter of all Dominican cane, selling it to the above-mentioned *ingenios*.

As will be seen below, a considerable number of new lands have been turned over to sugar production since the end of the Trujillo era, in particular, lands worked by the *colonos*. Though this must surely have led to an increase in the total sugar crop, exports have not grown. In 1960, 994,248 tonnes of sugar were exported, along with 366,456 tonnes of molasses. By 1979 the respective figures were 992,370 tonnes of sugar and 257,236 tonnes of molasses.[13]

For the past 25 years, the Dominican sugar industry has never been far from crisis. With the permanent instability of world pricing structures, and the ever-growing competition for markets at a time of declining consumption in the most developed countries, there have been periods of high profits but also many lean periods in which the market price has not met production costs. Over the past few years the crisis has reached its gravest proportions, apparently compounded by reports that the major consumer of Dominican sugar today — the United States — is now developing artificial sweeteners and sugar substitutes which in theory could enable it to eliminate sugar imports by the year 1990. In the Dominican Republic, as in all Caribbean producer countries which have been afflicted by plummeting prices, there is sporadic talk of diversifying out of sugar altogether.

For the Dominican Republic, this is nothing new. As long ago as 1962, according to the then US Ambassador to Santo Domingo, the Kennedy administration was attempting to tie new premiums and quotas for the Dominican crop to pledges by the Dominican government that the country would eventually diversify away from sugar.[14] It must be remembered that at this time the Dominican Republic enjoyed few of the benefits of the privileged US market. Ousted from this market by the world's two major sugar producers of this period, Cuba and the Philippines, it was the only large producer not to benefit from such preferential arrangements. Though it sold most of its crop at this time to the United Kingdom and Canada, it was also excluded from the benefits of the British Commonwealth. A Commonwealth Sugar Agreement (CSA) was drawn up in 1951, designating the UK and Canada as preferential markets for all Commonwealth countries which were given access at reduced rates of duty, and in return agreed to limit their exports. The CSA remained in force until the UK's entry into the European Economic Community, when it was replaced by a sugar protocol attached to the Lomé Agreement of 1975. The Lomé Agreement in turn provided for preferential access to EEC markets for the 13 African, Caribbean and Pacific signatories (which did not include any of the Latin American countries falling traditionally within the US sphere of influence).

Agreements similar in effect were concluded by the USSR with countries in its COMECON bloc. Though the Cubans lost access to the US market after 1961, the Cuban crop eventually found a ready outlet in the COMECON countries. After a disastrous experiment in rapid industrialisation and diversification away from sugar in the early 1960s, Cuba made a concerted effort to increase its production over the next decade. Its landmark of the "ten million tonne *zafra*" for 1970 was to be one of Cuba's most publicised, and yet most thwarted, economic goals.

The United States embargo on all Cuban products was perhaps the single most important factor that changed the face of Latin American agriculture in the decade after that. Favoured client states in the US backyard — Guatemala, Colombia and Nicaragua among others, apart from the Dominican Republic — now fought hard to get a larger share of the US market, and a sizeable chunk of the former Cuban sugar quota in the United States. For politicians and lobbyists in the US Congress, sugar became an important political instrument.

The political toings and froings after 1961 have been described in detail by John Bartlow Martin, US Ambassador to Santo Domingo at this time, and thus a well-placed witness of events.[15] In Washington itself, according to Martin, sugar policies were a bone of contention between Kennedy administration officials who wanted ideally to be rid of the country quotas for sugar, some Senators and Congressmen who wanted to retain the country quotas but limit their size, and other politicians and lobbyists who were in the pockets or pay of favoured governments or dictators. In the midst of this wrangling and lobbying, it was difficult for a country like the Dominican Republic to know exactly where it stood. For the first three months of 1962 the Dominicans received a generous quota which led them to believe they could sell as much as 900,000 tonnes at premium prices within the US market for the year as a whole. As total production for export was then in the region of one million tonnes, it was the best possible deal. Then the rot began to set in. The US Congress's Agricultural Committee, after rejecting a world quota bill suggested by the Kennedy administration, came out with its own projected bill giving the Dominican Republic a basic annual quota of only 200,000 tonnes, plus 150,000 tonnes of the former Cuban quota. Ambassador Martin himself was besieged by high-ranking Dominican government officials, who claimed that they would "have to close the sugar mills" and were "losing the fight against Communism" as the economy went to rack and ruin. Amid rumours of an impending military coup, Martin took up the Dominican case directly with Washington and lobbied for more favourable treatment.

When the US Sugar Amendments of 1962 were finally enacted, the Dominican Republic nevertheless ended up with a total quota of 319,000 tonnes. It was less than hoped for, but still more than the amount granted to any other Latin American country. Worldwide, only the Philippines received more. In the years after that the Dominican quota continued to rise, notably during the twelve-year rule of Dr Joaquín Balaguer, who received particularly favourable treatment from the United States (until the Carter administration persuaded him to accept electoral defeat in 1978) and who in turn was equally favourable to US commercial and political interests within the Dominican Republic. By the late 1960s the Dominican quota within the US was nearly 600,000 tonnes; in 1971 an amendment to the Sugar Act increased the Dominican share of the US market to 635,000 tonnes; and when the preferential US Sugar Act was terminated for some years in 1974 the Dominican quota had reached its highest ever level of 746,000 tonnes.[16]

In 1974, the repeal of the US Sugar Act spelled a potential new crisis for the Dominican sugar industry. In the long run, the sudden severance of a secure and privileged outlet was likely to have adverse, even catastrophic, consequences. At first, the effects were not felt at all, for the simple reason that the United States decision to end its preferential treatment coincided with an unprecedented rise in the price of sugar on the open world market. In 1974 there were unexpected setbacks in world production, above all in Western Europe, as a result of severe drought, and a sudden fall in global stocks. On top of this, the ending of the

Commonwealth Sugar Agreement in the same year fuelled speculation and a constant upsurge in prices. The world sugar price was 11.85 US cents per pound in December 1973, then soared throughout 1974 until it reached an unprecedented peak of 56.14 cents per pound by November of that year. In the following year, prices crept gradually down until they were under 14 cents per pound by December 1975 (though still several times higher than in the latest sugar crash of the mid 1980s). It was also in this year that the EEC enacted its Lomé Agreement, granting preferential treatment to some sugar-producing countries of Africa, the Caribbean and the Pacific.

During the days of the safe sugar quota, there had been an enormous temptation for landowners to turn their idle lands over to sugar, and needless to say the temptation to do so increased when the prices looked rosy on the world market. President Balaguer is reputed to have turned a blind eye to graft and corruption among his higher military officers, in order to keep them quiescent and ward off the ever-present dangers of a military coup. As one academic writer has commented:

> Senior officers enjoyed considerable success as farmers and businessmen, and their corruption was well known and commonly discussed. By the end of the Balaguer regime, high-ranking military men, with few exceptions, possessed important commercial interests and had invested in all economic sectors. . . . Officers were involved in enterprises of all kinds: large sugar plantations, hotel and casino ownership. . . . Most of Balaguer's generals were able to become multimillionaires through enterprises financed with government resources and through outright graft. More rich middle-grade officers were found by the end of the Balaguer era than rich generals under Trujillo.[17]

There was also said to be widespread corruption within the State Sugar Board (CEA). The Dominican Republic had been an inefficient sugar producer during the Trujillo era, and production costs were certainly no less after nationalisation. They most probably increased, as jobs were created on the state *ingenios* as political pay-offs. Thus when world prices began to fall again after the boom of the mid 1970s, CEA fell upon crisis after crisis, from which it has never recovered. By 1977, CEA's production costs were estimated at 10.3 cents per pound, while the price its sugar fetched on export markets averaged only 9.4 cents. At the end of that harvest year the state industry registered a deficit of US$26.8 million — then its worst ever trading loss though the situation has deteriorated far more in the 1980s.[18]

At this time, the Dominican Republic again felt compelled to seek alternative markets; but the crisis was compounded by the difficulties it had in securing an adequate export quota under the terms of a new International Sugar Agreement. The new international agreement was concluded in 1977, after protracted wrangling among the 24 major producer countries, and a special world conference held under the auspices of the United Nations Conference on Trade and Development (UNCTAD) in Geneva. The new ISA was essentially a price support mechanism, designed to stabilise the world price at between 11 and 21 cents per pound. The Dominican Republic had been a member of the International Sugar Organisation since its inception in 1953, and had ratified the earlier ISAs of 1953 and 1968. However, the USA was not a ratifying country at that time, and its preferential quota system had made the earlier ISAs of less significance to the Dominican Republic itself. In 1977 and 1978, however, the Dominicans were the most bitter critics of the new agreement. Originally allocated only 935,000 tons for exports, they protested that this was far less than half the quota allocated to neighbouring Cuba, which only produced twice as much sugar for the free world market. The Dominican quota was only 70 per cent of its average production for recent years, and would have led to annual surpluses well in excess of domestic consumption and the country's storage facilities.

The private sector was shielded from the harsher effects of this crisis period, through Gulf and Western's extensive contacts with refineries and trading houses within the United States, as well as its familiarity with the elaborate and uncertain world of the New York stock exchange. Under long-term contracts, the Central Romana arranged to deliver one million tonnes to US refineries between 1977 and 1980, and under a separate contract pledged between 75,000 and 100,000 tonnes per year to Colonial Sugar between 1976 and 1981.[19] This would account for the whole of the Central Romana's average production during this period. Moreover Gulf and Western realised considerable profits through its speculation with CEA's sugar on the New York stock exchange during the boom years of 1975 and 1976, in a move which was reportedly kept secret from the Dominican government itself, which later soured relations between Gulf and the Dominican government, and which caused a public scandal when the facts were revealed by the US Securities and Exchange Commission in 1979.

After the repeal of the US Sugar Act in 1974, the bulk of Dominican sugar had been sold through US trading houses. Sales could be made either at a fixed price, at the time when the contract was drawn up, or on the average of the "spot" price between the time of contract and the moment of delivery. In futures trading, millions can be made or lost by choosing the right moment and the most opportune form of sale, but producer governments tend not to be active members of the most active sugar trading markets in London and New York. Private companies such as Gulf and Western reap much of their profits through astute speculation. According to the Securities and Exchange Commission's 1979 report, Gulf and Western's president, Charles Bluhdorn, struck a verbal deal with Dominican officials to speculate with Dominican sugar on the futures market. The agreement was said to be that the Dominican government should receive 60 per cent of any profits, corresponding to the approximate amount of state sugar involved. Selling dear when the price was at its peak, and purchasing cheap when it had begun to fall, Bluhdorn realised an immense profit of US$64,534,126. In accordance with the verbal agreement, $38,721,000 of this amount should have gone to the Dominican government. Only half of it was apparently mentioned to the Dominicans, but even this reduced amount was not at first paid over to them. It took months of angry negotiations in 1979, including a threat by the new Dominican President Antonio Guzmán to sue Gulf and Western, before an out-of-court settlement was reached. Gulf never paid over the money, but pledged to spend an equivalent amount in infrastructural projects "of social value to the country". The use to which some of these funds were eventually put — including an idiosyncratic facsimile of an Italian village in the luxurious tourist belt near the Central Romana, not to mention a Miss

Universe contest — did not help improve Gulf's image in the five years before it sold off all its Dominican holdings.[20]

Even without such windfall gains, the Dominican CEA did reap substantial profits during the brief boom period of the mid 1970s. This money should have been utilised for both social and economic improvements within the sugar industry. In 1975 a special legislative decree was enacted, stipulating that sugar companies should establish a special fund for modernisation of the industry and improvement of labour conditions. This law, Decree No. 602 of February 1975, contained the sound provisions that the funds should be spent on "works that lead to the improvement of living standards of workers in the sugar industry, and investments which lead to greater productivity levels, as a precaution against an eventual decline in the world price of sugar".[21] Doubtless a sensible precaution, but one wonders where the funds went. Two years later the government saw fit to freeze wages on all twelve of the state *ingenios* when the price had begun to fall and there was nothing left in its coffers to make the customary incentive payments.

When President Antonio Guzmán, of the centrist Dominican Revolutionary Party (PRD), took office in August 1978, there were many promises that things would change on the *ingenios*. There were government pledges that CEA would no longer be used "to fund political campaigns, and to enrich officials and the military", but the severe decapitalisation of the sugar industry was the most urgent issue that the new government had to tackle. In May 1979, CEA claimed to have lost over $68 million over the past two harvests. An emergency project was submitted to the World Bank, for a $35 million loan offset by an equivalent Dominican contribution to finance modernisation of the *ingenios* and transport facilities; but the Dominican Congress questioned the wisdom of a multimillion-dollar investment at a time of spiralling national debt, when the returns were all too dubious. Later in 1979, a new upsurge in the world market price for sugar appeared to provide a breathing space. It rose from 11 cents per pound in October to 15 cents in December, then rose rapidly in the first months of 1980, reaching almost 32 cents by August. For the Dominican Republic, ironically, the price advantages were wiped out by a natural disaster, when the savage Hurricane David struck the island in August 1979. Exports fell from over a million tonnes in 1979, to 792,734 in 1980, and 864,034 in 1981.[22] Having complained bitterly about its low export quota in 1977, and received emergency supplements over the next two years, the Dominican Republic now found itself unable to match its original world quota figures.

As Dominican sugar production gradually recovered after the hurricane, world prices once again plummeted, to reach a new trough of under 6 cents per pound by autumn 1982, before falling to approximately 3 cents per pound by 1985. To make matters worse for the traditional Third World producers, the US government came under strong pressure from its domestic beet and cane sugar producers to provide new subsidies for domestic producers and impose tariff barriers on all imports in order to prevent a flood of cheap foreign sugar from altogether destroying the North American industry. By this time world sugar production — if compared with overall consumption demands — was reaching almost insane proportions. During the entire decade of the 1970s, global production increased by an estimated 22 per cent. Much of the growth took place in Western Europe, as the result of the expansionary beet production strategy adopted during the enlargement of the European Economic Community. With generous subsidies provided to European producers under the terms of the EEC's Common Agricultural Policy (CAP), European production tripled in the five years between 1975 and 1980. By 1979, instead of remaining a major world importer, Europe accounted for just under 18 per cent of worldwide sugar *exports*. While the European Community allows in approximately 1.3 million tonnes of cane sugar from favoured Third World countries under the terms of the present Lomé Agreement, to be purchased at the current preferential European price, it has also begun to compete with the traditional cane producers for exports to such countries as Algeria. Economically, this policy of subsidising sugar beet exports is costly to the European tax-payer; in human terms, this irrationally subsidised production has quite devastating effects on living standards in the more impoverished Third World producer countries.

Protectionism in Europe fuelled similar protectionist attitudes in the United States. Moreover, North American sugar consumption was now declining quite significantly, because of health concerns and new dietary habits, and because a series of sugar substitutes were now being developed as artificial sweeteners. During the 1970s, per capita consumption of non-sugar corn sweeteners rose from 19.3 lbs per head in 1970 to 37.2 lbs in 1979. The most significant increase was in high fructose corn syrup (HFCS), up from a niggardly 0.7 lbs per head in 1970 to no less than 15.4 lbs in 1979. In the meantime, consumption of refined sugar had decreased from 88 per cent of all sweeteners in 1960 to only 70 per cent in 1980. The Carter and Reagan administrations in turn took a series of measures which proved a slap in the face for the traditional overseas suppliers of the US market. Late in 1980 both a fee and tariffs were imposed on foreign sugar entering the US market. In 1981 draft bills were sent to the Senate and Congress, which would establish a minimum price of 19.6 cents per pound for domestic sugar crops between 1982 and 1985, and statutory tariff barriers against all sugar imports. As the London-based Latin American Commodities Report commented, the bill would have drastic consequences for Latin American sugar exporters:

> A necessary corollary to the loan programme would be the erection of rigid barriers against imports, either through quotas or high duties and fees. The effect on imports would be "horrendous", according to Nick Kominus, head of the US Cane Sugar Refiners Association; by 1985 imports from Latin America could be cut by more than fifty per cent. Last year Latin American exports to the US totalled 2.75 million tonnes and accounted for 72% of all US imports.[23]

The Dominican Republic was to be hit particularly hard by the new measures. Under a generalised system of preferences, some of the smaller Latin American sugar producers were to be liable to tariff exemption, but not the Dominican Republic which then had the largest share of the US market. The Dominicans, together with other Latin American republics, now strove for a return to the old country quota system, without which they could see no way to survive the new discriminatory treatment. In October 1981, in his meetings with US Vice-President George Bush, President Guzmán urged the US to set an annual import quota for the Dominican Republic at a price in line with that paid to domestic US sugar producers.

Eventually, this is what occurred. In May 1982 the United States again opted out of the free world market system, and reintroduced its country quotas. It began with quarterly quotas, with the intention of switching to annual quotas as of October 1982. The lobbying now began in earnest once again, as in the 1960s. The Dominicans had good reason to be optimistic. The US, now caught up in bloody civil wars in its Central American backyard, looked favourably upon the moderate pro-US democracy since the PRD had won free and fair elections in 1978. In May 1982 a moderate lawyer and businessman, Dr Salvador Jorge Blanco, won the latest presidential elections in the Dominican Republic, also on a PRD ticket. While the PRD continued to oversee a period of political liberalisation, there was no talk of nationalisation, or of any social and economic transformations which might be perceived as damaging to US interests. It was also at this time that Washington launched its Caribbean Basin Initiative (CBI) with a fanfare of publicity. Though its emphasis was on financial assistance to the private sector, to fit in with the ideology of the Reagan administration, there were clauses on trade benefits and tariff concessions. It was hoped that the Dominican Republic would now benefit like some of the small Central American republics from the US generalised system of preferences, enabling its sugar to enter the US market duty free. In his first visit to Washington in July 1982, President-elect Jorge Blanco pleaded with the Reagan administration to raise the current restrictive amounts of the Dominican sugar quota. In the same month, CEA announced gloomily that it expected to make losses of between $50 and $60 million for the current year, and that it had presented plans for the closure of a full third of its *ingenios* (namely, Amistad, Catarey, Esperanza and Montellanos).

Nevertheless, when the US announced its annual sugar quotas for 1983 at the beginning of October, they were far lower than expected. Total sugar imports for the next fiscal year would be only 2.8 million tonnes. The fee charged on raw sugar was to be reduced to zero in the short run, but the tariffs were to be retained. The Dominican quota was the highest for Latin America — as expected — but it was still only 447,040 tonnes, or less than half the amount that had been sold in the USA a few years previously under the free market system.

In these bleak circumstances, it seemed that countries like the Dominican Republic, which had pinned their hopes on the sugar industry for the past hundred years, would have to face the dismal facts squarely. Diversification is difficult and costly, but in the long run there could be no alternative. As the *Far Eastern Economic Review* warned in its cover story of November 1982,

> The writing is on the wall for Third World sugar producers: brisk export growth is a thing of the past, and prices may recover substantially only at the cost of sharp production cutbacks in tropical growing areas. Smart developing countries should start planning now to get out of this declining industry by 1990.[24]

In fact, the Jorge Blanco government did all it could to seek diversification away from sugar, but mainly by turning over to new export crops. In the Dominican Republic exports of sugar and sugar products declined from 47 to 36 per cent of total merchandise exports between 1981 and 1984, and it is predicted that this figure will fall further to under 25 per cent before 1990. In the meantime, new vegetable and fruit crops are beginning to replace sugar, now that exporters are taking advantage of the duty-free entry provided under the Caribbean Basin Initiative. Official statistics show that 21 new agro–industrial projects got under way in 1985, as against 13 in 1984 and none whatsoever in 1983. In the two years between September 1983 and 1985 49 new agro–industries were set up in the Dominican Republic, 21 of them as joint ventures between Dominican and foreign capital. It is estimated that they could earn up to US$70 million for the Dominican Republic by 1987 — about the same amount that is lost annually by the Dominican sugar industry.

For the immediate future, US policies will dictate the rapidity with which the sugar industries of the Dominican Republic and other Caribbean countries decline. Somewhat ironically the Reagan administration, having presided over measures that brought Caribbean sugar to the brink of collapse, was reported to be considering a last-ditch policy change that might raise hopes once again. In 1985, total Caribbean exports to the United States fell by no less than 23 per cent. At the same time, a new Farm Security Act in the US mandated a further 32 per cent cut in imported sugar during the 1986/87 cycle. At his meeting with eight Caribbean heads of state in February 1986, President Reagan was left in no doubt that an improved market for sugar was the number one point on the Caribbean agenda. At the time of writing, the Reagan administration was reportedly studying a proposal for an increase in the US sugar import quota for Caribbean states in return for increased imports of surplus US agricultural produce. However, as one leading magazine has reported, "What form the final sugar package will take is still guesswork. The US Department of Agriculture has been given the apparently impossible task of increasing imports of sugar from the Caribbean while preserving protection for US sugar producers as mandated by Congress."[25]

For the Dominican Republic, the protectionist whims of the US Congress are certainly no joke. In September 1985 its US quota was slashed overnight by a staggering 43.6 per cent. How could any Third World country cope with such circumstances?

Notes

1. Ian Bell, *The Dominican Republic* (Westview Press, Boulder, Colo., 1981), p. 282.

2. Quoted in Solon Barraclough, *Agrarian Reform Programmes for the Dominican Republic*, Consultancy report prepared for the United States Agency for International Development (USAID), April 1970.

3. Ian Bell, op. cit., p. 285.

4. For a good summary on changing land use during this period, see in particular Argelia Tejada y Anguela, "Estado y Desarrollo Capitalista de la Agricultura Dominicana, 1966–1978", *Estudios Dominicanos*, Year 1, No. 2, May–August 1984, pp. 9–67.

5. See Carlos Doré y Cabral, *Problemas de la Estructura Agraria Dominicana* (Ediciones Taller, Santo Domingo, 1979).

6. Ibid. See also *Ley de Registro de Tierras con sus Modificaciones* (Publicaciones America S.A., Santo Domingo, 1978).

7. Solon Barraclough and Peter Marchetti, "Agrarian Transformation and Food Security in the Caribbean Basin" (unpublished document submitted at a workshop on "Alternative Policy for Central America and the Caribbean", Institute of Social Studies, The Hague, Netherlands, June 1983).

8. Guillermo Bendezú Alvarado, "La Realidad Campesina y sus Posibilidades de Desarrollo" (conference paper, Santo Domingo, March 1982).

9. These official statistics are cited in several articles published by the special edition of *Estudios Dominicanos* on the national agrarian problem in the Dominican Republic (Year 1, No. 2, May–August 1984).

10. Bell, op. cit., p. 295.

11. From Frank Oleo, "Crisis Agraria", *Estudios Dominicanos*, Year 1, No. 2, May–August 1984, pp. 151–64.

12. Ibid., p. 160.

13. *La Industria Azucarera y el Desarrollo Dominicano* (Universidad Central del Este, San Pedro Macoris, Dominican Republic, 1980), p. 76.

14. See Barraclough, op. cit.

15. John Bartlow Martin, *Overtaken by Events: The Dominican Crisis from the Fall of Trujillo to the Civil War* (Doubleday and Co., New York, 1966), passim.

16. Lloyd Chilvers and Robin Foster, "The International Sugar Market: Prospects for the 1980s", Economist Intelligence Unit special report, No. 106, London, September 1981, p. 22.

17. G. Pope Atkins, *Arms and Politics in the Dominican Republic* (Westview Special Studies on Latin America and the Caribbean, Boulder, Colo., 1981), p. 29.

18. Bell, op. cit., p. 311.

19. Chilvers and Foster, op. cit., p. 24.

20. Henry Frundt, *Objecciones de Accionistas Cristianos contra la Gulf and Western en la República Dominicana* (Publicaciones Estudios Sociales, Santo Domingo, 1980), p. 130–2.

21. FENAZUCAR press release, April 1982.

22. International Sugar Organisation, *Sugar Yearbook* (1980).

23. Latin America Commodities Report, *Latin America Newsletters*, London, Report 81–13, 3 July 1981.

24. *Far Eastern Economic Review*, 5 November 1982.

25. *Latin America Monitor*, London, Vol. 3, No. 2, March 1986.

4 The Haitian Débâcle: From Ancient to Modern Slavery

"It is modern Haiti which has garnered the most terrible harvest of the Atlantic slave trade."
(*The Slave Trade*, by Oliver Ransford[1])

While plantation society prospered in the Dominican Republic in the late 19th century, in Haiti it collapsed altogether. But the nation of prosperous smallholders — the dream of such early liberators as Aléxandre Pétion — never emerged. Long before the Duvalier regimes made Haiti a byword for graft and corruption in the second half of the 20th century, it had become a uniquely exploitative state. Elsewhere in Latin America, an aristocratic Creole élite grabbed the land, formed large plantations, and turned the traditional peasantry into peons. In Haiti the élite left the peasants on the land, taxed their produce and lived off the proceeds. Over 150 years ago Haiti's liberated slaves invaded the western part of the island as proud conquerers. Today, driven by desperation, they flood into the Dominican Republic as near slaves.

This chapter asks how such a situation has come about. What were the reasons for the Haitian collapse? How did the first free republic in the Americas evolve into such a catastrophic society by the present day?

The 19th Century

We saw earlier that the short-term effect of Haiti's independence struggle, after the massacre of virtually every white planter in Saint-Domingue, was the complete disruption of the former colonial plantation system, followed by the emergence of a new smallholder society, virtually cut off from the outside world. And when the new republic did eventually secure recognition as an independent nation-state, it had to pay for it dearly. In 1825 France recognised Haiti, but at the cost of a crippling indemnity of 150 million French francs to cover lost and confiscated assets. There was only one way to service the debt. A 30-million-franc loan was floated in France to service the first instalment, and the Haitian economy was saddled with the burden of this unpayable debt for most of the century. In 1838, the outstanding 120 million francs was halved to 60 million, to be paid off over the next 30 years. But by the 1870s an estimated 20 per cent of government revenues were still tied to the service of the original debt, and in some years as much as 60 per cent of total customs revenues were taken up with the debt service.[2]

On top of the debt burden, the civil wars and the 20-year occupation of the western part of Hispaniola called for a large standing army. Soldiers were rewarded with land grants at the end of campaigns, but the army still had to be maintained in the meantime. Around 1850, military expenditure absorbed over 50 per cent of the national budget. The picture throughout the 19th century is of an over-militarised, unproductive and debt-ridden society which gradually relapsed into economic and political chaos. And the brunt of the debt service obligations was then borne by the peasant economy. Government revenue was derived almost exclusively from the taxation of peasant produce, primarily the coffee cultivated on small plots, which has provided the bulk of agricultural exports from then until the present day. Political power was shared and competed for by the mulatto and black "aristocracy" who enjoyed no economic base of their own apart from their taxation of the small farmer and — more importantly — their control of the export trade.

The fragmentation of agricultural land occurred only gradually. Of the early independence leaders, first Toussaint L'Ouverture and Dessalines, then Henry Christophe in the north of the country during the civil wars against Aléxandre Pétion's south, had endeavoured to keep the former plantation system intact. While technically abolishing black slavery, they legislated for forcible tied labour on the nationalised plantations. Dessalines only leased out the government land. Henry Christophe began to hand out land titles to his more privileged supporters, selling or granting land to them instead of merely leasing out the government land. In the south, Pétion pushed through his first land reforms aimed at the creation of a free peasantry, but nevertheless prohibited land sales in parcels of less than 15 acres.[3] There was nothing too radical about Pétion's reforms, which had markedly political ends and were essentially tailored to the need for support against the feudal regime of Henry Christophe in the north. As historian James Leyburn observed,

> Those who would read into Pétion's democratisation of land tenure the liberal convictions of a far-sighted statesman must ignore the evidence of his earliest land acts. For two or three years nothing was so apparent as that Pétion wished to please his friends, the mulatto aristocrats. He not only had the Senate restore to their former owners all lands of which Dessalines had despoiled them, but he also agreed to a law authorising a cash payment up to the full value of crops planted and then lost during the last year of the Emperor's rule.[4]

But Pétion paved the way for a more sweeping distribution of the former nationalised lands. During the last ten years of his rule, he distributed some 100,000 acres to approximately 10,000 beneficiaries — far more than a narrow clique of soldiers within his army. More important than the amounts themselves, he had paved the way for an agrarian structure free of feudal ties, and the precedent was eventually to have far-reaching consequences. Many of the large private estates now began to be leased to the former slaves under a variety of crop-sharing arrangements, while their legal owners remained in the towns.

Following the reunification of Haiti after Pétion's death, a new president, Jean-Pierre Boyer, made the last concerted attempt to turn back the clock and revive the plantation system. Once again, this called for highly coercive measures to drag the now free peasants back to the rigours of plantation life. An authoritarian *Code Rural* was enacted in 1826, which basically aimed to restore the conditions of serfdom and slavery. By law, it bound every Haitian except for officials, aristocrats and soldiers to the former plantations. There were provisions for the creation of a rural police force, to act as inspectors of the plantations and their workers. Soldiers were to be assigned to each plantation, receiving their living from it in return for the preservation of order and the punishment of vagrancy acts. Soldiers were to be responsible "not to any civil authority but only to their military superiors".

Such coercive measures were by then incapable of real enforcement. To judge from the few production figures available, there was virtually no sugar being produced anyway. After the years of revolution, the reaction against slavery was too strong to contain. Moreover, while much of the plantation land had been turned over to subsistence crops, there was also ample alternative land on which to settle, away from the clutches of the police and the army. The stern measures of the *Code Rural* were most probably prompted by the government's need for foreign exchange, to service a loan agreement finalised with France the previous year; but policies aimed at a return to plantation life were doomed to failure.

Coffee was to prove the only export crop to ride this early storm. It could be grown alongside subsistence crops on small plots. Whereas it had been grown on large plantations during the colonial era — the French colony of Saint-Domingue had once provided as much as 60 per cent of world coffee[5] — this did not have to be the case. Coffee exports fell sharply in the civil strife at the turn of the century, but revived quite rapidly after that. Overall production had been 68 million lbs in 1791, down to 20 million by 1818, then up again to 36 million by 1825 and over 43 million lbs by 1839. By contrast, sugar production was down from 163 million lbs in 1791 to an officially registered 2,020 lbs in 1825; indigo from 930,000 lbs in 1791 to nil in 1825: and cotton from over six million lbs in 1791 to under one million in 1825.[6]

Bowing to economic and social realities, the surviving mulatto landowner class also began to favour small-scale coffee production under share tenancy arrangements. With wage or tied labour in short supply, the well-tended plantations of the French colonial era had virtually ceased to exist. As with sugar, the plantations had generally been broken up into small parcels, leased out to peasant families. Generally speaking, there was no wage labour as such. In the words of one author, "In any season, from a quarter to a half of the gross receipts of the estates was to go to the workers, the exact proportion in any year to be determined by the government."[7] The percentage received by the workers appears to have varied on the smaller private plantations, depending on whether or not food was provided by the landowner. James Leyburn describes two common arrangements. Under one, the labourers worked in return for half of the produce of the estate, raising their own subsistence food in gardens provided by the landowner. Under the other, they worked for a quarter of the total produce, the proprietor guaranteeing to look after their food needs.

In time, even the smaller private plantations were broken up, as the crop-sharing system gave way to widespread squatting. Plantation land is useless without a guaranteed labour supply, and the lack of labour and ready markets provoked a sharp decline in land values. As their value sank, it became more and more pointless to prevent squatting, and smaller and smaller land parcels became the norm. The system of land ownership in itself became highly ambiguous. Under the civil legislation of the 1820s, legal title to the land could be acquired by 20 years' uninterrupted occupancy, or an even shorter time, when the occupant could prove his legal title. But land titles were not registered, and customary ownership through occupancy became the norm.

In the 1860s the legal registration of land titles was attempted unsuccessfully by President Fabre Geffrard who was by then reconciled to the predominance of small farm ownership, and actually legislated against the furtherance of larger land-holdings. His bill stipulated that henceforth state lands were not to be sold in parcels larger than five *carreaux*. Government lands could be alienated only through sales and grants, and no one was to squat on government property without legal rights. President Geffrard's government did its utmost to induce existing squatters to register formal claims to their land. However, as Mats Lundahl has observed, "The suspiciousness of the peasantry against legal documents and government officials turned this effort into a complete failure. The peasants continued to squat on government lands or abandoned estates, and no further organised measures were taken to prevent them."[8]

Towards the end of the 19th century, in 1883, President Lysius Salomon made a renewed effort to regulate land tenure systems, and also to encourage the cultivation of new cash crops. Peasants willing to cultivate export crops were to receive between five and eight *carreaux* of government land for a limited period of up to five years, and could then receive permanent title if up to three-quarters of the lands were adequately cultivated. No financial assistance was provided by the state to encourage such endeavours, and the move was a demonstrable failure for reasons not hard to guess. The specified commercial crops were mainly sugar, coffee, cotton, cocoa and tobacco. Most of these crops require a substantial initial investment, or take years to mature before any dividends are earned. Without financial backing from the state, the project proved a non-starter. There were some 1,700 applications in the first two years after 1883, and then they ceased altogether.

By the turn of the century almost all cultivation of coffee, the major export crop, was by small peasants with 5 hectares of land or less. It is interesting to draw some comparisons between the Haitian agrarian structure at this juncture and that of the remaining countries in Central America and the Spanish Caribbean. In the latter half of the 19th century the agrarian economies of the entire region were integrated more heavily within the world market. Almost everywhere there was a pronounced rise in commercial farming for export, most particularly of coffee, sugar and bananas; and a similar pattern of land accumulation by a small group of national and foreign capitalists. As has already been seen, it was at this time that the modern sugar *ingenios* of Cuba and the Dominican Republic began their expansion. Further afield, in El Salvador and Guatemala, massive coffee plantations ended up in a few hands, at the expense of the indigenous peasantry who were dispossessed summarily of their communal lands. Such land grabbing provided the basis for the formation of new national oligarchies, such as El Salvador's notorious "fourteen families".

In Haiti, this never occurred. The larger mulatto and smaller black élite showed little interest in landownership *per se*. As in all of Latin America, there was factional infighting for the spoils of political office among sectors of the local élite, in Haiti often divided along racial lines. Between 1843 and the eve of the United States occupation of the country in 1915, there were 22 different presidents and 14 palace coups. The frequent political changes inevitably affected land distribution. As French author Paul Moral has argued in a classic study on the Haitian peasantry,[9] land distribution became more politically motivated after the mid-19th century. Nevertheless there was no significant land accumulation, even though coffee production increased by some 30 per cent between 1860 and 1890, at precisely that historical period when rising demand for coffee in the developed countries had created vast fortunes almost overnight. Yet there was a large army and sizeable state bureaucracy, and the upper echelons of Port-au-Prince society enjoyed a lavish lifestyle. There was no industry to speak of, and no tax on agricultural land. How were state revenues collected?

Though there was no tax on land itself, there was plenty on agricultural produce. The first independence leaders had gained revenue by slapping a tax on crops equal to one-quarter of all agricultural production. During the civil war in the south, Pétion abolished the quarter-crop tax there, but replaced it with a monetary levy on coffee exports. As early as 1811, coffee is reported to have provided the bulk of national revenue. As Mats Lundahl has demonstrated in his meticulous historical survey of Haitian public finance, "Public outlays have been concentrated on debt-service, army and police wages and salaries for the administration, while much of the revenue derives from taxes levied on products produced or consumed by the peasants."[10] When world coffee prices fell, the Haitian regimes became increasingly oppressive towards the peasantry. In the 1860s a government report conceded that only the taxes imposed on coffee enabled it to save its face internationally. And, as Paul Moral has laconically observed, the collection of the coffee crop became so important that revolutions took place only in the hot season between the harvests.[11] Thus the élite gained its income by taxing the poor peasant producer at source, with the backing of a military and police apparatus which kept the rural population in check, and then by controlling the export trade. It was a convenient system for them in a small and backward economy, and was the major reason why land tenure and land distribution did not evolve along the same lines as in neighbouring countries.

The US Occupation of Haiti, 1915–34

The bare facts of US expansionism in the Caribbean in the early 20th century, together with the economic and geopolitical reasons for it, have been looked at briefly in the preceding chapter. The US marines landed in Haiti in 1915, and remained for two decades until 1934. It was a far lengthier occupation than in the Dominican Republic, and in the long run had perhaps more definitive consequences. The pretext for invasion was much the same in the two instances. The US government was replacing France and other European countries as Haiti's foremost creditor, and had been attempting to negotiate a treaty whereby it should have direct authority for the collection of Haiti's customs revenue. A more immediate catalyst was the outbreak of new political violence, and the murder of the Haitian president, Guillaume Sam, by an angry nationalist crowd.

In Haiti the underlying aims of the US occupation in the economic field were predictably the same as in the Dominican Republic. To create favourable conditions for foreign investment, land had to be registered with private title, and turned into a commodity which could be bought and sold. The Constitution then in force, still reflecting the sentiments of the black slave rebellion, hardly reflected US interests. It read textually that, "No white person of any nation shall set foot in this country as master or proprietor, nor hereafter acquire any property." The new Constitution of 1918, passed over the heads of a powerless Haitian Congress, contained the decidedly different provision that, "The right to ownership of agrarian property is granted to foreigners resident in Haiti, and to associations formed by foreigners for the needs of residential, agricultural, commercial, industrial and educational purposes."

Attempts to revive plantation agriculture were part of the strategy. They met with very limited success. Agricultural modernisation under the American plan required a major road construction programme, and the "corvée" system of forced labour was once again brought to Haiti. Workers were roped together in chain-gangs to build the first modern highway from Port-au-Prince to the northern coastal town of Cap Haïtien. Paul Moral describes how the brutality of the US marines under this forced labour system — it was legally abolished in 1918, but remained widespread after that nevertheless — was the major factor sparking off a rural uprising that lasted well into the 1920s.[12]

There were two large agro–industrial initiatives. The United States-owned Haitian American Sugar Company (HASCO) acquired 7,000 acres of sugar-cane land near the capital, and commenced production in 1918. The United West Indies Corporation acquired a 16,000-acre plantation by the mid 1920s. And the Haitian American Development Corporation built up its large sisal-producing Plantation Dauphin towards the end of the decade. Altogether, ten US agricultural companies tried to set up operations between 1915 and 1930, but only HASCO and the Plantation Dauphin survived by the time the Americans left in 1934. Compared with events in Cuba and the Dominican Republic, it was "small fry".

Instead of investing much in Haiti itself, the US government and, above all, the private US companies saw Haiti as the ideal source of cheap labour for their burgeoning concerns elsewhere in the Caribbean. During the occupations, the American administration oversaw a new regional division of labour which has been the general pattern ever since. The flow of Haitian migrant labour was solicited actively from both Cuba and the Dominican Republic, with the Haitian cane cutters often paying their own way. For example, of over 11,000 Haitians who left for the Cuban sugar mills in 1923, 86 per cent are recorded as having paid their own passage.[13] And in the neighbouring Dominican Republic, Haitian cane cutters who left their country legally had to pay an emigration tax, the proceeds of which "were mainly used to liquidate the Haitian foreign debt which had been consolidated during the occupation into American hands".[14] As Paul Moral claims, the head tax on the seasonal emigration of Haitian cane cutters turned out to be the chief source of internal revenue for several years.[15] In addition, the larger private companies now arrived in Haiti to carry out their direct recruitment campaigns. For example, agents from the United Fruit Company and General Sugar came to Haiti in the mid 1920s, and induced some 20,000 Haitians to migrate to Cuba for seasonal work at a dollar a day.[16] The emigration gathered pace so rapidly that it was made illegal in 1928, but to little effect. Haiti was considered to be overpopulated anyway, and emigration to Cuba only slackened when the depression and falling sugar prices curbed the demand for imported cheap Haitian labour.

Though few of the foreign agro–industrial initiatives survived the US occupation, it nevertheless left its effects on land tenure patterns. The Union Nationaliste, the vocal political opposition, denounced the "brutal expulsion from their lands" of thousands of peasants in the north. Such allegations were substantiated by a delegation from the Women's International League for Peace and Freedom (WILPF) which visited Haiti in 1926. Its subsequent report, *Occupied Haiti*,[17] provided both a balanced account of contemporary conditions and a savage indictment of the occupation itself. As the authors stated, some Haitians tended to believe that the "nub of the whole American policy towards Haiti was the desire to open up Haitian land for foreign land speculation, and see in this its chief purposes and menace". They also criticised new legislation which increased the rental charges for state-owned land, observing that:

> A landless class, with all that this would mean in a country like Haiti, would seem to be the natural consequence of the investment of capital on large agricultural estates got together by buying out or otherwise dispossessing small owners and tenants, even if all purchases were quite voluntary and on fair terms — conditions by no means certain to be secured.

In the critical area of taxation, the WILPF delegation expressed some optimism. Noting that the tariff laws had weighed far more heavily on the peasantry than on the "well to do classes of the city", it observed that the US administration was planning to amend the existing system. One draft law aimed to increase the "duties upon such luxuries as perfume, and decrease both the import taxes upon necessities and the export taxes upon commodities which are raised by the peasantry". If such a law ever saw the light of day, it did not last long beyond the occupation.

With canny prescience, the WILPF delegation criticised the training given to the élite "Garde d'Haïti", the military organisation established by the US occupation forces with responsibility for law enforcement throughout the country. It speculated as to what the effect of such an élite force would be after a US withdrawal: "One possible result is self-maintenance in power of whomsoever has control of this force, subject only to the development of a situation where, like the Pretorian guard, the soldiers sell themselves to the highest bidder."

As Mats Lundahl has written, "After the occupation, the road to the presidency and to a large extent the spoils went via the Garde d'Haïti." The Americans certainly left behind them a more militarised and centrally controlled society. Some attempts were made to improve the efficiency of small farm production, through technical inputs and assistance. Agricultural extension services were provided for the first time, but modernisation brought few benefits to the traditional peasantry.

In the highly authoritarian society that Haiti had come to be, external agents were likely to have a policeman's heart under a technician's coat. Thus the first United Nations technical assistance mission had to recommend, 15 years after the Americans had left the country, that:

> Any connections between the functions of the rural police and the Ministry of Agriculture be definitely severed, and the agricultural extension agents be relieved of all responsibility other than that required by law of all citizens, for reporting infractions of police regulations by the rural inhabitants.[18]

Safe bureaucratic language, but the point is clear. It was a short step from this to the age of Papa Doc's Tontons Macoutes.

From the Occupation to Duvalier, 1934–57

Immediately after the occupation, the new government still pinned its agrarian strategy on measures aimed at the expansion of export crops. In 1934 President Vincent enacted new laws offering up to 5 hectares of state land to peasants pledging to plant half the land area with exportable produce, and in the following year the US-owned Standard Fruit Company was granted a monopoly over the export of bananas. Then during the Second World War, an expensive experiment in large-scale rubber production led to widespread peasant eviction, and ended in complete fiasco. When the US entered the war, and found its traditional rubber supply threatened by the Japanese occupation of much of South-East Asia, a Haitian–American joint venture by the name of SHADA received a US$5 million loan from the Export-Import Bank to start cultivation of an indigenous vine rubber. Mats Lundahl has described the disastrous outcome of the project:

> The company had obtained jurisdiction over more than 100,000 hectares from which a large number of peasants had been evicted, their homes, fields and fruit trees being destroyed in the process. The productive results were zero. In spite of heavy spending on the project (6.7 million dollars by 1945) no rubber was ever exported. The Haitian government had guaranteed the repayment of the Export–Import Bank loan, but in view of the negligible results of the project this term had to be prolonged until 1961 and actual payment continued even beyond this date.[19]

By the end of the Second World War the panorama of contemporary Haiti had taken shape. The 1949 report of the United Nations development mission describes a picture similar to that of the present day. At the apex of the social structure was the small élite, people of essentially European culture and outlook. At the other end of the scale was the impoverished mass of the peasantry, with a cash income of next to nothing, no access to state credit, and thus always at the mercy of the *spéculateur* (local moneylender) who charged some 25 per cent interest for short-term loans at the time of most critical scarcity before the harvest season. Agricultural taxation systems were described in the UN report as follows:

> On the national scale the export of agricultural products is heavily taxed as a

means of providing revenue for the general expenditures of government. Thus for example coffee, a major item of export, whose curve of production closely parallels the curve of general prosperity in Haiti, is subject to taxes which may total some 25 centimes against a purchase price to the peasant of about 60 centimes per pound. Because of the demands of other chapters of the national budget, little of this revenue returns as a benefit to the peasant producer of coffee, and the curve of production of coffee shows a persistent downward trend.[20]

The UN report highlighted the longstanding and continuing conflict between the subsistence requirements of the peasant sector on the one hand, and the perceived needs of the government and exporting sector "whose attention is directed primarily to the production of commercial crops which can, through exportation, provide Haiti with goods from abroad which are essential to the country's existence in the modern world". But the average peasant knew about as much of the modern world as he did in the isolationist days immediately after the black slave revolutions.

Writing in the 1950s, Paul Moral gave the bare statistics of average land holdings. As many as 20 per cent of peasant families now had less than one *carreau*, another 60 per cent had less than two *carreaux*. In these conditions it is surprising that the Haitian could afford to utilise any of his land area for export-crop production. But the statistics show that he did: 34.4 per cent of coffee was produced on farms of less than one *carreau*, and much of the crop was destined for the market. A further 30 per cent was cultivated on plots between one and two *carreaux*, and only 11 per cent on holdings of more than five *carreaux*. Even in the sugar industry — by now reviving somewhat with the *ingenios* refurbished during the US occupation — 25 per cent was produced on lands under one *carreau*, and a further 28 per cent on farms between one and two *carreaux*. Though Haitian families might have several different plots, perhaps several miles apart, the fact remains that the average peasant family still produced very largely for the commercial market. Only sisal was produced primarily on large estates: cotton, cocoa and also most bananas were farmed on the tiny plots. The Haitian peasant was well into a cash economy; and many of the staple foods bought on the open market, such as flour, rice and oils, were imported produce.

For rural labour, the legal minimum wage was 3.5 Haitian gourdes (or US$0.7) in 1949. The effective daily wage was still the same when I visited rural Haiti in 1982. Average monthly wages were found by Moral to be between $30 and $40 per family on an independent small farm, and $25 on the plantations. Incomes were believed to have declined sharply over one generation, as land was constantly subdivided among all male heirs of the peasant family.[21]

The Duvalier Decades, 1957–86

In 1957 President François Duvalier came to power. Later elected "Président à vie" (president for life), he died in 1971, whereupon his son Jean-Claude was promptly named life president after him. The gruesome atrocities perpetrated by the regime of the father "Papa Doc" earned him international notoriety. They have been described most graphically by the novelist Graham Greene in *The Comedians*, and the facts of repression need not be repeated here. Papa Doc Duvalier, a black middle-class doctor, began as a populist politician, promising to defend the interests of the urban and rural poor against the entrenched mulatto aristocracy. His repressive government drove many of the well-to-do mulattos out of the country, together with most of the professional class. But he did nothing for the poor, merely refining the notion of the "predatory state" through his unabated graft. Relying only partly on the professional Garde d'Haïti, Dr Duvalier built up a new paramilitary organisation officially named the "Volontiers de Securité Nationale", but universally known as the dreaded Tontons Macoutes. Outposts of the Tontons were set up in every hamlet and except in the higher echelons the recruits were unpaid. They lived by graft and corruption, extortion and intimidation.

In his 14 years of rule, François Duvalier managed to amass an immense personal fortune from an impoverished nation. The International Commission of Jurists has estimated that the Duvalier family extorted some $10 million a year from the Haitian treasury; other sources have estimated the personal fortune of the Duvalier family at between $180 to $200 million, most of it clandestinely salted away in Swiss bank accounts. One of the most lucrative sources is said to have been the infamous Régie du Tabac, the government's tobacco monopoly for which no figures were ever published. Reportedly, the Régie also collected taxes on sugar, cement, flour, soap, textiles, alcoholic beverages, edible oils, dairy products and a host of other products which were part of the basic consumer basket.

Another source of income was the official contract signed with the Dominican Republic in 1952 for the annual import of Haitian cane cutters. As Mats Lundahl has written on this point (which is further discussed in Chapter 10),

> Between 1957 and 1963 an estimated 30,000 workers crossed the border each year. Allegedly the flow was maintained by means of various payments to Haiti's president, François Duvalier. "Dominican sugar mills . . . paid Duvalier's contractors first of all 15 US dollars per head for each cane cutter delivered. Half of each cane worker's wages was then paid to him in Dominican pesos and half was sent to Haiti in dollars". There it was kept by the Duvalier officials.[22]

François Duvalier died in 1971. When his son Jean-Claude was installed as life president, the United States began to present him as a clear break with the past, and the US government began to press for a resumption of extensive aid to Haiti (which had been broken off during the final years of Papa Doc's rule). For example William Luers, Deputy Assistant Secretary in the US Department of State, informed Congress at human rights hearings on Haiti, held in 1975, that

> Although the state of human rights still leaves much to be desired, the judgment of our embassy in Port-au-Prince is that the present situation represents a clear break with the past patterns of repression. Tontons Macoutes have been reduced in number and have had their activities circumscribed significantly.[23]

And a 1974 report from the US Senate's Committee on Appropriations, by Senator

Edward Brooke, was submitted to the same congressional hearings. It stated that Haiti now needed substantial aid from external sources if it was to "improve the lot of its people" and observed that "President Jean-Claude Duvalier appears to be genuinely committed to improving economic conditions for his people." Using language now familiar in Reagan's Washington, it drew a distinction between authoritarian and totalitarian regimes, and reached the somewhat extraordinary conclusion that,

> The political apparatus, although authoritarian, does not have a totalitarian impact on society. It neither has the capacity nor apparently the desire to obtain absolute mastery over the lives of the Haitians. Thus, in the immediate future both the Haitian political and economic systems will have limited impact on Haitian lives. This is especially the case in regard to rural Haiti.

Anyone familiar with the Haitian fiscal system, or with the reality of the Tontons' continuing control over every aspect of the Haitian peasants' everyday life, would have laughed bitterly at such a statement. At any rate international development assistance began once more to pour into Haiti, most of it earmarked for rural development and food aid projects. The United States took the lead, through its Agency for International Development (AID). The Canadian, French, West German and Israeli governments among others also increased their bilateral aid programmes. Of the multilateral financial institutions, the Inter-American Development Bank approved a $6 million loan for agricultural and industrial credit; the World Bank an $8 million loan in 1976 for a regional development programme, and the UN's Food and Agriculture Organisation approximately $11 million in technical assistance between 1972 and 1976.

No one can question seriously the urgent need to channel international development assistance into Haiti. And a series of devastating droughts in the mid 1970s redoubled that need. By the end of the 1970s, statistics on poverty and malnutrition in Haiti made desperate reading. Average per capita income in rural areas was US$55 per year according to World Bank figures, and 90 per cent of the people were believed to earn no more than $40 per head. Infant mortality was as high as 150 deaths per 1,000 children born, as against 43 per 1,000 in the neighbouring Dominican Republic. While education was free and compulsory by law, barely 20 per cent of the adult population were literate. And yet there were other statistics revealing huge inequalities in the distribution of wealth and income. While the vast majority had to make do with derisory annual incomes, approximately 7,000 families earned some $50,000 per year, and about 3,000 of these families enjoyed twice that amount. Thus the key issue for Haiti was still that of income distribution. How to tax the rich more, and the poor less?

As the overseas aid began to flow, the United States Agency for International Development hired a consulting economist, Clarence Zuvekas from the US Department of Agriculture, to evaluate its assistance programme. Like his predecessors, Zuvekas reserved his strongest criticism for the government's monopoly powers, and the outrageous inequalities of the fiscal system. Citing a wide range of official documents, he concluded that conditions in rural areas were continuing to deteriorate sharply, and that real per capita incomes were still declining. Per capita agricultural production was 11 per cent lower in the mid 1970s than in 1960. And for the first time, there were indications that absolute rural landlessness was becoming a real problem in Haiti. With an average daily wage rate of only $0.50, providing for the subsistence needs of the rural family was well nigh impossible, and migration to Port-au-Prince "or to another country would seem to be a more attractive option than staying in rural areas looking for work". The number of absolutely landless persons, he estimated, was likely to be in excess of 200,000.

While advocating significant tax reforms, Zuvekas realised that they were hardly likely in the current political environment. His comments on this are worth quoting at some length:

> tax and price policy . . . are constraints that can be overcome with small real resource costs to both foreign donors and Haiti. There is a strong case for attaching high priority to reforms in these areas. However, such reforms, though having low costs to the Haitian economy as a whole, imply a significant redistribution of resources to farmers at the expense of the national treasury and of relatively affluent private groups such as exporters and processors. Since the latter groups wield more power than farmers, policy changes in these areas will be strongly resisted. But these reforms would be very effective means of achieving the government's stated goal of narrowing income inequalities . . . if the impact of public policies on rural living standards is to be significantly greater, there will have to be a reallocation of domestic resources within the public sector from urban to rural areas. Reforms in tax and price policy would have to be important components of such a strategy, which would also have to include sharply high spending on rural health and education. There is little evidence that such steps are being contemplated.[24]

In his final comments, Clarence Zuvekas predicted that living standards for many Haitian families were likely to continue falling for many years to come, and stated unambiguously that improvements would not come without radical changes along the lines mentioned in his earlier recommendations. These may seem obvious enough comments, but it was important that an official US government report of this kind could recognise the futility of international development assistance without widespread structural change. It was at least a refreshing change from the earlier statements by US diplomatic representatives that life was getting better for the Haitians under "Baby Doc".

It was also arrant nonsense that the human rights situation — in the strict sense of civil and political rights — was improving under Jean-Claude Duvalier. There may have been the most marginal improvements in the early 1970s, as some of Papa Doc's long-term prisoners were released. But under Jean-Claude serious political opposition was tolerated no more than in the days of his father. In the rural areas, it was "plus ça change . . .". As the New York-based Lawyers Committee for International Human Rights reported in 1981,

> In Haiti today there continues to be broadscale government corruption and mismanagement of public funds . . . this pattern of corruption affects the country's rural population particularly harshly. In rural areas, Civilian Security Forces engage in a pattern of wholesale extortion and forced expropriation of private land. In these areas the Haitian Government has given these forces license to extort with impunity.[25]

In the late 1970s, an embryonic protest movement emerged in Port-au-Prince itself. During the days of the Carter administration in Washington, there was diplomatic pressure from the United States Embassy for the release of political prisoners, fair trial procedures, the right to form political parties and practise independent journalism, and the right to organise in trade unions. For a brief two-year period the Christian Democrat World Conference of Labour — a moderate and staunchly anti-Communist international workers' confederation — was able to do the previously unthinkable, and establish the rudiments of a Haitian affiliate in urban areas. A Christian Democrat opposition party was also created, and began to make its presence felt in Washington's political corridors. Washington still hedged its bets, and continued its military training for an élite counter-insurgency unit known as the Leopards. But the Carter administration meanwhile began to exercise pressure in the delicate area of fiscal policy.

In Haiti, as elsewhere in the US backyard, the election of Republican President Ronald Reagan seemed to spell an end to whatever political liberalisation had appeared during the years of Carter's diplomatic pressure. In November 1980, the very month of Reagan's election, there were extensive round-ups of the fledgling Haitian political opposition. At the end of the month, "approximately one hundred and twenty five persons, including virtually all Haitian human rights activists, most independent journalists, and many defence lawyers, were detained and imprisoned by the Haitian military police without explanation."[26] They included the founder of the Haitian Social Christian Party, Grégoire Eugene; the owner of Haiti's largest independent radio station, Jean Dominique; and several editors of the independent weekly newspaper, *Petit Samedi Soir*. The general secretary of the Haitian League for Human Rights, Lafontant Joseph, was held in the army's Casernes Dessalines for six weeks, tortured during interrogation, and was then, one of the luckier victims, set free. A host of small newspapers and radio stations, including Radio Haiti Inter, Radio Métropole, Radio Cacique, *Fraternité*, *La Conviction*, *Regard*, *Coquerico* and *Inter-Jeune*, were closed down or taken over by the government.

While the political liberalisation was over, the international lending agencies nevertheless stepped up their pressure for fiscal reforms. Eventually, they secured the appointment as Finance Minister of Marc Bazin, a former World Bank official whose Haitian salary was reportedly paid by the World Bank itself during his brief tenure of office. Western nations had given Haiti over $600 million of aid funds since Jean-Claude Duvalier's taking office, but were becoming increasingly restless about the use of their funds. As a journalist from the *Christian Science Monitor* reported from Port-au-Prince about the brief Bazin interlude:

> most of the money has been siphoned off in a number of ingenious, but fraudulent, ways. Before Bazin introduced proper bookkeeping, up to 15 million dollars a month was diverted for "extra-budgetary expenses" — including Duvalier's own Swiss bank accounts. When the International Monetary Fund voted Haiti 20 million dollars in standby credit last December, six million dollars disappeared. . . . Foreign donors reacted sharply to such abuse. The Canadian International Development Agency abruptly closed an eight million dollar rural development programme last January, after it learned that half the 700 employees did not work. The United States and West Germany also froze

aid allotments, though some non-governmental agencies have continued their work. After Bazin's appointment in April, it seemed that matters might improve. He met IMF public spending targets by slashing payrolls. But as he edged closer to Duvalier's bank accounts, and those of the president's father-in-law Ernest Bennet, Haiti's coffee monopolist, his fate was sealed.[27]

Marc Bazin did not last. His appointment had been in response to an ultimatum from Western donors, reportedly as a precondition for the continuation of US$100 million of development aid for the fiscal year of 1982, but by July 1982 he had been ousted. Among the Haitian political mafia there was no room for honest technocrats.

Nevertheless, the old corrupt system could not go on indefinitely. By 1982, all Latin American nations were feeling the pinch, as the advanced Western nations, the private banks and the international financial institutions cut back on their lending, and demanded budget-balancing operations from the debtor nations. Though Haiti was a small debtor nation, the IMF in particular put its foot down, and made unequivocal demands for the rationalisation of fiscal policies. In August 1982 a 13-month standby agreement was signed with the IMF only after the Haitian government had agreed to carry out a stabilisation programme aimed at the reduction of treasury spending and the raising of revenue through fiscal reforms. The notorious Régie du Tabac was brought under the control of the Central Bank in 1982, and finally abolished in February 1985 when a new central tax department was created.[28] But as IMF targets continued to be met up to 1985, the brunt of new tax increases was again felt by poor consumers no less than the old élite. As the value added tax was raised on several consumer goods, additional duties were also imposed on such items as fuel, cigarettes, alcohol and soft drinks.

At the same time nothing effective was done to stimulate the production of basic food items. The production of corn, millet, rice and beans fell between 1980 and 1984. To make matters worse, pigs were slaughtered throughout the country after a major outbreak of African swine fever in the early 1980s. Overnight, hundreds of thousands of Haitian peasant families lost their only nutritious food source over and above the bare subsistence items. More and more, the country depended on food imports and charitable food donations. In 1981 the US PL–480 food aid programme — involving mainly the distribution of surplus US wheat throughout the Third World — was budgeted at slightly over US$30 million; by 1985 this was up to $45 million and total food imports were estimated at over $75 million. Furthermore, an aid agency report indicated in 1982 that 250,000 children were being fed daily through overseas aid programmes.[29]

Worsening economic conditions for the urban and rural poor ultimately generated a series of social protests that proved too much for the security forces and the Tontons to handle. As in the Dominican Republic, food riots broke out in 1984 in key towns throughout the republic. Sporadic violence over the next months persuaded Duvalier to make new gestures towards political liberalisation. In June 1985, a new law allowed political parties — albeit with stringent limitations by which a party had to obtain the signatures of over 15,000 people before it could be legally recognised. But Duvalier was still "Président à vie" — or so he thought. Early in 1986 a further rise in protests, spreading now through the streets of

Port-au-Prince, persuaded his Washington backers that it was finally time for Duvalier to go, before the protests erupted into open revolution. In March 1986 his abrupt departure for exile in France spelled the end of an era.

The Haitian Exodus

Extensive emigration has been part and parcel of Haitian life for more than a century. We saw earlier that Haitian cane cutters were found in the *ingenios* of the Dominican Republic as long ago as the 1880s. For 50 years after that, the most favoured destination was Cuba. In particular during the years of the US occupation, they were actively encouraged to seek work on sugar plantations elsewhere in the Caribbean. Some paid their own way, some were recruited by US agents. Though in theory they left for only the duration of the Cuban and Dominican sugar harvests, tens and perhaps hundreds of thousands never returned. The depression of the 1930s brought a summary end to the first Haitian flood. The Cuban outlet was closed, and Trujillo's grim massacre of the Haitian population in the Dominican Republic — saving only those on the foreign-owned plantations — in 1932, provided a temporary deterrent to further moves to the west of the island. We also saw that things again changed when Trujillo moved more seriously into the sugar industry. Trujillo himself, at once mass murderer of Haitians and trafficker in Haitian labour, embodied the essential paradox of Dominican nationalism that has prevailed until the present day. "Dominicanisation" of society, and the quest for a pliant and cheap labour force, were contradictory objectives that could not easily be reconciled.

In later chapters, the situation of Haitians in the Dominican Republic will be examined in more detail. The Dominican Republic has certainly been in the front line of a modern diaspora, which shocked the world when a new generation of Haitian boat people took to the Caribbean seas in the late 1970s. At that time there was first a trickle, and then a flood, of spontaneous migration to Florida. Those would-be emigrants with some resources sold whatever land and assets they possessed, paying high fees to boat owners who offered them an illegal passage to the United States. Many others without the wherewithal to pay the exorbitant fees demanded of them had to use their own makeshift boats, the unluckiest dying of exposure and thirst before reaching their destination. Thousands ended up in internment camps in Florida and Puerto Rico, with little chance of avoiding deportation unless they could prove under US refugee law that their flight was "politically motivated". Nor was the USA the only destination. As the Puerto Rico-based Ecumenical Center for Human Rights described the phenomenon:

> From Guyana to Canada, or by way of Guadeloupe, the Dominican Republic, the Bahamas and Florida, the Haitian emigration washes up on many strands . . . the Haitian people have now undertaken a second migration, as though in answer to their first migration which brought them from their home in Africa to Hispaniola. They are leaving their country by any route which will take them out, however painful the voyage, in search of another way of life. Bateyes, ranchos, slums, taudis — you find them everywhere, like a new tribe of nomads

which has decided to start again from scratch now they have lost their tribal garden.[30]

Until the late 1970s the steady flow of Haitians away from their country had never made much news. A sizeable proportion of the professional classes took up residence in the USA, either as political exiles from Papa Doc's dictatorship, or more simply because there was money to be made abroad. There was a smaller trickle of the urban poor to the ghettos of New York, the Haitians outnumbered by the hundreds of thousands of new immigrants to the United States from Cuba, the Dominican Republic and Puerto Rico. Haitians also went in considerable numbers to the Bahamas. The majority were illegal immigrants, but in practice it made little difference. There was at first a strong demand-pull factor. As the Haitian population accepted the most arduous conditions abroad without complaint, the cheap and industrious labour force was widely welcomed.

But in recent years there has been a new element of desperation in the attempts to get out of Haiti, at the same time as there have been more stringent measures to keep them out of the wealthier neighbouring countries. For the second time this century the poorest people in the hemisphere have felt the brunt of a new world depression. Following their violent evictions from Cuba and the Dominican Republic in the 1930s, they have been mercilessly dealt with once again as immigration policies change in the 1970s and 1980s. In June 1978, for example, the Bahaman Royal Police moved against the estimated 40,000 Haitian residents in the Bahamas. As the newspaper *La Voz* described one such incident, 279 Haitians were arrested at 3 a.m. on 11 June 1978. Their houses were ransacked by an anti-Haitian crowd, and some women were raped. The Haitians panicked, and many of them tried to cross the sea to Florida. "That is how, on July 18 1978 after their boat capsized, twenty three bodies of men, women and children from Abaco and Grand Bahama were recovered."[31]

Two years later, in an incident on the small Bahaman islet of Cayo Lobos, over 100 Haitian boat people were shipwrecked. They pleaded for asylum, but the Bahaman police were determined to be rid of them. US cameramen filmed a detachment of the Bahaman Royal Police beating those who resisted arrest and repatriation. As the *Miami Herald* later portrayed their pathetic resistance:

> But the 108 weak and emaciated Haitians, twenty five of them women, two of them pregnant, didn't move. They clung to each other, seated with their backs against the island's solitary lighthouse. They didn't speak. The police tried to pull them away. The Haitians kept their position. Out came the batons. They cracked the Haitians on the arms, the legs. Still the Haitians sat impassively, unmoving. One man held on to a lighthouse pillar. The police officers hit them on the arms and head with their batons.[32]

When they made it to Florida, the Haitians fared little better. The Carter administration, under pressure to grant treatment to the Haitians equal to that given to the thousands of boat people who left Cuba at the time of the Mariel saga,[33] first announced that all Haitians who had arrived before October 1980 would benefit from an amnesty. As thousands more plied their way to the beaches of Florida, a swift change of policy ensued. Boats full of coastguards were sent to cut them off, those who made their way in were arrested and held behind barbed wire in military camps. Eventually over 2,000 Haitians were despatched away from the public eye to Fort Allen in Puerto Rico, where they were held for over a year behind barbed wire.

This Haitian exodus had been unique in the Western hemisphere. In other large refugee movements, the determining factors have been different. When up to a million Cubans fled their island in the 1960s, there had been drastic post-revolutionary changes in the political system, and — more importantly — a US refugee policy actively encouraging the immigration. When Cuban boat people suddenly took to the seas at Mariel in 1980, it was at the instigation of Fidel Castro himself, who actively encouraged the flow as a taunting response to Jimmy Carter's plea that the Cuban President relax his emigration restrictions. And in South-East Asia, Afghanistan or Central America today, the refugee flood has come during or after the ravages of civil war.

In Haiti it was different. There had been no directly political upheavals, no change in the political system for over 20 years. President Duvalier claimed to oppose the exodus, while other governments did everything in their power to halt it. While the US authorities took measures of increased vigilance at home, they were now equally concerned with an assessment of the causes in Haiti itself.

The US government created a special task force to deal with the Caribbean refugee situation. USAID hired a consultant to investigate the background to the current Haitian emigration, interviewing Haitians both in the Florida refugee camps and in some of Haiti's poorest regions with the highest emigration levels. Her report listed a range of political, economic and social factors, together with natural disasters such as the devastation wreaked by Hurricane Allen in 1980, drought conditions and the drastic erosion which had by now rendered much of Haiti's mountainous terrain agriculturally useless. It was clearly hard to put a finger on any overriding cause. Haitian observers, said the report, had noted that even educated people from the capital city of Port-au-Prince were sometimes willing to risk the illegal boat journey. For the poorer classes the reasons given were sometimes the "dire necessity of survival", sometimes the lack of any opportunity for economic and social advancement. In one region of north-western Haiti, where the ill-fated SHADA experiment in rubber planting had taken place some 30 years previously, the project was still singled out as the root of the economic decline, and the major factor precipitating the current emigration.

> Three years after its inauguration, SHADA closed the rubber plantation when the war ended. A local source cited its folding as the beginning of Port Margot's economic decline as many people lost their jobs, did not have land to return to farm, and large tracts of former plantation land were left standing with rubber trees which still remained unexploited. Squatters have gradually taken over some of the tract, but the land stands virtually unused and unproductive.[34]

One point, however, stands out from the survey. While dire economic straights were inevitably given as causes prompting emigration, over half the Haitians interviewed — either by the USAID consultant herself or by officials from the Immigration and Naturalisation Service (INS) in the USA — listed the growing interference of the Tontons Macoutes in their daily life as one factor motivating their decision to leave. In this sense, the report certainly pointed to the futility of distinguishing between "political" and "economic" refugees in a situation such as that of Haiti under the Duvaliers. Haiti was not only a militarised society, but one in which militarisation was utilised for outright graft.

In Duvalier's Haiti, the country was divided into 27 separate *arrondissements* (each of them controlled by both an army commander and a commander of the Tontons Macoutes), subdivided into communes presided over by a mayor and by Tontons Macoutes officers reporting to their commanders. The communes were divided further into *sections rurales*, each of them containing their own *chef de section*. Travelling around rural Haiti in 1982, I could feel the measure and extent of this control. At each town in the interior, cars were stopped at military checkpoints, and their number plates recorded. The names of drivers and their passengers were written down, and all outsiders asked the purpose of their visit. In the smaller villages the huts of the Tontons could be picked out easily enough, the national flag flying above them, and Duvalier portraits ostentatiously draped all over the walls. I was reliably informed that the number of the Tontons was then growing rapidly. So too, as the economic crisis worsened, were the reports of widespread extortion of peasants' lands. In the south of the country, one foreign priest described how a Tonton-backed local politician had accumulated no less than 30,000 *carreaux* in recent years, through litigation, compulsory purchase and intimidation. In these circumstances to quibble over whether refugees are "political" or "economic" is at best irrelevant nit-picking, and at worst deliberate distortion in order to gloss over the excesses of a corrupt and totalitarian system.

For Duvalier's Haiti, the mass exodus may have been a political embarrassment. It was also a useful source of foreign exchange and a safety valve against social unrest. When the outlet was cut off to everywhere except the Dominican Republic, the Haitian people had no alternative but to seek change — at whatever cost — within their own society.

Notes

1. Oliver Ransford, *The Slave Trade* (John Murray, London, 1971), p. 270.
2. Facts taken from Mats Lundahl, *Peasants and Poverty: A Study of Haiti* (Croom Helm, London, 1979), pp. 366–7.
3. James G. Leyburn, *The Haitian People* (Yale University Press, 1941), p. 94.
4. Ibid., p. 54.
5. Lundahl, op. cit., p. 40.
6. Figures from Leyburn, op. cit., p. 320.
7. Ibid., p. 68.
8. Lundahl, op. cit., p. 265.
9. Paul Moral, *Le Paysan Haïtien* (Editions Fardin, Port-au-Prince, Haiti, 1978), p. 50.
10. Lundahl, op. cit., p. 24 ff.
11. Moral, op. cit., p. 51.

12. Ibid., p. 66.

13. Franklin W. Knight, "Jamaican Migrants and the Cuban Sugar Industry, 1900–1934", Manuel Moreno Fraginals and others (eds) *Between Slavery and Free Labour: The Spanish-Speaking Caribbean in the Nineteenth Century* (Johns Hopkins University Press, Baltimore and London, 1985), p. 104.

14. Mats Lundahl, *The Haitian Economy, Man, Land and Markets* (Croom Helm, London, 1983), p. 121.

15. Moral, op. cit., p. 69.

16. Hans Schmidt, *The Occupation of Haiti: 1915–1934* (New Brunswick, 1971), p. 171.

17. Emily Greene Balch (ed.) *Occupied Haiti* (The Writers Publishing Company, Inc., New York, 1927).

18. United Nations, *Mission to Haiti* (New York, 1949).

19. Lundahl, 1979, op. cit., p. 306.

20. United Nations, op. cit., p. 96.

21. Moral, op. cit., p. 207.

22. Lundahl, 1983, op. cit., p. 126.

23. "Human Rights in Haiti", Hearing before the Subcommittee on International Organisations of the Committee on International Relations, House of Representatives, Washington, DC, 1975.

24. Clarence Zuvekas, *Agricultural Development in Haiti; an Assessment of Sector Problems, Policies and Prospects under Conditions of Severe Soil Erosion*. Prepared for USAID/Haiti, May 1978, pp. 286–7.

25. Lawyers Committee for International Human Rights, *Report on Mission to Haiti* (New York, 1981).

26. Ibid., p. 6.

27. Iain Guest, *Christian Science Monitor*.

28. *Haiti: Family Business* (Latin America Bureau, London, 1985), p. 52.

29. Ibid., p. 42.

30. *La Voz*, Puerto Rico, September 1980 (Publication of the Ecumenical Center for Human Rights).

31. *La Voz*, December 1980, p. 7.

32. *Miami Herald*, 13 November 1980.

33. In 1980 Cuban President Fidel Castro, when criticised by US President Jimmy Carter for preventing Cubans from leaving the island, responded by telling all those who wanted to emigrate that they could leave from the Cuban port of Mariel over the next few days. Altogether, an estimated 125,000 Cubans left the country at this time.

34. Dr Susan H. Buchanan, *Haitian Emigration: The Perspective from South Florida and Haiti* (Consultancy Report prepared for the United States Agency for International Development, 1981).

5 Modern Helots: Haitian Workers in the Dominican Republic

The nationalisation of Trujillo's twelve *ingenios* in 1961 brought no benefits to the labour force in the Dominican sugar industry. When CEA was created by Law No. 7 of 4 August 1966, there were statutory provisions to guarantee both worker representation in the management of the sugar industry, and worker participation in profits. The third article stipulated that there were to be two worker representatives on CEA's governing body, one representing the factory workers, another the field workers. Article 12 was the root of the constant and often violent conflicts between the government and organised labour since then. It stated that out of the year's net profit, 40 per cent was to be shared by the work-force after various deductions had been made upon the recommendations of the advisory body, "deductions needed for improvements on the plantations, for its efficient running, maintenance and expansion, along with taxation and rental dues".

In the early 1960s there were manifold strikes in the sugar industry, in the state-owned plantations and, above all, in the privately owned Central Romana. The *Central de Trabajadores Dominicanos*, under the control of Juan Bosch's PRD, was influential on the state *ingenios*. But the strongest of the independent unions was the *Sindicato Unido* of the Central Romana, which carried out technically illegal but successful strikes in the early and mid 1960s, with support from Haitian as well as Dominican cane cutters. The *Sindicato Unido* was forcibly broken up after the purchase of the Central Romana by Gulf and Western in 1967. Eighty-three of the union leaders were summarily dismissed: and its general secretary, Guido Gil, "disappeared" after being abducted by the local police. The leftist trade unions were also subject to brutal repression following the military coup which toppled President Bosch. A Decree passed in October 1963 — and only repealed in 1978 — prohibited all "Communist" activities, making them subject to imprisonment, and many sugar workers with a militant past spent much of their lives behind bars until the late 1970s.

Doubtless to curb worker militancy, as well as to cut labour costs, the Dominican government had ever greater recourse to Haitian labour. In 1952 and 1957 Trujillo had drawn up his contracts with the Duvalier dictatorship for the purchase of Haitian cane cutters. It was in 1966, the year of CEA's creation, that a third such agreement was made. It was signed in November 1966, approved by Dominican National Congress in December, and promulgated by President Balaguer the following day. It dealt in general terms with arrangements for the recruitment of workers in Haiti for a limited period of work in agricultural or industrial undertakings within the Dominican Republic. From then until 1978 — with the exception of two years at the end of the 1960s when border tensions between the two countries reached a high point — further contracts were drawn up on an annual basis between CEA and the government of Haiti. Though it was these annual contracts which regulated the exact rights of the Haitian workers, as well as the amount to be paid over to the Haitian government, they remained confidential. It was only after a change of government in 1978 that the terms of the annual contracts have been made available to the public at large, and — more importantly — to those Haitian workers who were in theory protected by them.

In popular jargon, the workers officially recruited from Haiti under the bilateral contract are known as the "Kongos". Their number was 14,000 for the 1966–67 harvest, down to 10,000 the following year, then 12,000 between 1969 and 1977. The following year no Haitians were recruited officially. Under the government of Antonio Guzmán, between 1978 and 1982, the number increased progressively to 15,000, then 16,000 and ultimately to 19,000.

The Kongos have never been more than a small percentage of the total Haitian labour force in the Dominican Republic. The vast majority, popularly known as the *viejos* (old-timers), are the Haitians who have resided illegally in the Dominican Republic for many years, perhaps on the sugar plantations themselves, perhaps living elsewhere in the country for the out-of-season months only to be dragooned forcibly on to the sugar plantations during the harvest season. A third category is known in the trade as the *ambafiles* (literally, below the wire): they are the Haitians who enter the country clandestinely every year, perhaps voluntarily and perhaps perforce, to find work on the sugar plantations.

There are no reliable statistics concerning the number of Haitian workers and their family members in the Dominican Republic today. As long ago as 1967, it was officially estimated that three-quarters of the agricultural labour force on the *ingenios* were Haitians.[1] But by 1980 government figures placed the figure at over 90 per cent.[2] Dominican politicians and writers, when warning of the dimensions of the "Haitian threat", give a figure of upwards of half a million Haitians. In 1979, the Anti Slavery Society estimated that the number was in the region of 280,000 out of a total population of just over six million,[3] but this is likely to prove a conservative estimate. As the ILO has noted, the great bulk of contemporary Haitian residents comprises persons without residence permission, who continue to have the status of illegal immigrants. The Minister of the Interior informed the ILO's Commission of Enquiry in 1983 that only 10,000 Haitian residents had lawful status; 7,000 of these were at the Romana plantation, the remainder were scattered about the country. Many others were born in the Dominican Republic and, although entitled by law to Dominican nationality, had been unable to get hold of identity papers and were therefore treated in practice as illegals.

For the sugar industry at least, official statistics are provided sporadically. In 1980 the Dominican National Planning Office (ONAPLAN) estimated that there were 85,000 Haitians among the 110,000 persons residing all the year round on the sugar plantations. There were 26,500 Haitians among the active work-force (15,000 on the state-owned plantations and 11,500 on the private estates), leaving some

60,000 accompanying family members. But the number of Haitian cane cutters soars during the harvest season. The state sector alone requires upwards of 70,000 agricultural labourers, and the Central Romana a further 20,000 during the six months of the harvest. And then there are the thousands of *colonos* or outgrowers who also depend almost exclusively on Haitian labour. In the sugar industry alone, the demand for Haitian workers easily exceeds 100,000. Thus if there are 26,500 living semi-permanently on the plantations, and up to 19,000 imported officially from Haiti, there is still an annual shortfall of over 50,000. It is the way that this latter group are recruited which continues to cause international scandal, and which will be described in greater detail later in this chapter.

But the sugar industry is not the only one to utilise cheap imported labour. In particular in recent years there has been growing use of Haitian workers in other agricultural sectors, and to a lesser extent in construction and other non-agricultural activities. In 1981 ONAPLAN calculated that 15,634 of just under 55,000 workers employed on coffee farms were Haitians.[4] In cotton and tobacco, large numbers of Haitians are also to be found. Even small farmers in the border areas opt for Haitians willing to undercut Dominican salaries by at least 100 per cent. In general, Dominican farmers, large and small alike, will opt for cheap Haitian labour for as long as they can get away with it.

Official documents in the National Planning Department in CEA, as well as regular editorials in the Dominican press, contain countless blueprints for the "Dominicanisation" of the sugar harvest, and for overall agrarian policies that would reduce the dependency on Haitian labour. Foreign technicians have been brought in by the score, advocating policies of mechanisation, new harvesting techniques, or sanctions against private employers who utilise cheap imported labour to the detriment of Dominican nationals. But for as long as the Dominican agrarian structure evolves along its present lines, most of these projects are likely to prove an ambitious pipe-dream. Before turning to the facts of Haitian exploitation today, it is useful to reflect on the role that these Haitians play in the overall agrarian structure.

Agriculture's Changing Faces: Haitians and the Agrarian Structure

Until the middle of the 1970s, the Dominican Republic had its own safety valve. It has been estimated that as many as one million Dominicans left their country for the United States. Put somewhat crudely, the face of Dominican society changed. Light-skinned mulattos left the island whenever they could, for the ghettos of New York and elsewhere. Haitians were welcomed in the Dominican Republic, because they would work for next to nothing, and because they had absolutely no rights whatsoever under Dominican law. They could be tolerated for as long as there was a demand for their labour. And because they were illegals, they could be repatriated arbitrarily whenever their presence proved to be unnecessary.

If Dominicans point to the paradox of the growing Haitian presence at a time of growing landlessness and fragmentation of Dominican lands, it is a paradox which can be explained easily enough — at least from the perspective of the wealthier strata of Dominican society. As seen earlier, two agrarian reform laws have been enacted, a very moderate one in 1962 and a potentially more effective one in 1972. Furthermore, labour legislation after the 1950s established the right to organise, and also provided for minimum wage agreements for urban and rural workers alike. We also noted that agrarian and labour laws enacted throughout Latin America after the 1950s provided for the abolition of "semi-feudal" land and labour relations, and paved the way for more commercialised and capital-intensive systems of agricultural production, through private farms producing for the domestic and overseas markets. Within this reformist model, the land and labour laws were themselves closely related, and in certain cases the strict application of labour legislation could have a strong redistributive effect on systems of property ownership. As one academic author has commented on this issue,

> Labor legislation may be considered part of the rural property system itself. When such legislation exists (minimum wages, health codes, social security, tenancy law, unionisation provisions) it imposes legal limits on proprietorship, which must be considered, from the point of view of the landowner, as impositions on the scope or domain of the authority vested in him as proprietor of rural land.[5]

Some of the effects of these reformist provisions throughout Latin America have already been analysed in the preceding chapter. But it is useful at this stage to distinguish between those agrarian societies where the prevailing model was the traditional *latifundio* and where there was only limited production for export; and the more typically "agro-export economies", in which much of the national land and labour was already involved in production for export. In many Andean countries there had been far less emphasis on production for export. By the 1960s the traditional Andean *latifundio* — with its large number of tied labourers producing for subsistence, its underutilisation of land and limited capital investment — was earmarked by social reformists and agrarian capitalists alike as a serious obstacle to progress. Thus, while there was strong pressure from below for redistributive land reforms in the interests of social justice, there was also much consensus from above for the transformation of the backward agrarian structure. With financial support from the state, landowners could now invest in greater agricultural productivity, relying on capital-intensive techniques which greatly reduced their labour requirements. Former debt peons and squatters were often evicted from their subsistence plots on the fringes of the large estates, as an increasing percentage of the land area was used for commercial crop production. In these countries, limited redistributive land reforms could take place without threatening unduly the labour supply in the commercial sector of agriculture.

The other end of the spectrum was the plantation economies of the small Central American republics. Here, the best agricultural land had already been taken up with large-scale commercial production for export, primarily of coffee and bananas, since the late 19th century. Coffee required a vast seasonal labour force, which had to be provided nationally. Thus land concentration and peasant dispossession proceeded in tandem. And as Central American landowners developed new commercial crops — in particular cotton and sugar — after the Second World War, the competition for subsistence land and cheap agricultural labour became more intense. Before then, the coffee magnates had allowed the dispossessed indigenous peasantry to grow subsistence crops on small plots made available to them on the fringes of the coffee plantations, in exchange for the provision of cheap labour during the harvest season. But as landowners increased the land acreage under intensive coffee cultivation, or diversified further into new export crops, peasants were evicted violently from their squatter plots and the level of absolute rural landlessness reached alarming proportions. Though land reform laws existed in such countries as El Salvador, and although labour codes in all Central American republics recognised the rights of organisation and minimum wages after the 1950s, any attempt to demand the enforcement of these "paper rights" was repressed ruthlessly. Denied access to their legal rights through peaceful means, the peasants of El Salvador and Guatemala finally turned to armed rebellion. The underlying social tensions in these repressive agro–export societies finally escalated into today's violent Central American conflicts.

The Dominican situation was of course different. The availability of cheap labour from across the border made it possible for the plantation and smallholder economies to coexist more easily. While there was pressure for land, there was no corresponding need to drive the smallholders off their land in order to find a cheap labour force. The problems were to arise when *either* the Haitian illegals began to compete with Dominican peasants for subsistence plots, *or* the increasing use of cheap Haitian labour was to deprive the Dominicans of cash incomes on which they had come to depend. These problems were to be compounded further by the ending of emigration possibilities for Dominican nationals, and the inevitable growth of Dominican rural landlessness within the framework of this agrarian model, producing rising social tension and a potential new eruption of anti-Haitian sentiment.

As elsewhere in Latin America, evolving norms of land and labour rights were to have their effects on the agrarian structure of the Dominican Republic. Peasants and rural workers tried to organise around demands for their enforcement: landowners and the state sugar sector did everything possible to evade their legal obligations.

The Dominican Republic's first Labour Code was enacted during the Trujillo era, in 1952. Generally speaking, Dominican labour law provides for less generous conditions for agricultural labourers than for all other categories of worker. For example, field workers in an enterprise with less than ten salaried employees are considered to be outside its scope. Furthermore, field workers are not protected by the eight-hour day, which is applicable in all other sectors of the economy. But agricultural workers are covered by the provisions of minimum wage laws. In the present Labour Code, there are provisions to limit the number of foreign workers, but there are also exceptions. Article 125 of the Code stipulates that at least 70 per cent of the total number of workers in any enterprise must be of Dominican nationality. Article 135 provides the exception, stating that "The Executive Power can grant permits, valid for no more than one year, for the employment in agro–industrial enterprises of foreign *braceros* in excess of the legal amount." Laws on social security and accident benefits are applicable to all agricultural workers, whether seasonal or permanent, whether Dominicans or foreigners. However, one difference between the Dominican social security system and the British one, for example, is that in the Dominican Republic social security benefits are contingent on regular payments by individual employers. There is no unemployment benefit.

Of the agrarian laws, it was the legalised abolition of tenancy arrangements, together with the obligation to hand over tenured lands to the former tenants, that almost certainly did most to encourage the use of Haitian labour in the non-sugar sector. No detailed studies have been made of the gradual rise in the proportion of Haitian labour in coffee, cotton, rice and tobacco. But there would seem to be a definite correlation between the agrarian reform laws of the early 1970s and the preference for illegals. Data on share-cropping are hard to come by, but it had reached a high level by the late 1960s. In 1969 an agricultural consultant to USAID observed that it was the second most prevalent form of tenancy. He distinguished between the larger share-tenants, those producing commercial crops for a large landowner, and those with the use of a small parcel of land with obligations to supply labour to the owner.[6]

The ONAPLAN figures cited earlier have demonstrated the importance of Haitian labour on coffee plantations. Travelling around medium-sized coffee plantations in the western district of Barahona in 1982, I found small settlements on coffee estates occupied by Haitian families exclusively. The predominant use of Haitian labour has spread to other regions of the country, notably the rich agricultural region of Cibao in the north-east, and commercial farming areas of the north-west near the Haitian border. There has been ample denunciation by agricultural spokesmen and government authorities of its adverse effect on the national economy and employment prospects, and the denunciations have been followed by regular forcible repatriations with ample press publicity. But there is a general feeling that the purpose of such measures is to confirm the illegal status of the Haitians, to reinforce their feeling of instability and powerlessness, rather than to effect any real changes in the structure of illegal immigration. Any attempt to do so would certainly meet with strong resistance from the landowners themselves.

From late 1980, the Dominican press carried a series of attacks on the pernicious effects of the use of Haitian labour, often containing racial undertones. In September 1980 an influential coffee planter from Cibao lamented that the Haitians were displacing the abundant national labour supply available in his area. The reasons given were predictable enough — the Haitians were more docile and cheaper. There were complaints about hygiene and population growth, because "the Haitians are very fertile and increase the population in a region which has high levels of population growth."[7] The invective grew in the following year, particularly following the publication of the ONAPLAN study on the widespread use of Haitian labour in commercial agriculture. Ex-President Balaguer added fuel to the fire, by insinuating that the ruling PRD was planning to garner illegal votes from resident Haitians in the forthcoming presidential elections. Then at the end of June, the government's migration department published full-page advertisements in the press, warning that all "businessmen, industrialists, ranchers, farmers, tradesmen and other employers" would be taken to court for violation of the country's migration laws if they made any use whatsoever of illegal foreign labour — which "directly prejudices Dominican workers". "From the first of July", read the communiqué, "officials of the Migration Department and other authorities will carry out searches to detect the different places where use is being made of illegal foreign labour, especially Haitian nationals, in order to take proceedings against them."[8] Proceedings were never taken against any Dominican national. But over the next couple of months there was a sharp increase in cases of arbitrary arrest and repatriation of Haitians. In July 1981 one newspaper reported a pitiful case, in which several elderly Haitians resident in Ingenio Haina for over 40 years expressed fear that they would be included in the current wave of deportations.[9] In the following month of August, another daily editorialised in its plea for more humane treatment:

> It seems that the Dominican authorities are ignoring certain norms of respect for human dignity, in their repatriation of Haitians. Recently undocumented foreigners were warned that they would be repatriated, and on the very next day the authorities scoured the streets of Santiago and other towns, picked up hundreds of Haitians, and locked them up to despatch them later to Haiti. The operation is indiscriminate, reaching the extreme that dark-skinned Dominicans have been detained to be sent to our neighbouring country.[10]

In the same month the bishop and priests of the north-western diocese of Mao-Montecristi claimed that over 4,000 Haitians had been arbitrarily repatriated through the Dajabón border post. As the bishop protested, "The Dominican Republic has the honour of being the only Latin American country to initiate mass deportations without prior humanitarian steps, without debate, evaluation, consideration and preparation, and without taking into account the respect that the individual deserves." The bishop pointed out that the law now being invoked to justify the deportations had been effectively in disuse for the past 20 years. For this reason, Haitians who had been in the Dominican Republic for up to a lifetime had done nothing to regularise their status, and probably had no idea what procedures were in existence to do so. He pleaded for emergency legislation in order to deal with special cases and longstanding immigrants.[11]

It was not only the church, humanitarian agencies and the press that lambasted the arbitrary measures. Many landowners expressed desperation. "Rice harvest endangered by repatriation of Haitians", read one newspaper headline. It cited large landowners from the northern towns of Jicome and Esperanza as claiming that over 50,000 *tareas* worth of rice, coffee and other crops would now be lost through lack of available labour. If it had not been for Haitian labour, the entire coffee harvest would have been lost in the previous year. Eighty per cent of all agricultural work in the region was now carried out by Haitians. Dominican peasants, said the informant, simply refused to do the work.[12]

The wave of deportations in 1981 was particularly severe, and there is no guarantee that it will not be repeated. As the ILO's Commission of Enquiry reported in 1983,

> Particularly in the Northern region, the Commission received testimony of arrests and harassment of the kind alleged, involving both forcible transport to the State-owned plantations in the area and confiscation of workers' money and

belongings by members of the armed forces. In that region, there appeared to
exist an organised atmosphere of repression on the part of the military, in
concert with the local employers of labour, to keep the Haitians on the
plantations and to force them to work there under threat of deportation . . . this
situation is contrary to the obligations of the Dominican Republic under the two
[ILO] Conventions relating to forced labour.[13]

Until now, there has been a very clear consonance of interests between the
government, landowners and military in maintaining this reserve of Haitian labour.
All have stood to gain, but only through the use of coercive measures which are a
flagrant denial of the basic rights of the Haitian community.

Notes

1. Taken from *Tecnología, Empleo y Distribución de Ingresos en la Industria
Azucarera de la República Dominicana* (study published by the ILO's Regional
Employment Programme for Latin America and the Caribbean (PREALC), 1978).
2. Figures taken from report by ONAPLAN (National Statistics Office),
*Participación de la Mano de Obra Haitiana en el Mercado Laboral: los Casos de la
Caña y el Café* (Santo Domingo, 1981).
3. Report of the Anti Slavery Society to the UN Working Group on Slavery,
1979.
4. ONAPLAN, op. cit.
5. From Brian Loveman, *Struggle in the Countryside* (Indiana University Press,
1976).
6. Solon Barraclough, *Agrarian Reform Programmes for the Dominican Republic*,
Consultancy report prepared for USAID, 1970.
7. *El Sol*, 13 September 1980.
8. Dirección General de Migración, 29 June 1981.
9. *El Sol*, 11 July 1981.
10. *El Día*, 19 August 1981.
11. *El Sol*, 26 August 1981.
12. *El Día*, 27 August 1981.
13. *ILO Official Bulletin*, Vol. LXVI, Report of Commission of Enquiry, 1983,
p. 135.

6 Modern Slavery: Haitian Forced Labour in the Dominican Republic, 1976–86

It was in May 1975, on my first visit to the region, that I first encountered Haitian cane cutters on the Dominican plantations. Then I had only fleeting glimpses of lines of black workers cutting the cane in the evening sun, then returning in silence to their miserable barracks. I asked only a few questions, and was told that they lived like slaves, were locked in their barracks at night, and were never free to leave the immediate compounds on which they worked. This was enough to arouse my concern, and I hoped to return one day to carry out a more serious investigation.

In those days, few facts came out in the open. The Dominican press was less free, and, though it was widely rumoured that the military were involved extensively in the traffic in Haitians, few journalists risked a serious investigation that might reveal conspiracy by high-level military officers. One exception was the lawyer and columnist from Santiago, Dr Ramón Antonio Veras, who has proved the most outspoken critic of the abuses within the official contract system. In May 1976 Dr Veras published an article in the Santo Domingo newspaper *El Nacional de Ahora*, denouncing a veritable "slave industry" in which captured Haitians were sold for between 3 and 10 pesos apiece, and then trucked to the purchaser's region:

> The person who buys a Haitian has the right to take him on his farm and put him to work without pay; he needs only to furnish the slave with basic needs, that is, take care of him so that he can cut sugar cane . . . it's unbelievable that in the twentieth century human beings are still being sold."

In the following year, during the 1977–78 sugar harvest, the bilateral contract with Haiti was not renewed for the first time in a decade. It was rumoured that the Dominicans refused to capitulate to Jean-Claude Duvalier's demand for an increase in the purchase price for Haitians from 60 to 70 Dominican pesos per head; but the severe financial crisis of the Dominican sugar industry, following the sharp drop in world market sugar prices, was doubtless a contributory factor. In June 1978, a brief report by a Dominican Republic Task Force in New York made further allegations of traffic in Haitians along the border regions:

> Clandestine entry is a costly process, which often puts Haitians deeply into debt. They must obtain medical certificates, identification documents, and finance bribes of the military on both sides of the border in order to cross into the Dominican Republic. The clandestine route entails an exchange of Haitians at

the border between Haitian and Dominican military onto trucks which cart Haitians to the southwest Barahona region. There, in a large fenced-in area, Haitians wait to be purchased by *colonos* or representatives from the three main sugar producers in the country. . . . At this point Haitian workers are sold for ten pesos per person, and then trucked to the purchasers' region. These workers are most likely to stay in the country, both out of preference and due to the nature of the agreement with the employers.[1]

Colonel Patrick Montgomery, then General Secretary of the London-based Anti Slavery Society, took the Haitians' case before the United Nations. In August 1979, appearing before the United Nations Working Group on Slavery in Geneva, Montgomery delivered a brief but influential report in which he concluded that "the condition of Haitian migrant workers could be compared only with slavery". His denunciation, which was widely reported in the world press, was to spark off a wave of international reporting and to culminate in the ILO's 1983 Commission of Enquiry.

Anti Slavery Society Report: The Dominican Response

In the Dominican Republic itself, Montgomery's allegations also received wide coverage in the national press, now freer since the moderate PRD had come to power the previous year. Most editorials rejected the use of the term "slavery", but nevertheless accepted that conditions were unacceptable. "Slaves no, but maltreated yes", read the headline in one newspaper, *El Nacional de Ahora*, on 22 August 1979. The paper stressed its "most vigorous rejection of the false accusation that our country maintains a system of slavery", but insisted that both Haiti and the Dominican Republic conduct an urgent investigation into the methods of recruitment and repatriation of Haitian migrants. Another editorial was more sympathetic to the Anti Slavery Society. "Though not on the scandalous scale, or in the volume and slavery conditions of other epochs", it proclaimed, "traces of this situation still last to the present day . . . cane-cutters continue to be victims of exploitation on both sides of the frontier. So we understand the denunciation that has been made against our country in Geneva." A small left-wing newspaper, *El Socialista*, went further still in an editorial of 25 August 1979:

> The Foreign Ministers of Haiti and the Dominican Republic have come from a meeting, denouncing as false the Anti Slavery Society's claim before the United Nations that every year 12,000 Haitians are sold as slaves by officials of the Duvalier dictatorship, to cut cane in our country. There's no need to fall into legalistic pedantry, as to whether or not they are slaves; one thing is certain, that every year corrupt officials reap massive profits from the Haitian labour force. These Haitian workers are the victims of extreme exploitation by the sugar companies, sugar producers and private farmers of varying "social strata", and they are then robbed of their miserable savings when they return home . . . the denunciation made by the Anti Slavery Society is positive, because it brings into the open a theme which is "tabu" in the bourgeois press: the inhuman exploitation of Haitian workers.

The widespread coverage given to the Anti Slavery Society's report elicited pledges from the new Dominican government that the forced labour would be terminated, but to little concrete effect. One newspaper reported in 1979:

> President Guzmán has given specific instructions that there should be no forcible recruitment of Haitians. Nevertheless, from Enriquillo, Oviedo and Paraiso in the south, to some regions of Mao in the north, there have been reports of repression against the Haitians. There is talk of beating and shooting in the air. Officially, the military authorities of the country have said nothing about the matter.[2]

Forced Labour Continues

Whatever President Guzmán's public stance, it soon became clear that the raids were conducted on the basis of orders from high-ranking government officials. According to another report, the military acknowledged that sweeping arrests were taking place, but insisted that they had "specific orders from above to arrest the Haitians and prevent them by any means from escaping".[3] At least 200 Haitians were arrested in the region of Mao, and forcibly removed to the CEA *ingenios*. The victims were described as illegal residents working on the private farms of well-known landowners in the region. The raid was described as brutal, with shots fired at those Haitians who took flight upon the military's arrival. Other reports attributed the severity of the raids to serious shortfalls in labour, caused by delays in signing the bilateral agreement. But even when the Kongos began to arrive, the arrests and kidnappings continued.

In January 1980 a journalist from the Santo Domingo daily *El Sol* filed a report from the southern town of Barahona. All Haitians in the zone, she reported, lived in perpetual fear of arrest, and transfer to cut cane in the *ingenios* of the eastern side of the country. Witnesses within the precincts of Ingenio Barahona itself related their experiences:

> In this *ingenio*, throughout the past few weeks and still at the present time, there have been frequent arrests of Haitians and all dark-skinned people, who are taken in trucks to the east to cut cane. They explained that the arrests are not limited to the area of Ingenio Barahona itself. They extend throughout the south-western region, mainly in the border zones between the Dominican Republic and Haiti. . . . The arrests involve not only young Haitians but also pensioners. "Many went to collect their pension and were taken prisoner", was the expression used by the Haitian to make his denunciation. Other people revealed that some of the foreign *braceros* who were taken off to the east to cut cane have now returned to their places of residence. Those who did so, as *El Sol* established, returned after they were "tried" by the military themselves who charged them from 3 pesos upwards in order to set them free.[4]

The raids tended to take place twice a year — first at the beginning of the harvest season, then towards mid-harvest when new *ingenios* commenced operations. Furthermore, those unfortunate enough to be despatched to the CEA *ingenios* with the worst living and working conditions did their utmost to escape, and moved to places like Gulf and Western's La Romana where condition tended to be marginally better. After a lull in the victimisation, the papers were again full of reported atrocities, raids and beatings by March and April 1980. On 19 March 1980 *Listín Diario* reported on a new series of arrests and kidnappings near the town of Valverde, Mao province:

> Hundreds of Haitians are being subject to mass arrests here, to be taken to the sugar harvest. The Haitians, most of them legal residents, are captured by troops of the National Army in settlements, on private farms and taken to the military fortress "General Benito Monción". During the course of Sunday and yesterday more than five army lorries were seen full of Haitians, and it has been unofficially estimated that around 500 have been captured. The people responsible for the resettlement of these Haitians are CEA officials, according to information provided by the Governor of Valverde . . . the Governor asserted that as soon as these Haitians are captured, they are taken to the State *ingenios* to work in the sugar harvest.

This time, the assault continued for well over a month. In the following week, *La Noticia* described how combined troops of the National Army and Police arrested over 100 Haitians in the town of Esperanza, beat them, took away all their belongings, and threw them violently into a vehicle belonging to the Ministry of Agriculture.[5] At the beginning of April, *El Nacional* reported that a further 600 Haitian victims had been picked up and packed off to the east. The majority of victims were described as "small merchants, ticket-sellers, agricultural labourers", among others. Assessing the cause, it stated that "information has been received that there is a deficit of harvesters on the CEA *ingenios*, above all in Montellanos and Catarey, which has led to a decline in milling activities."[6]

From the press reports and other available accounts there seems to be no doubt that the measures, though carried out by the army, were instigated by the State Sugar Council itself. As the London-based *Latin American Newsletters* reported, "General Humberto Trifilio, commander of the army's second brigade, caused outrage in the press in Santo Domingo when he admitted recently that the practice [of capturing Haitians for sale to the sugar companies] was widespread. He added, though, that the troops were 'acting on orders'." CEA resorted to these desperate measures because, short of locking the Haitians in their barracks and maintaining tight vigilance through military patrols, there was probably no way of curbing the flight of Haitian *braceros* from the miserable conditions on the state properties to the private mills and other agricultural sectors. This much was evidently admitted in a press interview given by the administrator of Río Haina, CEA's largest *ingenio*, early in April 1980:

> The administrator of Ingenio Río Haina, agronomist César Polanco, urged the State Sugar Council to "humanise" the life of Dominican and Haitian *braceros* engaged in cane cutting. Polanco said that, in the *ingenio* under his charge, there is essentially a "real migration" of cane cutters towards other private mills where they receive better treatment. . . . Polanco warned that it is time for the State *ingenious* to be rid of the slavery treatment meted out to the can cutters. "The Dominican rejects cane cutting, not because it brings little earnings, but

because he wants to get it out of his life system", said the young official. He believes that when Dominicans enjoy certain comforts, they will have no objection to engaging in cane cutting. "I think that, for as long as the sugar economy depends on foreign labour, the problems will just keep on growing."[7]

In the 1980–81 harvest, the same pattern repeated itself. On 3 February 1981 *Listín Diario* reported — in language and circumstances almost identical to those of the previous year — that:

> Troops of the National Army stationed in Benito Monción fortress here, have arrested around 300 Haitian citizens to make them work in the various *bateyes* in this province. According to reports, CEA officials have requested this measure, as a consequence of the shortage of labour for cane cutting. National Army Colonel Astacio Meneses . . . said that "we have precise orders to arrest the undocumented *braceros*". . . . Once arrested, the *braceros* are taken to Benito Monción fortress. From there they are transferred to the sugar centrals of the east of the country. Some of the arrested *braceros*, questioned by reporters, refuse to work because the "humble salary does not suffice for subsistence needs". "We prefer to devote ourselves to agricultural work, where we receive a humane treatment", they declared.

Further arrests were described three days later, by the newspaper *La Noticia* on 6 February. Raids had taken place in a number of peasant communities in the province of Mao. Many of the victims, reported the article, had been violently removed by military and civilian personnel. Two days previously, a further 300 Haitians had been captured while engaged in work on private farms in the region. The newspapers *El Nacional de Ahora* and *Listín Diario* reported further incidents over the next ten days. Again the raids took place both on private farms and in urban settlements. The victims were said to have been taken to the eastern *ingenios* of Porvenir, San Luis and La Romana.

The mechanics of the clandestine traffic in Haitians at this time, and the dual complicity of CEA and the Dominican army, have been most meticulously described in two long articles published by the left-wing newspaper *Libertad*, the monthly organ of the *Movimiento Popular Dominicano* (MPD). The articles only appeared after my 1982 investigations and intervention before the United Nations, and were in fact prompted by my own interventions and the Dominican government's subsequent denials. As *Libertad* commented,

> In Geneva, Switzerland, the Anti Slavery Society has denounced before the United Nations the sale of Haitians by Dominican troops to the State Sugar Council (CEA). Roger Plant, the organisation's representative at the UN Human Rights Commission, also denounced the sub-human conditions of life and labour to which the Haitian agricultural workers are subjected. The Secretary of the Armed Forces, Imbert McGregor, together with senior CEA officials, have rejected Roger Plant's allegations. But our organisation has documents in its possession, providing irrefutable evidence that Dominican soldiers capture Haitians, and sell them to CEA. For the recruitment of these Haitians, the commanders of the military border posts make use of various "tontons macoutes" and other Haitians who perform the functions of "caliés" in the country.

The MPD had got hold of documents, most probably obtained through a leak in CEA itself, that gave the details of the "Haitian trade" in the one month of February 1981 when the abuses were at their worst. It calculated that approximately 4,400 Haitians were rounded up and sold to CEA during the 1980–81 harvest, most of them clandestine entrants and illegal residents in the border provinces of the south-west. The victims — usually rounded up in the rice, cotton and coffee farms of these provinces — were taken to a staging post for a few days, where they were kept under lock and key. When sufficient numbers had been gathered, a lorry driver was contracted to truck them off to the CEA estates. The lorries, which travelled at night, were accompanied by armed guards who smoothed the transit through military check-points on the way to the eastern *ingenios*. The sale price was 20 pesos per head, most of which went to the higher-ranking officers who controlled the trade. The troops who guarded the convoys received between 7 and 10 pesos per head as a daily allowance, the amount being paid by the administration of the *ingenio* which received the *braceros*. But the troops could supplement this amount by pocketing the 0.50 pesos per head that was in theory to be allocated to the Haitians' daily subsistence needs.

The documents in question were transaction orders signed and stamped by the military officers, listing the names and number of the Haitians provided, and the lorry drivers whose services had been contracted; and receipts issued and signed by the administrators of the large Ingenio Río Haina (which, with its abysmal conditions, has customarily had the greatest difficulty in securing a sufficient labour force). One such document, entitled "List of *braceros* sent to CEA", and dated 5 February 1981, contained the names and ages of 40 Haitians who had been rounded up near the border town of Pedernales; it was signed by the military commander of Pedernales province. Another was a letter of 6 February 1981, signed by an army captain from Pedernales and addressed to the administrator of Ingenio Haina, and stating that

> I have the pleasure in informing you that Mr Tubides Ramírez Matos, C–5508–S–21, owner of the lorry Hino with number plates 536–846, was used by the undersigned on the days of February 4–7, transporting *braceros* from the mountains and (military) outposts to this Barracks. For which payment should be made in this office, for an amount to be agreed amongst yourselves.

A further document, signed by a lieutenant-colonel and military commander of Mao-Valverde province, and likewise addressed to the administrator of Ingenio Haina, contains the words:

> I respectfully inform you that I am sending you under guard the quantity of 70 Haitian nationals, in the Nissan lorry with number plates 534–419, driven by Mr Roberto Suárez, C–6393–S–34. These Haitians were found by troops of this (battalion), wandering around in this zone and in the town of Santiago Rodríguez. I annex a list of their names.

There are several similar documents, all of which are careful to list the number and names of the Haitians provided. As the MPD notes, there is often a discrepancy between the number of Haitians said to be provided by the army, and the number whose receipt is acknowledged by CEA. "What," it asks, "happened to the remainder?"

The documents provide no concrete evidence of money changing hands between CEA and the military officers. It is common knowledge that it does. One can only speculate that the financial benefits to be derived from this Haitian merchandise are the reasons for the fairly rigid accounting procedures. The *Libertad* articles estimated that the going rate was 20 pesos per head. On this basis it calculated that one army colonel from Mao and Valverde, who provided 238 Haitian "slaves" between 6 and 21 February 1981, would have received more than 4,000 Dominican pesos — or US$4,000 at the official rate of exchange at that time. It was a lucrative business.

It was at the end of this harvest season, in June 1981, that the worker delegates to the ILO's International Labour Conference in Geneva filed their complaints against the governments of Haiti and the Dominican Republic, on the basis of which the ILO Governing Body decided to set up its official Commission of Enquiry. For both governments, it was to be the first official international enquiry. Both Haiti and the Dominican Republic accepted an on-the-spot investigation, which was ultimately to take place in January 1983.

The ILO action began to have some limited effects. In August 1981 CEA's Executive Director, Secundino Gil Morales, published full details of official recruitment methods in the Dominican press. His statement focused only on the officially contracted Kongos, and painted a picture far rosier than the truth. But in the following year, at least, the army was held in check. When I visited the island between April and June 1982, on an unofficial visit sponsored by the Anti Slavery Society, there was less open evidence of the mass raids that had pervaded the previous harvest season. I talked with hundreds of Dominican and Haitian workers on 12 of the 16 sugar plantations, and received harrowing tales of violence, cheating over weights and salaries, harassment and threats, and also witnessed the grim physical conditions that are described later in this chapter. But there were no articles about mass raids and captures in the Dominican press; and several Haitians in the *bateyes* told me explicitly that this was the first year in which forcible recruitment within the country had not been a widespread and systematic practice.

It had certainly not been stamped out altogether, and the allegations continued. The newspaper *Libertad* claimed in August 1982 — without citing details or evidence — that as many as 3,500 captured Haitians were bought by CEA from the Dominican army in the course of the 1981–82 harvest season. And travelling in the south-western border regions around the town of Barahona, I heard accounts from Haitian male peasants who remained behind on the coffee plantations, and from the wives and children of those who had left for the harvest. In one village, Haitian family members described how the military patrols had reached their village as usual in December 1981. On this occasion they had not forced all able-bodied males to go with them, but had exacted a price for letting them stay behind. The rate was said to be in the region of 10 pesos a head. Further interviews throughout the south-western district suggested that the extortion of such bribes was still widespread. Several informants gave separate accounts of a chain of exploitation, whereby an ordinary soldier would either exact bribes or sell a captured worker to a superior for a few pesos, who would sell for a larger amount to a higher-ranking officer, who would in turn take his cut from a private landowner or *ingenio* recruiter. My informants insisted that, at least in the more isolated south-western region along the Haitian border, the trafficking system was still in force.

My impression at that time was that, as the international outcry escalated and the Dominican government came under more national and international press scrutiny, some directives must have gone out from the top to cut down wherever possible on the forcible recruitment. At the local level, the army was not going to lose the chance of quick profits, but it had not been put at CEA's unlimited disposal as in the past. To improve its image, the PRD government had both increased significantly the number of official Kongos, had marginally improved the daily wage on the state plantations, and had also devised new incentive payments to keep the Haitians on the *ingenios* to which they had originally been assigned. But in discussions with middle-level CEA bureaucrats, I also learned how the existing system had come to depend on forcible recruitment whenever there is a serious shortfall of Haitian labour in particular regions.

Recruitment takes many forms. In theory, the labour requirements for each of the 16 *ingenios* are calculated at the beginning of each harvest season. The top officials of the Romana enterprise, CEA and the Vicini family meet to calculate their anticipated labour deficit. There is also consultation with the federation of outgrowers, which is expected to calculate the needs of its own members. When the Kongos are brought over, they are assigned to a particular *ingenio*, though not necessarily to one of the CEA enterprises. Of the 16,000 brought over in 1979–80, for instance, 14,000 were originally assigned to CEA, 1,500 to Romana, and 500 to the Vicini group. By the middle of the harvest season, CEA tends to have the most serious deficit. The reasons are twofold, first the flight of many of the imported workers from the CEA properties reputed to have the most appalling conditions to other properties such as Romana where the conditions are generally believed to be better; secondly, the staggered nature of sugar production throughout the different regions of the country.

While flight from the CEA plantations can be prompted by the grotesque conditions on them, it can also be stimulated by active competition from CEA's competitors in the sugar industry, particularly at times of severe labour shortage. The Haitian workers who return year after year become familiar with the conditions in a number of different places. Though they may be unable to select the *ingenio* of their own choice, they may take advantage of the first opportunity to run away. And because the system works largely on the basis of illegals, no one will ask too many questions about identity papers if the cane is rotting in the fields and cane cutters are hard to find. Thus hundreds of workers try to run away from the dilapidated *bateyes* of the huge Haina complex near Santo Domingo, moving to the east of the country and particularly to Romana. Workers are not only brought in under the official contract; in addition each of the *ingenios* has its own recruiting agents, who tout for additional labour in both the Dominican Republic and Haiti. Regularly over the past few years CEA has taken paid advertisements in the national press, ordering the Haitians not to leave the place to which they were originally assigned, ordering the private sector not to recruit Haitians on the CEA plantations, and threatening reprisals against any recruiters who would do this. But the warnings appear to have had little effect. A CEA official from Ingenio Haina told me in May 1982 that 600 of the 2,000 Haitians assigned there had already deserted. I never found how they were replaced, if at all.

Such a system requires either financial inducements, or outright repression. And this is why the *bateyes* are like concentration camps, where the Haitians are not free to leave their immediate area. The PRD government claimed that the desertions were then increasing, precisely because it had relaxed the controls. Under the Balaguer government, they said, the *bateyes* were like prisons, with the Haitians padlocked in their barracks after the long hours of work. It may be that controls relaxed somewhat in the early 1980s, but the *bateyes* were still regularly patrolled by armed guards, and any Haitian moving around the country without a *cedula* (identification paper) was still liable to immediate arrest. Nor were the CEA plantation guards any more tolerant of Haitian protests about their living and working conditions. As the liberal newspaper *Nuevo Diario* reported in May 1982, when yet another Haitian cane cutter was killed in dubious circumstances:

> Beafil Bertonic. This was the name of the Haitian killed on the morning of May 20th, from a bullet in his head, in Villa Altagracia. According to news reports the police and rural guards arrested a further twenty friends of Beafil. All of them were protesting because of the excessive delays in paying the money which they had earned in cutting cane. . . . Beafil is yet one more name among those who die in so many ways, because of modern slavery, camouflaged slavery, institutionalised slavery.

Labour deficits also occur because milling and cane cutting start in different months, whereas the Kongos are brought in *en bloc* at the beginning of the harvest season. The Central Romana and the bulk of the CEA enterprises in the south-east of the country, together with Haina near Santo Domingo and Barahona in the south-west, tend to start production earlier, in December or January. The smaller mills of Amistad, Esperanza and Montellanos in the north begin to mill far later, in April or May, for climatic reasons. In principle CEA aims to move many of the Kongos up north when the earlier harvests are coming to an end. But the harvest often begins late in the south, in particular when there are problems in negotiating the contract with the Haitians. Competition for the available labour force then develops between the administrators of the twelve CEA enterprises themselves, as much as between CEA and the private sector. This is one reason why much of the forcible recruitment in the north of the country has occurred in the months of April and May, when the deficits have normally been at their highest.

In August 1982, I testified in the name of the Anti Slavery Society at that year's session of the UN Working Group on Slavery in Geneva. While trying to present a balanced picture, to mention the few improvements that had occurred including the possible reduction in systematic forcible recruitment and capture of Haitians within the Dominican Republic itself, I concluded that there had been no significant improvement in the Haitians' situation since Montgomery's testimony three years earlier. I had a wealth of written evidence to back up allegations of continuing forced labour, including eyewitness accounts that had already been published in such newspapers as the London *Guardian* and the *Washington Post*. Once again, the proceedings of the UN Working Group were picked up by the international press agencies, and quickly made new newspaper headlines in the Dominican Republic. Once again the Dominican authorities denied everything. Acting President Jacobo Majluta denied categorically that any such capture of Haitians had taken place; Armed Forces Chief Mario Imbert McGregor accused me of lying "in order to destroy the image of the Dominican Armed Forces". CEA Director Secundino Gil Morales affirmed more soberly that, "One cannot deny that the living conditions provided for contracted Haitian cane-cutters in our country have not been sufficiently adequate. Nevertheless, one can state that these conditions have now undergone fundamental change, in particular since the year in which the PRD took power under the presidency of Antonio Guzmán." The Armed Forces promised in the meantime that an investigation would be initiated concerning the alleged implication of soldiers in the capture and sale of Haitians entering the country clandestinely.

Two months later the ILO's Commission of Enquiry got seriously under way. In October 1982, preliminary hearings were held before the Commission in Geneva, at which I testified together with a member of the World Council of Churches who had visited the sugar plantations on several occasions, and French journalist Maurice Lemoine who had published his outstanding book *Sucre Amer (Bitter Sugar)* the previous year (a novel, based on fact, describing the plight of the contemporary Haitian cane cutters through the experiences of a Kongo).[8] Once again, the Dominican authorities continued to deny more or less everything. Concerning restrictions on freedom of movement the Dominican government representative stated that:

> at present freedom of movement existed in his country, and Haitian workers exercised this right to go to nearby compounds and villages, to make visits and purchases. The immigration laws however empowered the authorities to authorise foreigners to reside in the country for the purpose of carrying out certain tasks. While they enjoyed freedom of movement, the authorities had the right to know where they were.[9]

And concerning the specific allegations of forcible recruitment of Haitians in the Dominican Republic, he continued that:

> the present Dominican authorities had not been informed of any forced recruitment of Haitians for the sugar harvest, nor of any payments for the supply of such workers. Whatever might have been done in the past, the present Government condemned any practice of this kind. It was prepared to take measures to punish such abuses severely and to prevent a continuing increase in illegal immigration of foreigners.

The ILO Commission recalled that, according to statements made at the same session by a Haitian representative, the government of Haiti had transmitted protests to the Dominican Foreign Ministry concerning the round-up of Haitians by the security forces; the Dominican representative, however, denied all knowledge of this, concurring only that he was "merely aware of certain reports which had occurred in the Dominican press":

They referred to Haitians working in the coffee harvest, who had been arrested at the request of Dominican peasants because the latter's traditional source of employment had been affected. These arrests had not occurred during the period of the sugar harvest, and it was not a question of finding labour for the sugar plantations.[10]

In January 1983, the ILO Commission finally left to undertake its field enquiries in the Dominican Republic. On several occasions, it raised the issue of Haitian forced labour with CEA officials, other government officials, and administrators from the Romana plantation and the Vicini group. It also discussed the allegations with Dominican and Haitian trade unionists, and was able to visit many of the areas that I had visited one year previously. Together, the three members of the Commission visited the Haina plantation near Santo Domingo, and Romana in the east. They then divided into separate groups. One took CEA's Ingenio Porvenir, and the Vicini group's Cristóbal Colón, in the east. Another went to the south-western border, visiting the Ingenio Barahona. The third member went to the troubled Valverde region in the north of the country, visiting the two CEA *ingenios* of Esperanza and Montellanos. It was an intensive programme, which gave the Commission a comprehensive picture of conditions nationwide at that time.

With government officials and private employers, the Commission raised in particular the reports of forced labour which had been so widely published in the Dominican press between 1979 and 1981. As it reported subsequently:

> The above-mentioned allegations were generally denied by the authorities of the Dominican Republic, as well as by the Employers' Confederation and by the representatives of the plantations visited by the Commission. They observed that the press tended to distort, exaggerate and sensationalise. The representatives of the Ministry of Labour stated that there might be confusion between raids and efforts made by the State Sugar Board to persuade deserters to return to work if they did not want to be deported. The Minister of the Interior stated that the authorities arrested Haitians who were in the country as illegal immigrants with a view to sending them back, and confirmed that at certain times, particularly when there were complaints about this illegal immigration in the press or in political circles, these deportations had been intensified. The representatives of the State Sugar Board stated that the raids mentioned in the press might have occurred, but without any participation by the Board.[11]

In the south-western and northern areas of the country, the ILO Commission's findings were basically the same as my own of the previous year. At the Barahona plantation, the Commission spoke with various groups of workers who had entered the country illegally. Some stated that they had paid money to a Haitian to take them across the frontier, and had later been picked up by the army. One group stated that they had been kept for three days at the military barracks in Pedernales. The military had asked them for money, they had received nothing to eat, and finally they had been brought by lorry to the Barahona plantation at night. Several of them had tried to leave, but they had been arrested and brought back. They stated that it was impossible to leave on foot, because there were check-points at all the main crossroads. A recruiter interviewed by the Commission in Barahona stated that he went to military posts to collect Haitian workers detained after crossing the frontier.

In the northern regions the ILO's Commission member, Chief Justice Sir William Douglas of Barbados, found that "the presence and great influence of the military forces were very evident." Numerous informants, including workers interviewed on the CEA plantations, told him that the armed forces "persecuted and exploited the Haitian population in a totally arbitrary manner". It was observed that, because the Haitians had the status of illegal immigrants, they were in practice without any protection, and could be arrested at any time. Soldiers at the Benito Monción fortress carried out frequent raids "to extort money from them, rob them of their belongings, deport them or send them to work". Haitians apparently preferred to work on rice farms rather than the sugar plantations, but they were rounded up by the army when they were needed to cut cane. Douglas noted that the round-ups had happened "particularly in 1979, 1980 and 1981", but the atmosphere of fear and insecurity continued. One worker stated that at times the workers slept in the fields to avoid being rounded up by the army. Both Haitians and Dominicans also expressed their fear of informers.[12]

In conclusion, the ILO Commission of Enquiry affirmed that the exaction of forced labour from the Haitians normally resident in the Dominican Republic was a serious and ongoing problem, and it made a series of technical and other recommendations to bring about its abolition. The need to control the activities of the police and army was singled out for particular mention:

> The Government of the Dominican Republic should take measures to ensure that the military forces and the police act in strict accordance with the law and refrain from all arbitrary and oppressive conduct in relation to Haitian residents, whatever their status. In the light of the evidence received by the Commission, it recommends that the Government initiate a thorough study, by persons of recognised standing and impartiality, of means of ensuring observance of this standard of conduct by the security forces, including the provision of readily accessible and expeditious procedures for examining complaints and granting redress to victims of unlawful action by the security forces. Particular attention should be given, in this connection, to ensuring that the security forces do not use their law-enforcement powers as a means of pressure to meet manpower needs.[13]

Other recommendations concerned an end to measures which had "the effect of confining workers within the plantation or any part of the plantation," together with the establishment and rigorous enforcement of strict penal provisions for the violation of such principles; the establishment of placement offices and regular contracts for all Haitian workers employed in the sugar and other agricultural industries: and a programme with a view to the regularisation of the status of Haitians who had worked in the country for a given period of time.

The publication of the ILO's report in mid 1983 brought yet further rebuttals from the Dominican government. In its official reply, dated 15 September 1983, it rejected "as unfounded, baseless and false the accusations of alleged violations of various labour Conventions by the Dominican Republic," and stated briefly that "the charges concerning alleged violations of the Forced Labour Convention, which are the most serious, are completely cleared up by the reply we give." In fact the 19-page reply said nothing concerning the alleged forcible recruitment within the country, appearing deliberately to gloss over the issue.

In the meantime Dr Ramón Antonio Veras, now the scourge of CEA with his regular articles in *El Nacional de Ahora*, was raking up new evidence. In March 1983, only two months after the ILO Commission had left, he described a new series of round-ups in the northern town of Esperanza. As he wrote on 21 March, police and military troops had been carrying out fierce persecution against Haitian *braceros* working at the Ingenio Esperanza over the past few days:

> Information at my disposal, and also a photograph that I have in my possession, shows that a group of soldiers arrived in the town of Esperanza, indicating to the Haitian *braceros* that they would be transferred to the east of the country to work on private plantations. When the *braceros* refused, stating that they had been recruited to work on the CEA plantations, they were severely beaten, although they produced documents showing that they were working for CEA . . . one of the Haitians showed to the soldiers who beat and arrested him the receipts of payments from Ingenio Esperanza as evidence that he was currently employed there. According to my information, this Haitian is currently interned in a Santiago hospital recovering from the blows inflicted on him.

In a further article two days later Dr Veras produced more details, this time laying responsibility firmly at the door of the Vicini group:

> A letter from a Haitian defence organisation points to an operation for the buying and selling of Haitians, as well as the repression carried out against people from our next-door country. Among other things it says that since the end of December 1982 there has been open repression against the Haitian *braceros* in order to return them forcibly to Haiti. But since March this year the repression has changed its direction; now it is not to send them to Haiti, but to sell them to the private plantations in the east, in particular the Central Cristóbal Colón in San Pedro Macoris, and the Ingenio Catarey of San Cristóbal. On March 8 three jeeps and two lorries full of guards arrived in Valverde, Mao, fully armed, and carried out a raid in which they captured an indeterminate number of Haitians in Ingenio Esperanza, in such *bateyes* as Boca de Mao, Laguna Salada, Guayacanes, and *batey* Libertad. The Haitians were kicked and beaten, then despatched to the east, sold to work on the private farms. On March 9, at 5.45 in the morning, in Esperanza's *batey* no. 2, they took 50 Haitian cane cutters. Despite showing their papers, they were arrested by the soldiers and are now in the Ingenio Catarey working against their will.

This time Dr Veras gave details of a jeep with official number plates (No. 0–1795) that had been involved in one of the raids. One wonders whether any investigations were ever carried out.

Forced Labour Escalates: The 1985–86 Harvest

In May 1986, while completing the first draft of this book, I received allegations that there had been a new spate of forcible recruitment during the current harvest season. The *Central Unitaria de Trabajadores* (CUT), for example, had sent a communication to the International Labour Organisation, stating that

> following an announcement by the Government that there would be no organised recruiting of Haitian labourers for the 1985–6 sugar harvest, Haitian workers have been rounded up by organised groups, with the complicity of the Dominican authorities, and supplied to both state-owned and private plantations for money.[14]

If true, these allegations would imply that the past reports of the Anti Slavery Society and the ILO had borne no fruit, that the situation was as bad as ever. I decided to return to Haiti and the Dominican Republic for a follow-up enquiry. The following account is based on investigations in the Dominican Republic and Haiti, conducted in June 1986.

For the 1985–86 sugar harvest, negotiations with the Haitian government for a new contract had indeed got under way later than usual. Initially, the Dominican government of President Jorge Blanco had been reluctant to draw up a new contract with the now highly unstable Duvalier regime. But the main factor in the delay was the by now critical economic situation of the Dominican State Sugar Board. On 12 December, when the harvest should already have been under way, CEA's director Victor Manuel Báez announced that no Haitian *braceros* would be imported because of CEA's lack of resources, and that the *zafra* would be conducted "with the Haitians already in the country and with the Dominicans". Though admitting that the current sugar harvest was at risk, and that the *colonos* had not been paid because of the dire lack of funds, he insisted that CEA simply did not have at its disposal the US$3 million to finance an additional contract with the Haitian government. The CEA director's comments were followed by a wave of advertisements in the Dominican press, appealing to the Dominicans' sense of patriotism to cut their own cane. Slogans appeared throughout the country, pleading for the "Dominicanisation" of the *zafra*. And cartoons accompanying them portrayed a black-faced Dominican peasant, CEA badge on his lapel and machete at his side, carrying a model of a modern-looking sugar mill. On top of this, CEA promised better living and working conditions, and higher salaries for Dominican peasants who were willing to go to the cane fields.

The Dominican press itself remained sceptical, and did little to aid CEA's belated campaign. For example, *Ultima Hora* carried an article in late December, entitled "Situation in the *Bateyes* Obstructs Dominicanisation of the *Zafra*", in which it described the still appalling living conditions, and argued that the salary would still average only 8.5 pesos (approximately US$3) for a full day's gruelling work. On top of this, CEA had continuing problems with organised labourers on the *ingenios*. On 8 December 1985 54 trade unions from the twelve CEA *ingenios* adopted a manifesto, in which they threatened to paralyse the entire sugar industry if CEA did not at once grant seven demands, including 30 days' bonus pay from the previous harvest, a pledge to keep all twelve *ingenios* open, further pledges not to hand CEA properties over to private ownership and to carry out a labour-intensive diversification programme, and the back payment of social security earnings to registered Dominican workers.[15]

The influential Federation of Private Sugar Growers (FEDOCA) was equally sceptical. In a press statement issued in the second week of December, FEDOCA warned that the next sugar harvest would be a complete failure if Haitian *braceros* were not imported. Arguing that the livelihood of over one and a half million people would be placed at risk if the 1985–86 harvest failed to materialise, it urged the government to place eleven million pesos at CEA's immediate disposal to go ahead with the official recruitment programme.

Without a contract, the Dominican government seemed to know only one way to recruit cane cutters. As during past periods of acute labour shortage, it utilised the army to comb small villages known to be occupied by Haitian squatters, and round up the able-bodied males for forcible transfer to the sugar plantations. At Christmas time the Parish Council from the small town of Santa Ana de Enriquillo, near Barahona in the south-west of the country, declared that soldiers were "arresting and maltreating both Haitians and Dominicans of Haitian origin" who were then working in the coffee harvest.[16] The raids continued into the New Year. As the newspaper *Ultima Hora* reported on 3 January 1986,

> Troops from the national army have begun an operation to arrest the Haitian nationals found in the coffee-growing zones of this region, to transfer them to the Ingenio Barahona, where they are used as cane cutters in the harvest which is now getting under way. Arrests have flared up again in the communities of Enriquillo, Paraíso, La Ciénaga and other places where coffee is grown. The persons arrested are treated as prisoners, and trucked to different sugar fields of the local *ingenio*.[17]

Local sources confirmed that the arrests had taken place on a massive scale.

A similar wave of arrests was also reported in the north of the country, where the ILO had reported the most systematic capture of Haitians a few years beforehand. On 8 January one newspaper reported that 540 Haitians had been kidnapped by the army over the past few days, and transported to *ingenios* in the east. The newspaper attributed the arrests to the "interest of certain persons in charging 15 pesos for each Haitian taken to cut cane". The victims were said to include a prominent Haitian exile, Maslen Joseph, who had been residing in the Dominican Republic under UN protection since 1974.[18]

Such raids may have met the immediate needs of Ingenio Esperanza itself, and of the Barahona mill which was situated nearest to the Haitian border and had ready access to the largest amount of illegal Haitian immigrants. But desperate labour shortages apparently continued, above all on the CEA plantations in the east. On 17 January Néstor Julio Encarnación, the leader of the moderate and pro-government National Federation of Sugar-Workers' Unions (FENSA), once again warned that the present harvest would be a disaster without the customary imported Haitian labour. According to him only three of CEA's twelve sugar mills were then active, because the Haitians to be found in the country were working only on these three CEA properties: the vast Haina complex on the outskirts of Santo Domingo, as well as several small mills, would be unable to commence milling "because they have nobody to cut the cane". The FENSA General Secretary urged CEA to go ahead with the contract, affirming that his union "approves the wise and patriotic intention to Dominicanise the harvest, but feels that this is not the best moment to put such a precipitous measure into practice".[19]

Pressed by both employer and worker organisations in the sugar industry, and by the coffee growers who saw their own Haitian labour supply seriously threatened, President Jorge Blanco now capitulated to their demands and authorised the funds to finance a new contract with the Haitian government. On 18 January Haitian Ambassador Hervé Denis, accompanied by the two high-ranking CEA officials, left on a private flight for Port-au-Prince with his cargo of two suitcases each containing $1 million in cash. In a brief half-hour session with President Jean-Claude Duvalier in the National Palace, Mr Denis handed over the suitcases, received his instructions to arrange the details of the recruitment with Haitian police chief Albert Pierre, and returned to Santo Domingo.

But for the first time in recent years, the contract failed to materialise. Haiti was now in an advanced state of ferment, and Duvalier was rapidly losing control of the country. A nationwide protest movement led by discontented students and schoolchildren, and supported by the influential Catholic Church, had taken to the streets to demand an end to the Duvalier dictatorship. First in the major provincial towns, and then in Port-au-Prince itself, a wave of strikes led by the youth movement escalated with surprising rapidity into the national insurrection which was soon to spell the end of the Duvalier regime.

The protest movement was directed against the Duvalier family, against the repressive Duvalierist structure typified by the vast Tonton Macoute apparatus, and also against the corrupt practices associated with the Duvalier regime. And one very clear example of this corruption, and the degradation of Haitian society, was the contract with the Dominican Republic. Until 1986 there had been sporadic criticism of the contract, but Duvalier's tight control of the media had ensured that it remained muted. After the contract was signed and the initial payment made, the official Haitian radio stations had announced the dates on which aspiring cane cutters were to register for inscription, in the small towns of Leogane and Croix-des-Bouquets on the outskirts of Port-au-Prince. The official radio stations always painted a rosy picture of conditions to be anticipated on the Dominican plantations, suggesting that a diligent worker could earn several hundred dollars for his labours during the harvest season. With annual per capita incomes averaging little more than $50 in rural Haiti, there had often been strong competition among the impoverished peasants for the available places. From the dry Jacmel region on the south coast, landless rural workers and the sons of small farmers went to Leogane: and from the heavily eroded central plateau to the north, large numbers moved to Croix-des-Bouquets. As often as not there were more candidates than places available, and aspiring cane cutters had to bribe recruiting agents in order to be sure of a place.

But in the last months of the Duvalier regime some independent radio stations, in particular the Catholic Church's Radio Soleil and Radio Lumière, denounced the practice as an affront to national dignity. Their programmes, citing Dominican press accounts and the reports of international human rights organisations, had their effect on the anti-Duvalier opposition which now placed the issue of Haitian "slavery" in the Dominican cane fields high on the agenda of the protest movement. In early January 1986, students demonstrated outside the Dominican Embassy in Port-au-Prince, chanting "Jorge Blanco, cut your own cane", and leaving no doubt about the growing popular sentiment against the exploitative conditions on the other side of the border.

A more significant demonstration took place in Leogane at the end of the month. On 28 January 1986, following the official radio announcements, several thousand Haitian peasants made their way to the Leogane market-place, to register for the next harvest; but a large crowd of students and other demonstrators, estimated at between two and three thousand, simply prevented the registration from taking place. Hurling stones at the recruiting agents, they compelled them to run for cover in the local military outpost. Though the army was swiftly called in, and reinforcements sent from the Casernes Dessalines army headquarters in Port-au-Prince, the Haitian government eventually gave up. After two days of often violent demonstrations, in which three Haitian peasants were killed, and most of the remainder fled to the surrounding countryside, the government first announced that the recruiting operations would be switched to the nearby town of Jacmel. Exactly what happened after that has been difficult to determine. It appears that there were further skirmishes in Jacmel a few days later, but no further serious attempts were made by the Haitian authorities to get the recruitment operation under way. In Croix-des-Bouquets, one junior official at the registration point informed me that a few hundred Haitians did turn up for inscription, but by the beginning of February the provinces were in a state of rebellion. In both Leogane and Croix-des-Bouquets, informants told me that the recruitment operation had always been masterminded by the notorious Colonel Albert Pierre, head of Duvalier's secret police and a renowned torturer, who used it to make substantial profits for himself. But by the beginning of February Jean-Claude Duvalier had already made his first unsuccessful attempt to flee the country, before finally leaving for France on 7 February. Albert Pierre was doubtless more concerned to save his own skin than to extort a few thousand dollars from the contract operation, and he too fled the country for Brazil upon Duvalier's own departure. Thus the 1986 contract operation fizzled into nothing.

On the Dominican side, CEA was once again desperate. By the end of January the Dominicans had tightened up border controls, fearing that the effects of the Haitian unrest would spill over to the Dominican side, and declared the frontier closed for an indeterminate period. However, after an emergency meeting with leading CEA officials, on 5 February President Jorge Blanco made a specific exception for the *braceros*. The army commanders of the Third Brigade, in Mao, and the Fifth Brigade in San Juan de la Maguana, were instructed to facilitate their entry through strategic points on the border. Then, one day after Duvalier's flight from Haiti, two leading CEA officials left for the Jimaní–Malpasse border post to persuade Haiti's new National Council of Government (CNG) to respect its obligations under the terms of the contract signed with Duvalier, and to provide 12,000 cane cutters at the earliest opportunity. Although the Haitian Ambassador, Hervé Denis, had stated that the new government would "honour all its contractual obligations" with the Dominican Republic, the CEA delegation nevertheless returned home without a single *bracero*.

CEA's attempt to find patriotic Dominican cane cutters was by now a demonstrable failure. Though government officials were photographed machete in hand, the Dominicans had to resort to the army — the only sector of society unable to say no. Young soldiers were now stationed in at least six CEA *ingenios*, enabling the harvest to get under way in earnest. And while some soldiers went to the cane fields themselves, others now received orders to step up their witch hunt against Haitian immigrants everywhere in the country.

On the night of 11 February, only a few days after Duvalier's fall, the anti-Haitian raids reached Santo Domingo. Army and police units equipped with lanterns combed the Malecón — the long avenue bordering Santo Domingo's Caribbean coastline — searching for Haitians hiding in caves and inlets by the seashore. And behind the "model Market" in the centre of town, where Haitian pedlars and streetsellers tended to congregate, the victims were forced on to trucks under military custody even when they could show documents proving legal residence in the country. Outside the capital, similar raids now took place in the western towns of Dajabón, Elias Piña and Restauración: also in the eastern towns of La Romana, San Pedro Macoris and Higüey. At check-points and customs posts on the main roads, lorries and buses were thoroughly checked for dark-skinned persons suspected of Haitian origin, who were summarily removed. Reportedly, identity documents were taken from the captured Haitians, before they were taken away by the army.[20]

At first CEA simply denied that the raids were occurring, in spite of all the evidence to the contrary. But the denials became less and less convincing, as leading church figures added their voice to the protests now being made by journalists, politicians and pro-Haitian solidarity groups. In mid February Monseñor Fabio Mamerto Rivas, Diocesan Bishop of Barahona, denounced publicly the fact that countless Haitians were being arrested and beaten by the army, and demanded that the government set up a commission of enquiry into the army's brutal treatment of the Haitian population in the south-west of the country. The following week, eight Roman Catholic priests from San Pedro Macoris issued a press release, denouncing the forcible arrest of young Dominicans as well as Haitians, and claiming that the "entire population was terrified to leave their homes for fear of being detained by the Armed Forces". A group of journalists invited by the San Pedro priests to visit the *bateyes* of the region was able to receive eyewitness testimony of the arrests. One 39-year-old resident of Haitian origin, who had been eight years in the Dominican Republic, described how he had been grabbed from his village in Salcedo and taken to *batey* Cachena of Ingenio Consuelo, "without being allowed to go home and tell my family, and without even being able to pick up any clothes". Others described how they had been thrown violently into lorries, and given no money for ten days with which to purchase any food.[21]

In early March the Conference of Dominican Bishops spoke out in unison, urging the government to put an immediate end to the "scandalous outrages" against the Haitians. "To take the Haitians who live here, whether legally or illegally, against their will to cut cane is an act contrary to the most elementary justice, an indignity to our entire nation, and a thing which has impoverished our image overseas", said the bishops.

In a further denunciation on 22 February, independent Deputy Miguel Angel Velásquez attempted to provide some statistics. On the basis of information provided by a commission of Haitian citizens, Velásquez calculated that between two and three thousand Haitians in all had been taken from their homes, and forcibly transferred to the sugar plantations. As others before him, he cited allegations that the kidnappings were a lucrative enterprise, in that CEA paid "ten pesos for each Haitian" — an allegation which he made before the Human Rights Commission of the Dominican Chamber of Deputies in order to secure a parliamentary resolution against such corrupt practices. Around the same time, the lawyer Ramón Antonio Veras announced that he would take before the United Nations Working Group on Slavery the "savage treatment meted out to Haitian residents in the country, who are illegally arrested wherever they are found, and bound together with wire before their transfer to the cane fields".[22] According to Dr Veras, Haitian villages around the towns of Mao and Esperanza were now completely abandoned.

President Jorge Blanco wrote to the Bishops Conference, still blandly denying that it was government policy to force people into cane cutting against their will. But confirmation of the bishops' accusations came from an unexpected quarter. In February 1986 General Héctor Rafael Rojas Canaan, Commander of the Military Brigade in Mao, told journalists in a press conference that Haitians who could prove they were political exiles from the Duvalier regime had been and would be left alone, but that the "*braceros* and other Haitians who do not enjoy this status have been taken to different *ingenios*, in particular in the east of the country". The general gave no numbers, and insisted that the detained Haitians were well enough treated, but otherwise seemed to find nothing unduly wrong with a practice that was in flagrant violation of international law against forced labour.

In effect, whatever the government might say in its public relations statements, public opinion was easily persuaded that Haitians had no right to be in the country unless they cut cane. Either the sugar plantations, or back to Haiti: such was, and should be, the lot of the Haitian illegals. By late February, the Dominican government was once again threatening a new wave of mass deportations for those Haitians who evaded their "responsibilities" on the CEA plantations. Instead of the propaganda aiming to cajole Dominicans on to the plantations from patriotic motives, there was now a series of paid advertisements warning that illegal Haitian immigrants without documents would be repatriated within the next few days if they did not sign up for the harvest, the task "for which they have been permitted to enter the country".

A certain number of Haitians did accept work on the plantations after that, attracted by CEA's promise that the piece-work wage would be raised to 3 pesos per ton of cane cut. In the three months until the end of the harvest, there was no further talk of mass raids in the major towns. In the south-western border there were eyewitness accounts of the arrest of Haitians as late as June, and military check-points kept a tight control on movements around the country. But the recruitment system, as well as being brutal, also proved to be immensely inefficient. In March, official sources stated that there was still a deficit of some 10,000 cane cutters, and at the end of the season the harvest was the lowest in recent memory.

Notes

1. Dominican Republic Task Force, *Task Force Newsletter*, New York, June 1978.

2. *El Sol*, 17 December 1979.

3. *El Nacional de Ahora*, 16 December 1979.

4. *El Sol*, 18 January 1980.

5. *La Noticia* (Santo Domingo), 1980.

6. *El Nacional de Ahora* (date unknown).

7. *Ultima Hora*, 3 April 1980.

8. Maurice Lemoine, *Bitter Sugar* (Zed Books, London, 1985).

9. *ILO Official Bulletin*, Vol. LXVI, 1983 ("Report of the Commission of Enquiry to examine the observance of certain international labour Conventions by the Dominican Republic and Haiti with respect to the employment of Haitian workers on the sugar plantations of the Dominican Republic"), p. 53.

10. Ibid.

11. Ibid., p. 57.

12. Ibid., p. 59.

13. Ibid., p. 156.

14. "Report of the Committee of Experts on the Application of Conventions and Recommendations", International Labour Conference, 72nd Session, 1986, Report III, Part 4A, pp. 236–8.

15. *Unidad Sindical*, November–December 1985.

16. *El Nacional de Ahora*, 26 December 1985.

17. *Ultima Hora*, 3 January 1986.

18. *Nuevo Diario*, 8 January 1986.

19. *El Nacional de Ahora*, 18 January 1986.

20. Ibid., 12 February 1986.

21. *La Noticia*, 21 February 1986.

22. *Nuevo Diario*, 14 February 1986.

23. *El Nacional de Ahora*, 14 February 1986.

7   The Plight of the Kongos: The Bilateral Contract and Official Trade in Haitian Labour

It is now time to turn to the official bilateral contract drawn up almost every year between the governments of Haiti and the Dominican Republic at the beginning of the sugar harvest season. It is the abuses inherent in this contract labour system — and above all its confidential clauses, with the secret cash payments that have been made to the Duvalier regime — which have caused the greatest international scandal and allegations that the system is no more or less than modern-day slave traffic. But the problem lies not so much in the provisions of the contract itself. In fact they are generous, providing for adequate conditions of recruitment and repatriation, and for living and working conditions perhaps better than those enjoyed by the average Dominican rural worker. The problem is a different one. The contract is drawn up in such a way that, whatever rights the Haitian *braceros* may have on paper, there is no way that they can ensure the enforcement of these provisions. Until recently, the contract was drawn up in such secrecy that the Haitian workers involved were unaware what the text of the contractual agreement was. Though this has changed in recent years, the *braceros* have still had no means of fighting for its implementation. In theory, their rights have been guaranteed by a large number of Haitian inspectors and supervisors nominated by the Duvalier government to protect the workers' interests. In practice, as will be seen below, these official Haitian guardians have been more concerned with protecting Duvalier's and CEA's interests than in protesting against abusive treatment on the sugar plantations.

This chapter traces the evolution of the contract until the time of Duvalier's downfall when the recruiting arrangements collapsed altogether. First it looks at the early history of the inter-state agreements, and considers arguments for and against the validity of the contract agreements as legal instruments. Then it looks at the theory and practice of the contract's provisions during the eight years of the PRD government between 1978 and 1986. Finally it examines the reasons for the breakdown of the contract in 1985–86, and considers what may be done to humanise this migrant labour system in the years to come.

Early History, 1952–78

The first agreement with the Haitian government was drawn up in 1952. On 28

January of that year, General Trujillo addressed a letter to the Dominican Senate, expressing the "desire of the Governments of Haiti and the Dominican Republic to regulate the contracting of Haitian labourers to work temporarily in the Dominican Republic, in agricultural or agro–industrial enterprises", and explaining that, under the terms of this agreement, agricultural workers were to be repatriated by the enterprises employing them at the end of the harvest season. The agreement was to expire at the end of five years. In December 1959 a new and similar agreement was concluded, likewise to last for a five-year period. Under these two early inter-state agreements, the imported Haitian workers were to be given individual labour contracts on the agricultural enterprises to which they were assigned, and their basic rights and expectations were to be spelled out in these contracts somewhat more clearly than had been the case in recent years. At this time, it seems there was no mass traffic involved. The private sugar plantations, such as the Central Romana, had to file petitions for their own quotas of Haitian labour. Although the period was in theory to be limited to one year, it was easy enough for recruited Haitians to remain behind, and turn gradually into the *viejos* who have remained since then in their precarious situation in the Dominican Republic.

After Trujillo's fall, no further official agreement was drawn up until 14 November 1966, when a new agreement, also to last for a five-year period, was signed by the two governments and approved by Dominican Congress on 20 December 1966. As in the previous instances, it provided for individual labour contracts to be granted to the imported migrant workers. Since then, no further agreements have been signed between Haiti and the Dominican Republic, although annual contracts have normally been drawn up between the Dominican CEA and the Haitian Ministry of Social Affairs. They are stated to have been made in accordance with the terms of the 1966 agreement. However, they have never been submitted to Dominican Congress for approval, nor were the contents of any of these annual contracts available to the public until 1979. Though the matter of congressional approval may seem a technicality, in practice the absence of any parliamentary or other supervision was always likely to lead to severe abuse. Since CEA took responsibility on the Dominican side for the signing, operation and implementation of the contract, it has treated the imported Haitian workers *en bloc*, reserving the right to transfer them from one plantation to another at random throughout the harvest. Thus, when there was a severe deficit in the *ingenios* that began milling later in the harvest season, hundreds or thousands of *braceros* might be moved arbitrarily to a new plantation on the other side of the country, where conditions were infinitely worse than they had bargained for.

The number of *braceros* officially imported remained fairly steady throughout the twelve years of the Balaguer government from 1966 to 1978. For the 1966–67 harvest it was 14,000, then it fell to 10,000 in 1967–68. Between 1969 and 1977 it was recorded as 12,000, except for three years when the contract failed to materialise, usually as a result of border and other diplomatic tensions between the two governments.

The transport, living and working conditions were grotesque. According to one account in the mid 1960s,

Already at registration the prospective migrants are treated like chattels.. . . . The Dominican companies provide the transportation and give a dollar to every migrant for food on the trip. Then they are packed in trucks and taken to various parts of the Republic. The trip takes from two to four days depending on the location of the Dominican sugar plantation to which they are assigned. It is a sight to behold, according to a Dominican informant, to see these men arrive at their ultimate destination. Tired, dusty and hungry after several days of travelling, guarded by soldiers, they look more like the inmates of a concentration camp than voluntary workers. . . . The life of the Haitian migrant worker in the Dominican Republic is reminiscent of slavery days. Their work consists of cutting or carting cane from dawn until dusk.[1]

By the end of the Balaguer government, there had been no sign of change. By all accounts, the worst moment for the imported Haitian contingent was the end of the harvest, the time of repatriation. There were many claims that some Haitians tried to make their own way home but were stopped and sold off to private landowners for a few pesos each. If they were sent home, they might first have to wait several days until the harvest had been concluded in each *ingenio*. Then all their compatriots would be grouped together in one place until the repatriation could finally get under way. As one source described the Haitians' situation in 1977:

In early August of 1977, 10,000 contracted Haitians waited twelve days for their return transportation by the State Sugar Council (CEA). Gathered in the town of Haina, they were herded into a confined area of the street without food, housing facilities, fresh water, bedding or blankets. There, men and women were guarded by the military. Most of them subsisted on donations from local townspeople or spent their small savings on food. After twelve days of such mistreatment, they took to the streets angrily demanding repatriation. Only then did the buses arrive to transport them to the border.[2]

After 1978: The PRD and the Contract

The PRD came to power on a platform including pledges to respect human rights. There were manifold promises that "things would change on the *bateyes*", and the contract would be both humanised and enforced. In mid 1979, the Dominican government headed by President Antonio Guzmán was apparently incensed by the Anti Slavery Society's denunciation of the cane cutters' situation. PRD spokesmen protested that the accusations were both outdated and unfair, because the facts presented had taken place under the previous government. When the Anti Slavery Society's allegations were presented as evidence before the ILO's Commission of Enquiry, the Dominican government responded in strong and offended terms:

The statements in the reports concerned are guilty of a grave distortion, since it is untrue that the immigrants in question lack any protection under the law. Quite the contrary, labour in the Dominican Republic, in its broadest sense, is regulated by the Constitution and the laws, without distinction of any kind in respect of work carried out by aliens. . . . Since taking office on 16 August 1978, the Government of the Dominican Republic, presided over by His Excellency Don Silvestre Antonio Guzmán Fernández, has remained true to its undertaking regarding the observance of the rights and fundamental freedoms of the human person, and it is wrong, indeed calculatedly unjust, to subject this policy to public debate by making it the target of criticism, evidently in pursuit of particular interests. The Haitian workers in question come to work, not on estates owned by individuals (although they may do so exceptionally), but to cut cane on state-owned plantations and, in far small numbers, in privately financed plantations, since this is the source of employment which is most practicable for them and which has the least effect on the national labour force. They come protected, in all cases, by an appropriate contract of employment, supervised by the Government of Haiti itself. The assertion that slave labour exists in the Dominican Republic, involving foreigners or Haitian nationals, is devoid of truth. Freedom of association is fully ensured and the right to organise is protected, as it should be.[3]

In an attempt to protect its image, the one thing that the PRD government did now do was to publish, for the first time, the details of the bilateral contract for the 1979–80 harvest. Details of the 30 articles of the contract, dated 18 December 1979, were now published in the Dominican press and began to lead to widespread public debate. It would be useful to summarise the essential details, as the basic language was hardly to change in the annual contracts subsequently drawn up during the years of PRD government.

Under Article 1, CEA requested the Haitian government to provide 14,000 *braceros* for the 1979–80 harvest season. Article 2 then specified the ten pledges made by CEA, with regard to the overall treatment of these workers, namely: (a) that the recruitment should be carried out in Haiti, through CEA representatives in special recruiting centres, and should not last for more than 30 days; (b) that CEA should foot the costs of the medical checks demanded by the State Secretariat for Public Health and Social Assistance; (c) that CEA would assure transport to the Dominican work centres in buses "offering full guarantees of comfort and security" (the Haitian government having to pay transport costs as far as the Malpasse–Jimaní border post); (d) that CEA should pay the costs of food and lodging from the recruitment centre to the border, and also from the border to the work place in the Dominican Republic; (e) that salaries should be equal to those paid to Dominican workers for the same kind of work; (f) that the Haitian workers and their family members, from the date of arrival in the Dominican Republic until the date of departure, should have "lodging units or communal apartments offering the hygienic and sanitary conditions required by law, as well as furniture (table, chairs and bed); the roof of all lodging units was to be covered, in order to protect the workers from the rain"; (g) to facilitate visits by the Haitian Embassy's supervisors and inspectors to the places where the Haitian *braceros* were to live, before their arrival. Moreover, these living places were to be furnished with "metal beds with mattresses, drinking water, bathrooms and other conveniences". The installation of "adequate and hygienic dining rooms was compulsory", so that the workers could have convenient places for their daily meals; (h) to extend to the Haitian agricultural workers during their stay in the Dominican Republic, the benefit of Dominican laws on social security, compulsory sickness insurance, insurance against work accidents, weekly rest, maternity insurance, annual bonuses, etc. It was further understood that, at the moment of repatriation, an injured person would have the right to the costs of all subsequent treatment and legal benefits if he had not been passed fit by that time; (i) to pay the immigration tax in the Dominican Republic and matriculation costs to the Haitian Consulate; (j) to repatriate the Haitian *braceros* at the end of the harvest, with travel costs (for both food and travel) from the place of work to the Malpasse frontier. The Haitian Embassy was to be given 15 days' advance notice of the end of the harvest.

The remaining 28 articles of the 1979–80 contract elaborated further on the basic CEA commitments which had been spelled out in Article 2. Article 8 was concerned with the designated work place. It specified that "the Haitian agricultural worker recruited by CEA should work exclusively on the *ingenio* to which he had been assigned", and that "CEA commits itself, with the collaboration of the supervisors and inspectors nominated by the Haitian Embassy, to take the necessary measures to avoid the worker being transferred to another work place which has no obligation with the Haitian Government". Article 11 stipulated that CEA was authorised to discount one peso from the Haitians' fortnightly pay cheques, the discounted money to be converted into dollars and handed over to the Haitian Embassy for eventual payment to the *braceros* on their return to Haiti. Article 22 provided that Sunday should be a rest day, and that there should also be a daily break between midday and 1.30 p.m. Furthermore, CEA was to provide recreation centres organised by its Department of Social Affairs. Article 25 stated that, in the event of accidents, the Haitians should be provided with free transport to the medical centres where medical care was to be provided. Article 26 stipulated the remuneration as 1.55 Dominican pesos per ton of cane cut (in the event of the piece-rate being raised, the Haitians were also to benefit from this). Article 27 elaborated further that in the event of any devaluation of the Dominican peso during the current harvest season, both the *braceros* and the supervisors and inspectors would be compensated. Article 29 recognised the right of the Haitian *braceros* to bonus payments during the last weeks of the harvest, in the event that CEA should realise any profits, in accordance with the relevant legislation then in force. Under Article 30, CEA committed itself to ensuring that the savings of the Haitian *braceros* could be converted from Dominican pesos to US dollars at the moment of repatriation.

Several articles of the 1979–80 contract were concerned with the number and role of the Haitian supervisors and inspectors who had been introduced by President Guzmán the previous year (many claimed that this had been a condition made for the continuation of the contract by the Duvalier regime, which was then concerned at the implications of the democratic opening in the Dominican Republic for internal events in Haiti: Duvalier felt he needed to keep a close check on the *braceros*, to see that they were not influenced by the Haitian opposition movement, and did not become familiar with the concept of trade union freedoms). The Haitian Embassy was granted the right to nominate 80 inspectors and 17 supervisors in order to "protect the Haitian agricultural workers". The normal salary of a Haitian supervisor was to be 385 Dominican pesos per month, and of an inspector 220 pesos per month, "the salaries to be remitted by CEA every month directly to the Haitian Embassy, in accordance with instructions given by the Government of Haiti, to be handed over subsequently to the beneficiaries".

On the surface, there were now some improvements, above all in the highly visible process of transport and transfer of the *braceros* at the beginning of the harvest season. At the Jimaní border post, journalists noted that for the first time the Haitians were treated more or less like human beings. Whereas in the past they had been left out in the open before being removed to the *ingenios*, now they were taken in buses, in more organised fashion, to their final destination. But at the end of the harvest, the delays were as bad as ever before the final repatriation, leading to the same kind of protests as a few years previously. In July 1980, over 2,000 Haitians were left in an open-air camp 20 kilometres outside Santo Domingo, in the small village of Yaco. Cooped up with no food or sanitary facilities, they were kept waiting for the repatriation order for a full three weeks. The Dominican government blamed the delay on the Duvalier regime, which was reportedly holding out for higher bonus payments. After threatening to march on the Presidential Palace if they were not sent home immediately, some of the Haitians finally lost patience, openly rioted, and began to set fire to nearby cane fields. The army moved in swiftly, quelled the spontaneous demonstrations with tear gas and widespread beatings, and regained control.[4]

On this occasion, the press publicity had some effect, and may have been instrumental in persuading the government to change its methods of repatriation. Partly to keep the *braceros* away from the public eye, they were now moved in smaller groups from the *ingenios* to the Haitian frontier, as soon as their own task had been completed. In the following year, 1981, CEA's Executive Director published his own account of the repatriation process, describing an orderly transfer in "comfortable buses". Unfortunately for him, eyewitnesses could provide a different story. As a Catholic priest reported from a border village a few days later, "I have seen with my own eyes the repatriation of the Haitian workers. They pass through Elias Piña not in comfortable buses as the letter says, but in cane-carrying trucks like animals. They pass through by night — perhaps so that the Dominican people should not see the conditions of repatriation."

While professing to improve the conditions of recruitment and repatriation, the PRD also looked for other ways of stabilising the labour force during the harvest season. One of the problems it tried to address was the regular flight of Haitians from the CEA plantations to the private estates, where conditions were often reputed to be marginally better. To do this, it threatened reprisals against the private recruiters, who "stole" the Haitian *braceros* from the CEA *bateyes*, and it also changed the method of payment, to provide the Haitians with some incentive to remain on the CEA plantations to which they had originally been assigned. In December 1979, for example, one newspaper reported that several recruiting agents from the Central Romana had been arrested while engaging in clandestine recruitment on CEA's Ingenio Consuelo.[5] Nevertheless, the practice evidently continued. In May 1980, towards the end of the harvest season, CEA took out a full-page press advertisement warning

all private individuals or public entities who spirit away the workers contracted by the state *ingenios*, by false promises or any other mechanism, that CEA is increasing its vigilance against such acts which are in clear violation of the law, and that once the guilty persons are caught in the act or identified, they will be prosecuted.

The Haitian *braceros* who had now completed the harvest in the *ingenio* to which they had originally been assigned were ordered to report at once to the Haina plantation where there was currently a severe labour shortage. CEA warned that a census was about to be taken, to locate all those Haitians who had come officially to cut the cane under the bilateral contract. These threats did not come to much — as I was able to see for myself the following year. But CEA also devised a more practical method of persuading the *braceros* to stay on its own plantations. As stated above, in the 1979–80 contract Haitian labourers were given one piece-rate income, of which a peso was deducted every fortnight as compulsory savings, to be handed to them on return to Haiti (the *braceros* claimed that they never received this payment). The system was now changed, partly (according to CEA) to rid the contract of its slavery-like connotations, but also to provide a strong disincentive to those who deserted their post. All cane cutters were now to be paid 1.83 Dominican pesos per ton, plus a 50 cent incentive payment at the end of the harvest for each ton that they had cut. During the six months of the harvest they were given vouchers for each incentive payment, which could only be traded for cash during the last fortnight.

With regard to living conditions and the social infrastructure of the *bateyes*, the PRD government still did little, if anything. With the greater press freedom brought by the change of government, countless journalists went into the *bateyes* during the harvest. By and large, their reports produced a similar picture of tumbledown shacks without roofs, toilets, mattresses or, often, beds — let alone the innumerable comforts and appurtenances that had been mentioned in the much-publicised contract. In fact, the PRD attitude towards the labour force and labour conditions in the sugar industry was full of the most flagrant contradictions. On the one hand it made more noise than its predecessor about the "Dominicanisation" of the harvest, commissioning several studies to recommend measures that might bring Dominican peasants back on to the sugar plantations. On the other hand it consistently increased the number of *braceros* brought in under the contract, until it had reached its highest ever level of 23,000 in 1985.

In 1980 the National Planning Department (ONAPLAN) was instructed to undertake a major survey on current trends and future perspectives on employment in the national sugar industry. Its comprehensive report, *Empleo en la Zafra Azucarera Dominicana*,[6] was eventually published in April 1981. Noting that one out of every five Dominicans was currently unemployed, and that the underemployment figures were even greater, it asked the fundamental question why 90 per cent of the labour force in the industry was nevertheless Haitian, and why some 30,000 Haitian *braceros* had to be brought in every year (half of them officially, the other half through a variety of clandestine methods) at an apparently great cost to the Dominican economy. In assessing the reasons for this "paradox" it concluded that they could be broken down into economic factors (the low salaries and poor conditions in the *bateyes*), social factors (the lowly status of cane cutting, considered the work of a "slave" or a Haitian) and structural factors (the highly seasonal nature of the work involved). Of ONAPLAN's major conclusions, two stood out. The first was that, whereas CEA had been arguing that a "picador" (cane cutter) could harvest several tons a day and thus end up with a reasonable daily income, the average harvest under present conditions was no more than $1\frac{1}{2}$ tons per day, giving a miserable average daily income of only $2\frac{1}{2}$ Dominican pesos — far below both the legal minimum wage and average daily income in other sectors of the rural economy. The second was that, although the actual number of imported *braceros* was evidently higher, their percentage of total production costs was becoming progressively lower. For the 1979–80 harvest the imported Haitians had constituted 25 per cent of the estimated total labour force, but represented only 10 per cent of total labour costs and 4 per cent of total production costs. ONAPLAN nevertheless expressed its concern that the percentage of Dominicans in the cane-cutting labour force was steadily decreasing, and recommended a series of measures to improve productivity and overall living and working conditions. Its basic argument was that, whatever else might be done, Dominicans would only cut cane if salaries were far higher, and that salaries could only be raised if productivity was infinitely greater. It thus recommended new methods of organising the labour force, as well as a system of burning the cane before harvesting it in order to make the *bracero*'s task far easier.

The ONAPLAN study expressed some scepticism as to whether its report would lead anywhere. It pointed out that

> since 1964 there have been at least five advisory studies concerned with the rehabilitation of the sugar industry and the importation of *braceros* despite the levels of national unemployment. These have included studies by Italconsult, Parsons, Bookers, Downs and the World Bank. Although on the one hand it is comforting to know that almost all of our conclusions and recommendations have been anticipated in one or other of these studies, and thus confirm their seriousness, it is nevertheless disturbing that so few of them have been put into practice, so that the problems persist today without any apparent improvement.

For the short term at least, ONAPLAN's fears were to be vindicated. In the next harvest the number of *braceros* was up yet again, this time to 19,000.

1982: A Personal Testimony

It was during the following sugar harvest, between April and June 1982, that I carried out my own field investigations on behalf of the Anti Slavery Society in the Dominican Republic. During that visit, either alone or in the company of trade unionists, church workers, social workers, journalists and other pro-Haitian activists, I visited most of the CEA *ingenios* as well as many of the *bateyes* on the Central Romana and the private Vicini plantations. Of the CEA properties, I went to Barahona in the south-west, travelling to many remote *bateyes* around the nearby town of Tamayo. In the north I went to the older and dilapidated mills of Amistad and Montellanos, as well as Ingenio Esperanza and the Haitian settlements within the town of Esperanza itself. On several occasions I visited different *bateyes* of Ingenio Haina, which were tens of miles apart and often differed markedly in the conditions offered to the various groups of *braceros*. In the east I spent several days walking, motor-cycling or driving around the group of CEA *ingenios* (Consuelo, Porvenir and Quisqueya) which more or less adjoined each other, as well as to the Vicini group's Ingenio Cristóbal Colón and its Caei plantation to the south-west.

My findings, to those people familiar with the Haitians' situation, were perhaps nothing new; they served only to corroborate previous accounts of thousands of Haitian workers, often barefoot and clad in torn shirts, complaining of working from before dawn until the late evening for a pittance, well below their expectations, which allowed them the choice of returning without savings or half-starving for the six months of the harvest season. They gave endless accounts of threats and reprisals, of cheating over weights, of being compelled to work on official rest days. When I tried to discuss the provisions of the bilateral contract, I seemed to be wasting my time. Some *braceros* had heard of the contract, had heard mention of it over the Haitian national radio, but none of them said they were familiar with its detailed provisions. None of them had received a copy, and a Dominican church-run radio station which attempted to discuss it on the air had been closed down not long before my visit. Copies were not distributed, and, even if they had been, it might not have made much difference. Almost all the Haitians were illiterate, and those with a smattering of literacy understood only Haitian Creole — the contract had apparently never been translated into their national language. In some of the *ingenios*, most notably in Gulf and Western's La Romana, there were indications that old *bateyes* had been modernised and new ones built in the course of the past few years. However, as I soon found out, these were never where the Kongos (or imported *braceros*) were required to live. Either at the end of the Dominican quarters, or in separate and more remote quarters set aside specifically for the Kongos, there were rudimentary concrete rooms, usually equipped with metal beds and sometimes with old mattresses, but nothing else. Dining rooms, bathrooms, running water, recreation centres? Even CEA officials laughed when I mentioned them. Haitians cooked outside on primitive wood fires, walked several hundred yards to collect water from an evil-looking spigot, as often as not had no toilets, and in the worst cases lived in primitive wooden shacks with leaking roofs that must have been sheer hell when the rainy season began in early May.

In fairness, Haitians were not the only ones to suffer. Conditions were often abysmal for all, which is why many of the *ingenios* became predominantly Haitian enclaves. The Haitian workers might be perhaps second- or third-generation residents in the Dominican Republic who are unsure of their national allegiance, speak Spanish better than Creole, see their children saluting the Dominican flag at Dominican schools, but can nevertheless be treated as unwanted aliens when it suits the Dominican authorities. But the Kongos are always at the bottom of the pile, separated from the *viejos*, encouraged by the Guardacampestres and the Haitian inspectors to have nothing to do with their fellow workers. Before turning to specifics, and the huge discrepancy between the provisions of the contract and the reality of the conditions I encountered, it would be useful to give some idea of the social organisation of the average *ingenio*.

Many modern Dominican towns were actually built around the sugar industry, after the late 19th- or early 20th-century booms. Thus in Barahona, you can walk from the centre of town across a CEA check-point into the *ingenio* compound where the *batey central* is to be found. Likewise in San Pedro Macoris and La Romana to the east, and Esperanza to the north, the town itself serves as the central *batey*. Elsewhere, the central *batey* has generally expanded into a smaller town or large village. It is here that the middle-class Dominicans, the administrators or technicians of the sugar mill itself, are to be found. They may have modern subsidised housing, and in some cases — as in the compounds of the Central Romana — even luxury housing. On the outskirts of the central *batey*, as the housing and streets become more squalid, one reaches the quarters of the Haitian *viejos* and some Dominican families. The racial lines may break down.

Most sugar mills employ several hundred technicians at least. Some of them are high-level administrators and highly skilled scientists. Then there are the maintenance teams, both for the mill itself and for the complex transport and loading machinery. The larger mills have extensive rail networks, employing a range of *maquinistas, conductores, chuchoneros, fogoneros, jefes de patio* and others.

The Haitian *braceros'* domain is likely to be far away from this. On the larger plantations he may never see the central *batey* — except, perhaps, when he passes through it on the way to a distant cane field far from his normal *batey*. He comes into contact with the "Guardacampestre", the field guard who keeps a close eye on him, watching for signs of unrest and possible escape (these armed guards, often on horseback, patrol the *bateyes* 24 hours of the day, and are stationed at check-points near to the main roads). Then there is the *jefe de cuadrilla*, the chief of the particular brigade of cane cutters in which he works. The *jefes*, usually Dominicans but sometimes Haitian *viejos* with many years of residence, are the ones who bang on his *batey* door at 4 or 5 a.m., who decide the hours and pace of the day's work. Then there is the *pesador*, who weighs the cane at the weighing points scattered around the cane fields: the *tickeros*, who give out the payment vouchers in accordance with the amount of cane cut, and the *carreteros* or *wagoneros* driving the trucks that take the loaded cane on to the railways which finally deliver it to the sugar mill. In his *batey* he will also become familiar with the *tienderos*, the shopkeepers in the small stores who sell rice, beans, rum, eggs and a few other commodities (often at inflated prices), charging interest for the *vales* (vouchers) with which the *bracero* has to purchase subsistence items before he has any cash in hand. Finally, there are the Haitian inspectors, whom the *bracero* is meant to see as his saviours and protectors, but whom he often fears as much as any of the Dominicans above him.

In numerous interviews with the Kongos, I tried to make some estimates of average wages and remuneration. It should be remembered that the Haitians were to be granted treatment equal to that of Dominican workers, and should by rights have been guaranteed at least the daily minimum wage — at that time 3.50 Dominican pesos. For the 1981–82 harvest, as already noted, *braceros* were paid piece-rates of 1.83 pesos per ton, plus the 0.50 pesos incentive. As it happened, however, several persons informed me that the incentive had in many cases not been paid at the end of the previous harvest season. Small compulsory deductions were made for social security and medical insurance. Though rudimentary lodging was provided free of charge, all food had to be purchased. Though food was meant to be subsidised on the CEA plantations, through the Dominican state organisation INESPRE, I found that basic subsistence items (notably rice and beans) were often marked up beyond the official selling price — this being particularly the case in the small *tiendas* on the remote *bateyes* where the Haitian *braceros* normally lived. One of the most bitter complaints made by those Haitians who had come under previous contracts was that food prices had increased over the past year, whereas there had been no corresponding increase in the piece-rate paid to cane cutters. With official prices of 32 cents for a pound of rice, and 70 cents per pound of beans, even the daily purchase of these two staple foods would have cut heavily into the Haitians' earning potential.

Average remuneration was of course difficult to calculate. A small minority of those interviewed claimed that they could cut up to 3 tons of cane in a day lasting from 5 a.m. until 6 p.m. At the other end of the scale many others — notably youths in their mid to late teens who had crossed the border for the first time and had no previous experience of cane cutting — insisted that they could not even cut one ton per day. I was shown payment slips indicating daily incomes closer to 2 than 3 pesos.

ONAPLAN, it was noted earlier, had calculated average incomes of 2.50 pesos per day. But there were several reasons why the Kongos might not earn even that amount. First, they are paid only when the cane has been loaded on to trucks, and taken to CEA's weighing machines. On many occasions, I was told, the *braceros* had to wait for one or two days before their cane was loaded. Then there was the time lost while getting to the cane fields. The luckier ones, especially at the beginning of the harvest, might be assigned to a field only a few minutes' walk from their *batey*; the unlucky might have to walk for a full two hours before they could begin harvesting. There was no official transport to ferry them to the work place. And then almost all informants complained of endemic cheating over weights. Serving to line the pockets of the *tickero* and the *pesador*, this system of *engaño* or trickery has been one of the major complaints of the Haitian organisations, trade unions and human rights activists for many years. The *tickero* will write one ticket underestimating the amount cut, which he hands to the powerless Haitian worker, and another for the *carretero* who drives off with the cane, the two of them sharing the profits. If his *jefe de cuadrilla* allowed it, the *bracero* might be able to follow the trailer to the weighing post, doing his utmost to ensure that he was not tricked. But this in itself would be a time-consuming operation, perhaps losing him two or three hours of harvesting time to watch over his quota. Though some Haitians evidently did this, others appeared to accept the cheating as one of the tricks of the trade, and may have lost up to a third of their legitimate wages as a result. Occasionally, I was informed, the more voluble protests received the backing of Dominican trade union organisations. A couple of years ago, the Haitians on the Central Romana went on strike to protest against the alleged fixing of the company's weighing machines. The CGT, the most militant of the trade union organisations, protested publicly that Gulf and Western's *pesadores* reported no more than 3 tons for each 5 tons of cane harvested. Since then, one of CGT's demands had been for trade union representatives to check the weighing and report on any abuses to the CEA authorities. Their demands fell on predictably deaf ears.

A further problem was that, although the *fichas* (payment slips) were made out at the end of the day's labour, cash payments took place only once a fortnight, and sometimes even less frequently. The Haitian, who most likely arrives penniless in the first place, is quickly thrown on the mercy of moneylenders charging exorbitant rates of interest (I was told that interest rates can be as much as 25 per cent over a two-week period). Most of the *bateyes* have their moneylenders (the *jefe de cuadrilla* sometimes doubling up in this capacity), and the *tienda* keepers also reap their dividends by selling goods in advance at a premium.

All the Haitians interviewed had come with the expectation of realising significant savings. I received markedly different claims of the amounts that had been saved in the past, and which they expected to save during the current harvest. A few claimed to have put aside $200 or more. Others denied saving anything, or gave a figure in the region of 20 to 30 Dominican pesos. From my own estimates, the average saving at that time was a paltry sum of between 30 and 80 pesos for six months of back-breaking work.

The hours of work were invariably long, by most accounts a full twelve hours between departure from the *batey* in the early morning and the return at night — and sometimes far longer, if the *jefe de cuadrilla* woke them before dawn for a long tramp to a distant cane field. The Dominican Labour Code stipulates that the normal work day should not exceed eight hours, or 44 hours per week. For the Haitian *braceros*, an average week could easily be double that amount. The contract does not stipulate the maximum work period, listing only the 1½ hour break at midday and the Sunday rest day. In effect, there was no regular provision for a midday break as no lunch was provided and there were no cooking facilities in the middle of cane fields perhaps several miles from the residential *batey*. The Haitians stopped only for brief periods during the day, to munch the cane stalks that acted as food and drink during the heat of the long day. On Sundays, I regularly found the Haitian *cuadrillas* at work. On one occasion, an apparently embarrassed *jefe* dismissed his Haitians when I began to ask some awkward questions. But for the most part Sunday was considered a normal work day.

CEA officials showed little concern about the long hours of work, arguing that the Haitians themselves wished to work as much as they could, all seven days of the week, in order to maximise their earnings. I was told of at least one case, on a *batey* in Ingenio Barahona in April 1982, when guards broke into the Haitians' quarters on an official holiday, beat down the doors of recalcitrant workers, and forced them into the cane fields. But it was the only allegation of its kind that I heard in my travels around the *ingenios*. For the most part it seemed that the long hours of work were accepted by the Haitians, and were necessary to make ends meet. But it says little for the justice of the system if the *braceros* had no alternative but to work nearly 100 hours a week to earn the equivalent of £5 sterling.

On living conditions, perhaps enough has already been said above to give the general picture. Nowhere is the vast discrepancy between the social provisions of the contract and the stark reality more pitifully marked than in the housing provided for the Haitian migrants. Enough studies have been made, and the situation was known well enough by the CEA authorities. Some ten years before my own visit, in 1971, a CEA Medical Assistance Commission had carried out a systematic survey of living conditions on the CEA plantations. It reported enormous overcrowding, with ten or more people sleeping in the same room with little or no ventilation. The majority of the *bateyes* then had no drinking water, and latrines were almost always lacking. The barracks of the Kongos could be picked out easily enough in any of the *bateyes* I visited. They were usually of solid construction, and had perhaps been built during the previous decade. But no attempt had been made to provide them with amenities, over and above the basic beds and, sometimes, mattresses. Clothing, cooking utensils and a few other personal effects would be scattered around on the concrete or dirt floors.

But it was not so much the poverty of the living quarters that caught my attention, as the fact that no attempt had been made to provide the Haitians with any amenities which might make their life more bearable. The previous year when I had been in Nicaragua, I had seen one of the larger *ingenios* formerly owned by a member of the Somoza family and comprehensively remodelled after the 1979 revolution. A central dining hall had been built, providing adequate food for the seasonal workers during the harvest season, and showing what could be done by an impoverished country suffering as much as any other — perhaps more — from the collapse of sugar prices and unstable markets for its crop. In the CEA *bateyes*, nothing had been done to give the Haitian encampments anything but a prison-like atmosphere. The Haitians were housed in small cell-like rooms in long prefabricated concrete blocks, with doors that could be padlocked if need be.

In the area of health and social security, my findings were equally disturbing. The contract gives ample guarantees in this domain, pledging medical treatment and compensation for accidents and illness. I soon saw the importance of this: the cane cutter's task is immensely dangerous. During my own survey, I came across at least half a dozen *braceros* nursing serious wounds and deep gashes inflicted by an ill-directed machete, and many other ailments. There were endless complaints about the lack of treatment, or its rudimentary nature. In one case, a Haitian with an acute swelling on an infected hand had been fobbed off with two aspirins at the neighbouring health centre, being told there was "nothing else that could be done". Overall, the accident statistics are extraordinarily high. ONAPLAN figures over a four-year period in the 1970s revealed that, out of 11,670 accidents in the sugar industry, three-quarters occurred in the cane fields, most of them inflicted by the machete. And as these are only the reported accidents, one can surmise that the true figure may be far higher than that. All Haitians pay their social security dues, as the amount is deducted at source from their salaries. But the problem — as an official from the Dominican Social Security Institute (IDSS) informed me — is that many CEA *ingenios* are loath to pay up, and are sometimes years behind in their dues. In the event of more serious accidents, I was told, treatment is given though it is often inadequate. For cuts and ailments considered minor, the Haitian worker will be lucky to get any treatment. I heard innumerable complaints of "racist" attitudes on the part of IDSS officials, who made life as difficult as possible for the Haitians and produced a host of bureaucratic requirements including paperwork well beyond the comprehension of the largely illiterate Haitian workers. The major problem, as with everything else, seemed to be the time lost and the expense. As the Dominicans generally lived in or around the central *bateyes*, they had physical access to the IDSS facilities located there. The Haitian had to pay his own way there, or lose valuable time by going on foot.

The living conditions, with housing barely protected from the torrential rains that come at the end of the harvest, are bound to breed disease. When the rains come, the *bateyes* are quickly infested with malaria-carrying mosquitoes, and the disease invariably breaks out in the sugar regions. A National Service for the Eradication of Malaria carries out regular visits to spray the *bateyes*, but in recent years it has evidently been fighting a losing battle. Ironically, the presence of the disease in the Dominican Republic is blamed on the presence of the Haitians themselves in the regular outbursts of "anti-Haitianism" which pervade the Dominican press. For example, I came across the following passage in a savagely anti-Haitian book, published by the former President of the National Frontier Council:

> But there is another thing, the Haitian comes bearing disease. This is shown by the fact that the Dominican government — with the assistance of respected international organisations — managed to eradicate malaria at a cost of twenty million dollars. And when we have been rid of this for years the Haitians who come to cut our cane — brought over like beasts to the landowners — bring the malaria that is once again beginning to flourish.[7]

Such unbelievably crass statements masked the real cause of disease on the *bateyes*. It should be pointed out that, under the provisions of the contract, all *braceros* were to undergo rigorous medical checks before their arrival, in order to weed out all those carrying infectious diseases. As CEA officials were all too well aware, it was not so much the Haitian carriers as the conditions that bred disease. And it was not only malaria. There was a wide range of other ailments resulting directly from polluted water, lack of sewerage and refuse disposal systems, and the cramped living conditions. As a CEA medical commission had noted some years before, the lack of medical care had led to chronically high levels of diarrhoea and enteritis, intestinal parasitism, and typhoid and paratyphoid fever. And in the absence of subsistence food plots around the *ingenios*, both malnutrition and infant mortality had reached exceptionally high levels. When any curative or preventive health programmes did exist, they were the initiative of private, church and charitable organisations. I came across such non-governmental health projects in the *ingenios* of Montellanos in the north, Barahona and Haina. As I heard later, CEA had drawn up its own plans for improving its network of health centres as part of an ambitious new improvement programme for the *bateyes*. At the time of my visit, this only existed on paper. On the ground, there was very little indeed.

With regard to the supervisory system and labour inspection, I tried to find out more about the supervisors and inspectors nominated by the Haitian Embassy. What kind of people were they, what did they do, and how did they live? The Minister of Labour intimated that they had been brought in at the specific request of the Haitian government, which had been concerned at reports of abuse of Haitian nationals in the Dominican Republic. But other CEA officials made it clear that these Haitian officials had exclusive competence to represent the Haitian *braceros* before the Dominican authorities, in protests against abuse and demands for enforcement of the contract's provisions. When I asked why Dominican trade unionists could not monitor the contract, and themselves represent the Haitian workers, one CEA administrator told me that Dominican labour organisations had no competence in the case of workers who had been imported through a bilateral agreement with a foreign government. During my field research, it was difficult to find any of these Haitian officials. On several occasions I asked for them, and was told that they were "away" and "had not yet arrived". I began to suspect that they might even be a figment of the imagination: yet another device used by Duvalier to extort money — salaries paid to the Haitian Embassy for non-existent inspectors. But on Ingenio Haina, towards the end of my visit, I did come across two Haitians, one of whom admitted to being a supervisor, the other an inspector, and who responded to my questions with noticeable reluctance. The supervisor said he had been resident in the Dominican Republic for several years, had no specific training in labour administration, and had been selected for this position because he was bilingual in Spanish and Creole. When asked what he had done on behalf of the Haitians that year, he limited himself to stating that there were no problems at present and thus nothing to report to CEA — a remarkable statement if one compared the contract with the conditions around him. The main task of the supervisors and inspectors, it appeared, was to complement the work of the Dominican plantation guards in ensuring that the Haitians did not run away from the *bateyes* to which they had been assigned. And on the few occasions that they may have interpreted their duties more literally, the Haitian inspectors could themselves be at risk. Towards the end of that year the Haitian Embassy made a formal complaint to CEA that a Haitian inspector had been roughly handled by the area chief of the department of cane cutters and a rural guard, and put under arrest for having complained about the poor food distributed to a group of workers recently arrived at a camp on the Río Haina plantation.[8]

Dominican nationals — trade unionists, other *ingenio* employees, and even some of the CEA officials with whom I spoke — seemed to take it for granted that the Haitian supervisors and inspectors were there primarily to serve the interests of the Haitian government. In common parlance they were referred to by workers and management alike as the "Tontons", a reference to Duvalier's notorious "Volontiers de Securité Nationale". It was assumed that the unofficial function of these Haitian "guardians" was to spy on the Haitian Kongos, make sure that they did not get too close to the exiled opposition movement or the trade unions, and report any militancy to the Haitian Embassy in Santo Domingo. The two roles may have been combined, in that the Duvalier regime had a vested interest in securing some improvement in the *batey* conditions. CEA evidently saw the Haitian inspectorate system as an encumbrance, something to be tolerated but never encouraged. For the Haitian *braceros* it brought no dividends, adding yet another element to their sense of powerlessness and insecurity.

The Contract and International Law: The ILO's Findings, 1983

When the ILO's Commission of Enquiry visited Haiti and the Dominican Republic the following year, among other things it considered the contract from the perspective of international law. Both countries were legally bound to enforce the provisions of certain ILO Conventions that they had already ratified. The Dominican Republic had ratified ILO Conventions relating to forced labour, freedom of association and collective bargaining, and the protection of wages. Haiti had ratified the Conventions on forced labour and freedom of association and collective bargaining, but not the instrument on the protection of wages. Before turning to the ILO's findings and recommendations on the contract itself, it is important to understand the nature of these ILO instruments, and the obligations incurred by states which ratify them.

International Labour Conventions are legal instruments adopted by the ILO's International Labour Conference, which set standards of achievement in the area concerned, and which, when ratified, create binding international obligations for the countries concerned. Since its creation in 1919 the ILO has adopted over 150 of these Conventions, the most important of them being concerned with fundamental human rights. Ratifying states are obliged to report periodically on the measures taken to give effect to these obligations. Moreover, under the ILO's tripartite structure (with representation from government, employer and worker organisations) trade unions can petition the International Labour Conference and the ILO's Governing Body to establish a Commission of Enquiry in the event of alleged serious violation of a ratified Convention. This is what happened in the case of Haiti and the Dominican Republic: a number of trade union organisations presented allegations of widespread Haitian forced labour to the 1981 session of the International Labour Conference.

Both countries had ratified the ILO's most important Convention against forced labour (No. 105) in 1958, soon after its adoption by the International Labour Conference. It prohibits any use of forced labour, as a means of political coercion, as a method of mobilising and using labour for purposes of economic development, as a punishment for having participated in strikes, or as a means of racial, social, national or religious discrimination. Neither country, however, had adopted a more recent ILO Convention (No. 143 of 1975 concerning "Migrations in Abusive Conditions and the Promotion of Equality of Opportunity and Treatment of Migrant Workers") which is apparently more relevant for the protection of Haitian cane cutters in the Dominican Republic — it requires ratifying states to suppress the clandestine movement of migrants for employment and the illegal employment of migrants, and to take measures against "the organisers of illicit or clandestine movements of migrants for employment departing from, passing through or arriving in its territory, and against those who employ workers who have migrated in illegal conditions".

Nevertheless the ILO Commission, interpreting its mandate broadly, was able to probe deep into the internal operations of the contract, to demand access to documents and information which had previously been withheld from the public, and finally to publish a report which condemned almost every aspect of the existing contractual arrangements. It found that, although the 19,000 workers currently recruited for the harvest could be said

to voluntarily seek employment, and may return repeatedly . . . the workers are kept in ignorance of their conditions of employment. The annual recruiting contracts which regulate these conditions are not published and are not available to the workers and the trade unions. The Commission doubts whether the workers have given an effective consent to an engagement whose terms they do not know and which the Haitian authorities described as a collective contract concluded by the Government on their behalf.

Moreover, the Commission concluded that the recruited workers were obliged to stay for the duration of the sugar harvest at the plantation to which they were assigned and, if they tried to leave, "would be forcibly returned to their workplace — a practice contrary to the Abolition of Forced Labour Convention".[9]

The ILO Commission confirmed my own impressions, that there was no way the Haitians could even discover what their legal rights were, let alone press for their enforcement. Without exception, said the ILO report, recruited workers met on the Dominican plantations stated that they had not been informed of the conditions under which they would be employed. They had merely been informed that work was available in the sugar harvest and that pay and conditions would be good. The annual recruiting contracts, it noted, were not the subject of any official publication in either of the two countries concerned and were not available to anyone else. Although an individual contract was found to exist, and was apparently completed for each recruited worker, "the worker himself does not receive a copy. The form is, moreover, seriously defective as a statement of employment conditions, even omitting an indication of the rates of remuneration."[10] The Haitian Minister of Social Affairs, when asked by the Commission to comment on these facts, only stated

that the workers could not read and would be incapable of understanding the contracts. He observed that it was the Government's responsibility to conclude a collective contract for them and that officials of the Ministry of Social Affairs toured the country to make it known that the sugar harvest was about to start and to provide information about the recruiting arrangements.[11]

The ILO Commission, not surprisingly, found this an "inadequate explanation". The major problem, from the perspective of the forced labour Conventions, was that the worker was not free to terminate his employment, being bound to stay at his post on the plantation to which he had been assigned, under all circumstances. The Commission then examined the mechanisms by which the *braceros* were prevented from leaving. Under the 1966 Inter-State Agreement, employers were required to obtain for each worker a temporary residence permit in the Dominican Republic and a Dominican identity card. In practice, neither of these two documents was currently issued. The recruited workers had only an identity document issued by Haiti's Ministry of Social Affairs and valid for the period of the sugar harvest in question. But even this identity document was often retained by the plantation administration, and replaced by a new identity card issued by the plantation — thus ensuring that any fugitive could easily be recognised. CEA and Dominican government officials confirmed that any worker who abandoned his work would be treated like an illegal immigrant, liable to arrest and deportation. In practice, as the Commission concluded, when Haitian workers recruited for the sugar harvest left the plantation to which they had been assigned before the end of the harvest, the employer and the authorities usually returned them to the work place rather than expelling them from the country. Moreover, while this practice was itself in clear breach of the ILO's forced labour Conventions,

> This breach of the Convention is made more serious by the fact that, while the workers are made to carry out their obligations under their contract, the same is not true as regards observance of all the obligations resting on the employer, particularly with respect of wages, housing and living conditions, hours of work and rest, and social security matters.[12]

Much of the responsibility for the forced labour situation was laid firmly at the door of the Haitian government. Under the existing contract, certain clauses were seen to facilitate a *de facto* situation of forced labour, with the full connivance of the Haitian government: first, there was the fact that travel documents were removed from the workers and deposited at the Haitian Embassy; second, the fact that the Haitian government had reserved to itself important powers to verify the conditions of life and work of the Haitian recruited workers, and to seek the observance of the conditions of the contract. On this point, the ILO Commission noted the practical complicity of the Haitian supervisors and inspectors.

> The contracts also require the supervisors and inspectors appointed by the Haitian Embassy to see that workers are not transferred to other plantations. From information gathered by the Commission, it appears that this power is used as a means of preventing the unauthorised departure of workers rather than as a basis for protecting the workers against transfer by unilateral decision of the employer. . . . It is thus apparent that the Haitian authorities are associated in the measures which oblige the recruited workers to remain at their workplace for the duration of the harvest.[13]

Though the Haitian officials interviewed by the ILO Commission claimed to have protested on many occasions against such abuses as "cheating in the weighing of cane, the inadequate wages, serious deficiencies in medical care, and the whimsical and arbitrary application of social security legislation", the Commission members were informed at the Dominican Foreign Ministry that no such correspondence existed, and the Haitian government apparently proved unable to come up with the documents requested. The Commission was "therefore led to conclude that, although the Government of Haiti has been aware of the above-mentioned deficiencies and abuses, it has not shown that it has taken action to have them remedied. Nor does it appear that the supervisors and inspectors appointed by the Haitian Embassy have intervened on these matters."

In Port-au-Prince, the ILO raised the thorny issue of payments for the recruiting expenses. Their questions were clearly not welcomed by the Haitian Minister of Social Affairs. As the Commission subsequently reported:

> The Commission then proceeded to put a number of questions. However, he refused to answer one question. The Commission referred to the substantial payments made to the Government of Haiti by the State Sugar Board under the annual recruiting agreements to cover the costs of recruitment, and asked whether there were any accounts or other documents which showed the

expenses incurred. The Minister asked what authorised the Commission to put this question. The Commission pointed out that it concerned a specific allegation made in the complaint, that, according to information previously given to the Commission by a representative of the Haitian government, the payments were intended to cover the costs of medical examinations and administrative formalities, and that the Commission wished to have further particulars. The Minister stated that he was prepared to deal with facts, but not to answer allegations; the Commission was accepting the unsubstantiated allegation on this matter contained in the complaint and was asking the Government to provide proof of the expenses; its question was therefore abusive, and the Government reserved the right, in the absence of proof by the complainants of the allegation of a sale of workers, to contest that accusation before the International Court of Justice.[14]

The Commission nevertheless had to deal with the allegation made by the complainants that the payments vastly exceeded the real recruitment costs, and thus constituted a sale for profit by Duvalier to CEA. On the basis of information provided in the Dominican Republic, it came up with the following calculations. The most substantial payments had been in respect of recruitment expenses and the transport of workers from the recruitment centres to the frontier at Malpasse. The amount for this had been US$1,250,000 for the 1978–79 harvest, for 15,000 *braceros*; but for each of the 1982–83 and the 1983–84 contracts it was up to $2,250,000 for 19,000 *braceros*. Then there was the sum to be paid by CEA for the cost of transporting the workers, upon repatriation, from the frontier to the centres where they were recruited. This amount was also fixed, at $85,000 for the 15,000 workers in 1978–79, and $129,010 in the 19,000 workers in each of the last two harvest seasons. Finally, there were the salaries of the Haitian inspectors and supervisors, which also had to be met by CEA.[15] After the transport costs had been deducted, the 1982–83 payment worked out at $112 for each Haitian recruited. Haitian government representatives had informed the Commission that these payments covered the cost of organising information campaigns in the recruitment areas, and establishing and operating the recruitment centres. They stated that "the payments did not appear in the budget of the Republic, since they were not State receipts". Though unable to get precise information on the overall recruitment costs, the Commission was nevertheless satisfied that "these measures involve only limited expenditure, substantially less than the payments provided for in the recruiting contracts". And the Commission intimated moreover, albeit in veiled diplomatic language, that one of the Duvalier regime's major reasons for signing the contract was to extort money from the Dominicans. First, the Commission noted that it had been unable to obtain, from either the Dominican or the Haitian government, the confidential addenda to the recruiting contracts which regulated the annual financial payments. As it then continued:

> The contracts purport to lay down safeguards for the workers. The addenda, apart from fixing the payments to the Haitian government, contain additional clauses concerning the workers' monetary entitlements. There should therefore be no reason to seek to hide the contents of the contracts and their addenda from public view other than a desire not to reveal the payments made to the Haitian

government. It is furthermore incomprehensible that payments which purport to cover the cost of work performed by officials of a considerable number of different government departments should not appear in the State accounts. In the light of all these elements, the Commission has come to the conclusion that the payments received by the Government of Haiti on account of recruiting costs substantially exceed the actual expenses and thus constitute a consideration for permitting the engagement of Haitian labour by the Dominican State Sugar Board.[16]

On the Haitians' living and working conditions in the Dominican Republic, the ILO's findings were basically consistent with my own of the previous year. The Commission confirmed the excessively long work hours and concluded that in many instances, particularly on the state-owned plantations, the wages of cane cutters still did not exceed $2 per day, thus substantially below the minimum wage for a work day that was generally twelve hours and often more. On supervision, it criticised both the Haitian and Dominican inspectorate systems, concluding that "No evidence was provided of any action by the labour inspection service in relation to conditions of Haitian plantation workers or with a view to remedying abuses affecting the observance of the Conventions under enquiry."[17] On freedom of association the Commission observed that — although by law the Haitians enjoyed the same rights as Dominican nationals, and the Dominican government had pursued a policy encouraging the free exercise of trade union rights — practical difficulties stood in the way of Haitian workers, including the close vigilance to which recruited harvest workers were subject and fear of reprisals on return to Haiti.

At the end of its lengthy report, the ILO's Commission of Enquiry made a series of general and specific recommendations. The most important of these are summarised below. In the long run, it recommended measures aimed at the stabilisation of the labour force on the sugar plantations. In the meantime, it advocated improved guarantees for workers recruited from Haiti for so long as such recruiting was still undertaken (including conclusion of a basic new inter-state agreement valid for a fixed time period, and widely publicised in language which could be understood by all those interested including prospective recruits, trade unions, the press, members of the legal profession, and others concerned with the workers' welfare). It recommended the establishment of placement offices, where workers seeking employment in the Dominican sugar harvest outside the contractual recruitment arrangements could be hired, and the discontinuance of all measures having the effect of confining the Kongos within the plantations. It suggested that workers recruited in Haiti should, at the time of their engagement, receive individual contracts of employment clearly indicating the employer and the place of work for which they were engaged, the duration of the employment, the nature of the employment, the terms of remuneration and the other principal conditions of employment. Creole translations of the contract, of any inter-state agreement and other instruments regulating labour conditions should be either provided to each worker or be prominently displayed at each village or camp where these workers were hired. The present practice of retaining the Haitians' passports should be abolished. In future, each Haitian worker authorised to work in the

Dominican Republic should have the right to keep his own passport, together with a document issued by the Dominican authorities attesting to the legality of his residence for the duration of the authorised employment. There was a series of recommendations on the protection of wages, in particular requiring that cane cutters should be guaranteed the equivalent of the legal minimum wage, notwithstanding the amount of cane actually cut. It advocated the abolition of the deferred "incentive" payment currently utilised by CEA, recommending that CEA might instead offer material incentives distinct from the workers' wage. With regard to supervision, the Commission pointed out that primary responsibility must rest with the Dominican government, and urged that the national labour inspection services be developed into "an effective instrument for ensuring observance of labour laws and of the workers' rights on the sugar plantations". Noting that the Haitian inspectorate service "has not proved to be an effective means of protection", the Commission recommended instead that a small nucleus of properly qualified officials acting under the authority and control of the Haitian Embassy in Santo Domingo be empowered to visit all plantations. But the Commission also urged a greater role for the Haitian workers themselves:

> Pending greater unionisation of the Haitian labour force, measures should be taken, at least on the State-owned plantations, for the designation of representatives by the Haitian workers themselves who would be able to take up with management day-to-day problems and have defined responsibilities in defending the workers' interests. The Commission recommends that the Government of the Dominican Republic, in consultation with the managements and trade unions concerned, make the necessary arrangements to this end.[18]

The report of the ILO Commission of Enquiry had some immediate effects. On 11 May 1983 CEA established a special commission to "carry out studies and formulate recommendations with the objective, within a reasonable space of time, of trying to Dominicanise agricultural work on the State *ingenios* during the sugar harvest".[19] The recommendations were reportedly to be put into effect as of the 1983–84 harvest. Though there was talk of raising cane cutters' salaries, and of carrying out a comprehensive programme of physical improvements on the *bateyes*, CEA failed in its fundamental objectives: the number of imported cane cutters rose once again to 23,000. During the 1983 session of the International Labour Conference, the Dominican government also reported on a new range of measures to improve living, working and health conditions. For example, ambulances were provided to eight of the twelve CEA properties. A toilet installation programme got under way, to provide an exact number of 728 new toilet units. Drinking water was provided for 40 *bateyes* in all, and a programme was drawn up for installing potable water in 283 *bateyes* around the country. There was a sudden spate of decoration, and CEA could report that 1,900 collective housing units and 5,000 family units had now been painted. On Ingenio Porvenir, one entire *batey* was reconstructed, and 60 schools were refurbished throughout CEA's domain. Other state organisations were brought into the clean-up campaign. The national housing institute INVI was granted authority to devise new housing projects, and the Dominican Social Security Institute commenced a broad public health operation, looking out for signs of tuberculosis and other infectious diseases.

Overseas aid agencies, concerned by the international denunciations, also began to invest in programmes to humanise life in the *bateyes*, sometimes with non-governmental and church organisations in the Dominican Republic as their counterparts. A Norwegian agency, for example, signed a contract with the Protestant *Servicio Social de Iglesias Dominicanas*, worth an estimated $170,000, for nutrition programmes. The programme was also funded by private and governmental agencies from the USA, including USAID and Church World Service. But programmes evidently remained piecemeal, and fell short of the hundreds of millions of dollars that would by now have been required to make the sugar industry an attractive proposition for Dominicans who had anywhere else to go. As the newspaper *Ultima Hora* was still reporting in December 1985,

> A sugar *batey* is the living replica of misery. The wooden huts constructed by CEA threaten to collapse, and the workers cannot remember the last time that repairs were carried out in these housing units where cockroaches, rats and all kinds of insect dispute with human beings . . . some houses in these *bateyes* are supported by stones.

The paper also claimed that, even with the higher rate of 2.83 pesos per ton, it was still almost impossible for the cane cutter to reach the minimum legal wage.[20]

The ILO's Commission of Enquiry, after rigorous on-the-spot investigations, had made a number of pertinent recommendations, which — at least in theory — had been accepted by the governments of both the Dominican Republic and Haiti. The problem afterwards was to secure their adequate implementation. But in this area the ILO machinery has its limitations. Under the human rights machinery of the United Nations, a Special Rapporteur can be appointed at the annual meeting of the Human Rights Commission to carry out an investigation in any one country; in practice the UN's human rights investigators tend to make follow-up investigations year after year, at least until the UN Human Rights Commission is convinced that sufficient improvements have been made to render its Rapporteur no longer necessary. With the ILO it is different. The Commission of Enquiry submits its report to the ILO's Governing Body, and no further on-the-spot investigations are carried out *unless* the government specifically asks for further technical assistance from the ILO, *or* a new complaint or representation is filed against the governments inculpated. In practice, the ILO's investigations have tended to be one-off, and implementation of the Conventions is then again in the hands of the ILO's regular supervisory machinery. This works in the following way. An independent 20-member Committee of Experts on the Application of Conventions and Recommendations meets in Geneva in March, considers government reports on the application of Conventions, and then makes further comments either in the form of confidential "direct requests" or — in the case of possible violations of the Conventions — makes "observations" which, although published, in fact tend to receive little publicity. The meetings of this Committee of Experts are invariably held behind closed doors. In June a tripartite Conference Committee on the Application of Conventions and Recommendations then meets during the proceedings of the annual International Labour Conference, and gives particular consideration to some of those countries on which "observations" have previously been made by the independent experts' committee. Governments may be requested to report in detail concerning the application of specific Conventions to the June Conference Committee.

In practice, the Dominican Republic was asked to report in detail to the June Conference each year between 1984 and 1986, and public "observations" have been made each year concerning its implementation of the Conventions on Forced Labour and the Protection of Wages. Without a further complaint, this was the only supervisory mechanism open to the ILO. The practice may serve to keep a government on the alert, by asking awkward questions to which it is obliged to respond, and passing on comments furnished to the ILO by representative organisations of workers and employers. But at the end of the day the ILO can only repeat the government's comments. A brief survey of the ILO's observations made in 1986, concerning the Forced Labour and Protection of Wages Conventions, gives some idea of where things stood three years after the publication of the Commission of Enquiry's 1983 report.

First, the Forced Labour Convention (No. 105). In 1986, the ILO's Committee of Experts considered both the Dominican government's report, and comments which had been furnished by the *Central Unitaria de Trabajadores* (CUT).[21] The government had said that the 1984–85 and 1985–86 contracts had taken account of the ILO's recommendations — but the ILO had not even been sent a copy of these contracts. Thus the ILO could only "once more request(s) the Government to communicate copies of all agreements or contracts concluded since 1983, either by the Government or employers, in respect of recruiting workers in Haiti (including any supplementary documents fixing the details of their application)". Concerning payments to the government of Haiti in respect of recruiting operations, the government had said that "a careful review of the expenditure in question was made by these two Governments and that they concluded that these expenses were in accordance with the economic needs of recruiting." On this point the ILO's rejoinder was that

> the Committee would appreciate more detailed information on the nature and amount of the various expenses involved, since the financial aspects of recruiting of Haitian workers have a direct effect on the efforts initiated by the plantations to improve conditions of life and work and thus to obviate recourse to any form of constraint to keep the workers at their workplace.

With regard to information supplied to the Haitian workers concerning their conditions of employment, the government had stated only that "information is provided by means of loudspeaker vehicles". On this point the ILO's 1986 observation noted that

> However, the Government has not so far provided any relevant texts, except an individual employment contract in French which, as indicated in the Committee's observations of 1985, did not give sufficient indications concerning the conditions of employment. The Committee hopes that the necessary additional measures will be taken to make available to the workers concerned adequate written information on their conditions of employment, and that copies of the documents in question will be communicated to the ILO.

Concerning the prohibition of payments to officials and employees involved in recruiting Haitian workers, the government had previously stated that it was absolutely forbidden for officials and employees involved in this recruitment to demand or receive any benefits and that "severe penalties would be imposed if any such cases occurred". As the ILO countered on this issue,

> The Government refers in this connection to provisions issued by the State and undertakings, as well as to corresponding penal provisions. It has however failed to identify the legal provisions which lay down the prohibition in question. The Committee once more repeats its request for this information. In so far as the provisions are not contained in general legislation, it would appreciate receiving copies of the relevant texts.

With regard to the measures to prohibit infringements of workers' individual freedom, the Dominican government had also failed to come up with convincing guarantees. Thus the ILO commented that

> It has however omitted to furnish the information and documents requested by the Committee in the light of indications previously given by the Government, namely a copy of the instructions which, according to the Government, had been issued to the administrators of state-owned plantations to ensure the compliance by Haitian workers with their employment contracts, and indications concerning the penal provisions under which administrators of plantations or their agents could be punished if they sought to confine workers within the plantation or any part of the plantation. The Committee hopes that these indications will be communicated.

On supervisory measures, the government had stated generally that "the labour inspection service of the Ministry of Labour continues to make inspections", but had otherwise given no useful information concerning the extent to which the ILO's detailed recommendations had been implemented. Thus the ILO's Committee of Experts urged that

> The Committee would, in particular, appreciate information on any measures taken to investigate the allegations made in the comments addressed to the ILO in March 1985 by the CUT [Central Unitaria de Trabajadores], according to which the rights of Haitian workers on the sugar plantations were in many respects not being respected, a matter on which the Government has not so far presented any observations.

For the Protection of Wages Conventions, the ILO's Committee of Experts could detect more signs of progress by 1986. It noted, for example, the Dominican government's statements: (i) that the practice of paying wages by means of negotiable vouchers had been abolished on the CEA plantations; (ii) that an agreement had been concluded in January 1983 between CEA and the Price Stabilisation Institute (INESPRE), concerning the production of food crops to be made available to the workers at accessible prices, and the operation of pharmacies to provide medicines at reduced prices to workers requesting them; (iii) that the deferred payment of wages had been abolished on the CEA *ingenios* and replaced by an incentive paid to the Haitian workers and an allowance of US$55 for each

Haitian worker engaged under contract at the time of his departure. The Committee also noted with interest the information provided by the Dominican government to the effect that the legal minimum wage, which had previously been fixed at 5 pesos for a working day of eight hours for agricultural workers, had been raised to 6 pesos. It nevertheless expressed its concern that the provisions of the Labour Code relating to the protection of wages in agricultural enterprises had not yet been extended to those enterprises employing ten workers or less; and it reminded the government of its earlier recommendations to ensure that the Haitian cane cutters did indeed receive the equivalent of the legal minimum wage. It also reminded the government of the Commission of Enquiry's concerns with regard to alleged cheating over wages. On this point the government had stated in general terms that it considered that "the most effective method of checking the weight of the cane is the presence of the representatives of the workers, chosen by the workers themselves, and the supervision that these can exercise in weighing operations" — but it had not clarified what measures had so far been undertaken. Thus, the ILO's committee reiterated that it "would be grateful if the Government would continue to inform it concerning the measures adopted, and the regulations and orders decreed, both concerning state plantations and those owned privately, in order to give effect to this recommendation of the Commission of Enquiry."[22]

On the Haitian side, the ILO's follow-up comments in 1986 were concerned with the Abolition of Forced Labour Convention, and most particularly with the sensitive issue of government-to-government payments, and supervision of the contract by nominated Haitian officials. The Haitian government had apparently stated in its most recent report that note had been taken of the recommendations concerning payment, pending negotiation of a new agreement. With regard to supervision, the Haitian government had informed the ILO that a special section for social affairs had by now been created at the Haitian Embassy in Santo Domingo, with a view to improving the conditions of life and work of Haitian agricultural labourers in the Dominican Republic. The ILO's Committee thus limited itself to requesting further details "including the composition of the services concerned, statistics concerning their activities and particulars of complaints or irregularities brought to the attention of the Dominican authorities by the Government of Haiti or its officials". But by the time of the ILO's 1986 Committee of Experts, the Duvalier regime in Haiti had fallen, and the ILO thus offered technical assistance to the new government.

> The Committee would remind the Government that the International Labour Office is at its disposal for any assistance it may need in formulating legislation that will give effect to the Convention. It would, accordingly, invite the Government, should it consider it appropriate, to seek such assistance in the near future.[23]

It is a challenge which will hopefully be taken up. Events during the 1985–86 sugar harvest, both before and after the fall of Duvalier, were to show how little effect the ILO's 1983 report had had in Haiti until that time, and how strong the antipathy to the contract had become among the Haitian public at large.

Collapse of the Contract: The 1985–86 Sugar Harvest

In the previous chapter we saw, first, how CEA tried for a couple of months to do without the imported Haitians and then had to submit to pressure from the sugar-grower organisations; second, how the Haitian Ambassador left on his secret flight to Port-au-Prince carrying the $2 million in suitcases for personal delivery to President Duvalier on 18 January 1986; third, how the contract failed to get under way as the Haitian people demonstrated vigorously against its enforcement; and fourthly, how the Dominicans now suffered from a desperate labour shortage and resorted once again to massive capture of Haitians within the Dominican Republic in order to make up for the serious labour deficit.

It was in the second week of March, when Haitian Ambassador Hervé Denis made his sensational revelations to the Dominican press before his abrupt departure from Santo Domingo, that the squalid facts of the contractual negotiations came into the open. Ambassador Denis had not only owned up to his secret transactions, how he had taken the $2 million in cash to Duvalier. He also laid the blame squarely on CEA for permitting this state of affairs. On 11 March 1986 *Ultima Hora* reported part of Mr Denis's press statement as follows:

> The question of the *braceros* has never been the object of a state-to-state or government-to-government agreement, and cannot be related to an international agreement. Moreover, the practices utilised by CEA to carry out the payment of the financial compensation foreseen in the contract proves CEA's total complicity in this matter. For CEA has never consented to use modern financial methods that exist, such as cheques, bank transfers etc. . . . Far from putting an end to such practices, on the contrary, CEA has done everything to perfect them, even establishing, a few years ago, antennae in Haiti so as to deal directly with all issues relating to the contracting of agricultural workers and especially the financial clauses — clauses which I have denounced in several reports addressed to the previous government of Haiti, pointing out the importance of making all these operations public by means of fiscal accounting of the money received. I have always asked the Haitian government to do everything possible to normalise and legalise the status of the Haitian nationals in the Dominican Republic, I have never received a positive response to this. Haitian labour, it appears, was always considered as black, i.e. suitable, labour. . . . Nevertheless, whenever I have wished to see for myself what was happening in the *bateyes*, visiting them personally, the conservative media have created a scandal and asked through the press that I be declared *persona non grata*.

Ambassador Denis's revelations were bound to affect the chances of new *bracero* contracts in this and the coming harvest seasons. His press statements, and all the leaked correspondence between himself and CEA, were reproduced in the freer Haitian press, and led to a new wave of popular Haitian sentiment against the plight of the *braceros*. When I visited Haiti three months afterwards, I encountered very strong doubts that the contract would ever be concluded again. Haitian public opinion was then passionately against it. One popular leader interviewed in Leogane, the major recruitment centre in Haiti, cried out with some passion that "the people of Leogane will never permit this monstrous slavery to take place again". In the Haitian Ministry of Social Affairs — which, at least until 1986, had official responsibility on the Haitian side for drawing up the contract and monitoring its enforcement — a spokesman was equally adamant that the contract could never be repeated under existing conditions. There would, he felt, be no contract for the coming 1986–87 harvest season, for which negotiations were supposed to be getting under way at that time. In the long term, he said after consulting his superior, the contract would not be renewed until conditions were immeasurably improved, preferably with supervision by an international body and certainly with "full respect for international law". Leading church representatives in Haiti also expressed scepticism that the new Haitian government would be able to renew the contract, even if it wished to do so, given the welter of public sentiment against it.

And yet other informants, possibly more pragmatic, insisted that the few months of cash savings in the Dominican Republic had been, and still would be for the foreseeable future, a vital safety valve for the penniless Haitian peasant. It was the urban youth — as they pointed out — rather than the landless rural workers normally recruited, who had demonstrated so passionately against the 1986 recruiting operation. And at the time of my visit one branch of the then divided Haitian trade union movement (CATH) was actively considering ways in which it might monitor any future contract, and provide for more genuine representation of the *braceros'* interests through official worker organisations.

On the Dominican side, whatever the rhetoric of anti-Haitian and "patriotic" sentiment, the pressure for new contracts to import Haitian labour will continue. The incoming government of President Joaquín Balaguer, to take office in August 1986, was reported to be looking at all available alternatives, including the import of mechanical harvesters from Cuba, and the closure of the less productive *ingenios* as part of a diversification programme which may reduce labour requirements and turn some of the CEA lands over to the cultivation of new export crops. But for the next few years, the talk of either mechanisation or "Dominicanisation" is likely to remain a pipe-dream — and in the meantime the cane will still have to be cut. At the time of my June 1986 visit, much of the 1986–87 harvest had already been sold in advance on the US futures market, and tens of thousands of cane cutters would evidently have to be recruited for the next harvest season.

Thus the essential paradox will continue, in all of its aspects. Part of Dominican opinion still insists that the sugar industry is doomed, and that the country will have to find its way out of sugar altogether by the early 1990s. Another part wants to humanise the industry, to spend millions of dollars on modernisation of the technical component of the industry, and humanisation of its social components, while hoping against hope that world prices for cane sugar will somehow pick up in the years to come. Neither lobbying group is likely to countenance multi-million dollar investments in the current unstable climate.

What will this mean for the Haitian workers? Can there be any real hope that the Dominican government will approve and implement a better contract, which would guarantee adequate living and working conditions in accordance with the provisions of international law? In a country which has such widespread rural unemployment and underemployment, can it make social and economic sense for the Dominican government to provide *better* conditions for imported workers — at considerable cost to the national exchequer — than those available to the average Dominican worker in the agricultural sector? Or are the average living conditions of less importance in the long run than wages, incentives, trade union freedoms, and genuine protection against the brutality and abuse by CEA officials that has, among other things, caused Dominican workers to equate the life of a cane cutter with slavery?

We have seen the extent and the limitations of international pressure, from non-governmental organisations such as the Anti Slavery Society, and from an influential specialised agency of the United Nations, the International Labour Organisation. But international bodies can only complement the activities of domestic pressure groups, in this case particularly the organised labour groups within the Dominican sugar industry. As will now be seen, the attempts of sugar workers to organise in defence of their rights is another unending chapter of repression in the Dominican Republic.

Notes

1. Taken from Roland Wingfield, "Haiti. A case study of an underdeveloped area", Ph.D. thesis, Louisiana State University, 1966 (cited in Mats Lundahl, *The Haitian Economy: Man, Land and Markets* (Croom Helm, London, 1983), p. 130).
2. Nancy Fink, "The Haitian Cane Cutter: Notorious Dominican Racket" (Epica Task Force, New York, 1978).
3. Comments made to the ILO by the Attorney-General of the Dominican Republic, October 1981 (text reproduced in the report of the ILO Commission of Enquiry, 1983, pp. 184–5).
4. See, for example, *El Sol*, 24 July 1980.
5. *El Sol*, 6 December 1979.
6. *Empleo en la Zafra Azucarera Dominicana* (Secretariado Técnico de la Presidencia, Oficina Nacional de Planificación (ONAPLAN), Santo Domingo, April 1981).
7. See Carlos Cornielle, *Proceso Histórico Dominico–Haitiano: una Advertencia a la Juventud Dominicana* (Publicaciones América, Santo Domingo, 1980).
8. Cited in *ILO Official Bulletin*, Vol. LXVI (Report of the Commission of Enquiry), 1983, p. 99.
9. "Haitian Cane Cutters forced to work on Dominican Republic plantations, ILO Inquiry Commission reports", ILO press release, 17 June 1983.
10. *ILO Official Bulletin*, 1983, op. cit., p. 124.
11. Ibid.
12. Ibid., p. 126.
13. Ibid., pp. 126–7.
14. Ibid., pp. 20–1.
15. Ibid., p. 44.
16. Ibid., p. 129.
17. Ibid., p. 151.
18. Ibid., pp. 160–1.

19. CEA report, 21 June 1983.

20. *Ultima Hora*, 28 December 1985.

21. "Report of the Committee of Experts on the Application of Conventions and Recommendations", Report III (Part 4A), International Labour Conference, 72nd Session, 1986, pp. 236–8.

22. Ibid., pp. 197–200.

23. Ibid., pp. 246–8.

8 Pressure from Below: Trade Unions and the Dominican Sugar Industry

For the past 30 years, the Haitian *braceros* who came to the Dominican Republic had no knowledge of trade union rights. The most moderate attempts to organise the labour force had met with swift reprisals in Duvalier's Haiti, and labour activities had to take place underground. On the Dominican side, there has been a history of militant trade union activity, but also periods of repression as savage as anything on the Haitian side. During the Trujillo era, it was seen, the only labour activities permitted were sponsored by, and often acting in the interests of, the Trujillo regime. Under Balaguer too, many prominent trade unionists spent many years behind bars, and the trade unions which had known links with leftist political parties were banned. The PRD government between 1978 and 1986, as we saw, made great play of the widespread political and trade union freedoms it permitted on the sugar plantations as in all other sectors of the economy. The Communist Party was permitted to act openly for the first time in recent history, and militant unions with links to the Communist and other socialist parties grew rapidly in numbers. As will be seen below, however, there was much trade union repression even during the years of the PRD governments, when the unions declared unofficial strikes to support demands for bonus payments, higher salaries and other benefits, and launched countrywide strikes against the threatened closure of CEA's sugar mills. At the time of writing this chapter, a new situation has developed. The post-Duvalier *Conseil National de Gouvernement* (CNG) in Haiti has pledged respect for trade union rights, has recognised trade union federations, and has claimed that it will make a stand for the protection of the rights of the Haitian *braceros* in the Dominican Republic. In the meantime, some trade unionists in the Dominican Republic fear that the return to power of President Joaquín Balaguer may herald yet another period of severe repression of the union movement. Despite pledges by Balaguer that his fourth government will respect human rights, and that there will be no repeat of the widespread repression of the 1960s and 1970s, the sugar workers are understandably worried. They are determined to fight for the protection of their jobs, while knowing that the future of tens of thousands of sugar workers is highly uncertain. And many of them have taken a strong stand for the protection of Haitians' rights, at a time when Dr Joaquín Balaguer has himself been involved in a strong campaign against the Haitian presence in the Dominican Republic.

This chapter looks at the role played by organised labour in the Dominican sugar industry in protecting the rights of either Dominican or Haitian cane cutters. To what extent do the law and practice allow for effective worker participation in the industry, in either the state or the private sector? What constraints exist on freedom of trade union activity? In recent years, what improvements if any have been gained from the increased trade union activity? And to what extent have the Dominican worker organisations included the rights of Haitian *braceros* within their trade union activities?

When CEA was created by Law No. 7 of 4 August 1966, there were statutory provisions to guarantee worker representation in the management of the nationalised sugar industry, and also worker participation in profits. Article 3 of this law affirmed that there were to be two worker representatives on CEA's Governing Council — one representing the factory workers, another the field workers. Article 12 stipulated that:

> Out of the year's net profit, forty per cent is actually to be shared by workers after various deductions have been made upon the advice of the advisory body — deductions necessary for improvements on the plantations, for its efficient running, maintenance and expansion, along with taxation and rental dues.

It was an ambiguous guarantee, and everything depended on the profits that CEA declared for any one year. As the Dominican worker delegation noted in its report to an international sugar workers' conference held in Trinidad in 1977, "This confused wording of the article leaves the allocation of the sums of money for improvements, distribution among the workers, and subsequent use for social welfare in the hands of the authorities of the CEA."[1]

In the years since CEA's creation there have been bitter disputes, and often protracted strikes, to determine the amount of the bonus payments made to sugar workers — and often to determine whether any bonus payments should be paid at all. It would have taken a strong and independent worker organisation to press for implementation of this agreement to the advantage of the cane cutters; but throughout the Balaguer government the union movement was weak, repressed and politically fragmented. Socialists had gained control of much of the labour movement during Juan Bosch's brief tenure of the presidency in the early 1960s, but after his overthrow Marxist organisations were specifically outlawed by Act No. 6 of October 1963 (only repealed in 1978) which made all Communist activities liable to imprisonment. Before then, the strongest of the sugar workers' unions had been the *Sindicato Unido* on the Central Romana, which had carried out technically illegal but successful strikes in the early to mid 1960s with support from Haitian as well as Dominican cane cutters. But this union was forcibly broken up after the purchase of the Romana complex by the US-owned Gulf and Western conglomerate, and 83 of the union's leaders were summarily dismissed. Its General Secretary, Guido Gil, "disappeared" after being abducted by the local police.

In other *ingenios* too, the United States was evidently concerned to promote moderate unions, after its Dominican intervention of 1965. It was widely reported that the American Institute for Free Labour Development (AIFLD) devoted clandestine resources and personnel to building up pliant company unions (known variously as "yellow", "plant" or "sweetheart" unions), and to counteracting the influence of the more radical *Central de Trabajadores Dominicanos*, which was under the influence of former President Bosch and the PRD.[2] In the first years after the US intervention, trade union activity declined throughout the country, and the sugar plantations provided no exception. Most members of the "company" unions permitted at this time were the factory workers, technicians, transport workers and others who already enjoyed conditions better than the field workers and cane cutters. Leaders of the *sindicatos* within the separate *ingenios* limited their activities to seeking improved conditions for their own affiliated members, with little bargaining power behind them, under the system of *Pactos Colectivos* (collective contracts) which were provided for under the Labour Code dating from the Trujillo era, and which were generally renegotiated every two years. Solidarity strikes were banned by the existing Labour Code, thus preventing any nationwide protest activity for improved conditions. Haitians were unorganised, whether Kongos brought over through the contract, or the *viejos* who had been in the country for years or decades. Wages remained exceedingly low, and the growing recourse to illegal Haitian labour ensured that wages could be depressed through the regular availability of cheap imported labour.

In 1972 a number of breakaway unionists from the Christian Democratic CASC federation, together with leaders of the leftist FOUPSA–CESITRADO federation, formed the *Confederación General de Trabajadores* (CGT). Politically to the left, but nevertheless independent of both the Communist Party and the international trade union confederations, the CGT has been combative from its inception, fighting for structural changes including the nationalisation of wide sectors of the economy. Later it spawned its sugar workers' federation, FENAZUCAR, which rapidly increased its influence on both state-owned and private *ingenios*. While working like the other trade union federations for control of the company unions within the individual sugar mills, and for the renegotiation of collective agreements, FENAZUCAR has been more liable to challenge the government and CEA head on, in demanding higher salaries and more generous bonus payments at the end of each harvest season. By the late 1970s the CGT's FENAZUCAR claimed to have control of the plant unions on a number of CEA *ingenios* in the eastern sugar-producing centre of San Pedro Macoris, and in the northern sugar mill of Montellanos. In the large mill of Río Haina, where the allegiance of several separate unions was divided among different labour federations, FENAZUCAR could also claim significant support. The CGT has claimed furthermore that it was only deprived of control of the Central Romana's important company union by a private arrangement between Gulf and Western and the incoming PRD government in 1978. After reportedly fraudulent union elections, a new trade union was formed under the control of the PRD's recently formed *Unión General de Trabajadores Dominicanos* (UGTD), and a large number of CGT activists were summarily dismissed.

In November 1974 a new law (Law No. 80 of that year, enacted at the height of the boom in world sugar prices) had imposed a tax on refined sugar, and instructed CEA to use 15 per cent of the profits to increase cane cutters' salaries. As under Decree No. 602, there was endless wrangling over the amounts that CEA owed to the cane cutters, but only very small sums were actually paid out. By the end of the

Balaguer government in 1978, FENAZUCAR was claiming that the government was several millions of pesos in debt to the sugar workers under the provisions of this law, having failed to make the requisite payments for each of the past four years. The incoming government of President Antonio Guzmán was threatened with widespread strike action if adequate bonuses were not promptly paid over.

When the PRD finally took office in August 1978, and pledged to respect trade union freedoms, FENAZUCAR, together with the other sugar unions, moved fast to recruit rank-and-file members within the *bateyes*, and took advantage of the improved political climate to press their economic claims. It was unfortunate for the PRD that this coincided with the worst ever collapse of sugar prices on the world market, which has lasted ever since except for an all too brief upsurge in the early 1980s. Throughout the first four years of the PRD government, nationwide strike action and stoppages occurred at the beginning of each harvest, following sugar workers' demands for their annual bonus payments, and CEA's refusal to pay up on the grounds that no profits had been made. Though CEA published its annual accounts, pointing to multi-million dollar deficits each year, the sugar workers countered with allegations that the "books had been cooked". In the 1979–80 harvest, sugar workers stood out for bonus payments equivalent to 30 days' normal wages, and paralysed production on all the sugar plantations in the area of San Pedro Macoris. The government reacted strongly, sending troops into the *ingenios*, arresting trade union leaders including the CGT's General Secretary, and dismissing over 300 grassroots union activists from their jobs on the CEA plantations. The conflict was ended unsatisfactorily from the workers' perspective, with CEA finally agreeing to make a reduced and delayed payment equivalent to 15 days' earnings, effectively a loan to be made from any profits realised in the forthcoming harvest.

In the 1981–82 harvest, the phenomenon was repeated. This time a broad-based "National Coordinating Committee for the Struggle in the Sugar Sector" threatened strike action while it held out for a larger bonus equivalent to 90 days' pay. During the strike, while CEA was once again providing statistics pointing to unprecedented losses, opposition parties counter-claimed that CEA had in fact realised profits of over 20 million pesos during the past financial year. Strike action again broke out in the east, and was halted only when CEA agreed to make bonus payments equivalent to 33 days' normal work.

During my field research in 1982, I spent much time in the company of sugar workers' unionists. I was concerned mainly with the following questions. To what extent was trade union organisation effectively permitted, and were union activists still dismissed in large numbers for their grassroots organisational initiatives? To what extent did the unions take action on behalf of the Haitian *viejos* and Kongos? Were the Haitians ever included in the benefits deriving from the collective contracts agreed between the sugar workers and management?

The imported Haitian Kongos, I found, were invariably excluded from the collective bargaining over bonus payments, though small end-of-harvest bonuses for them had been provided for under the most recent contracts. For the remainder, the situation was more complex. The agreement reached between CEA and the sugar unions after the most recent strike had stipulated that year-round workers should receive the full bonus payments, and temporary workers (those engaged for the six months of the *zafra*) a pro rata percentage of this amount. As a large proportion even of the Dominican factory workers were engaged only for the duration of the sugar harvest, the reduced payments for the *temporeros* were strongly contested by some of the sugar workers' unions. The resident Haitians should in theory have been eligible for bonus payments. FENAZUCAR claimed that "as regards bonuses, when they exist, the majority never receive them."[3] Certainly, those Haitian *viejos* whom I asked about this claimed that their precarious status precluded them from claiming their legitimate benefits. Yet many of them were now being recruited within the unions for the first time. The CGT and FENAZUCAR in particular were making serious efforts to break down the racial barrier between Dominican and Haitian workers, and to recruit the Haitian *viejos* within their ranks. On both CEA and private sugar plantations, I met a number of Dominican CGT activists who had been dismissed over the previous year for their efforts to organise Haitian labour. Nevertheless, the recruitment efforts were clearly making some headway. As FENAZUCAR reported in its May 1982 newsletter:

> More than 300 cane cutters of Haitian nationality resident in the *bateyes* of Caraballo, Cangrejo, Pancho Mateo, Schevere, Muñoz and El Tamarindo have affiliated to the *Sindicato Autónomo* of the Ingenio Montellano, which is in turn affiliated to our federation. This important step taken by our Haitian brothers is a result of the educational and organisational effort made by our trade union leaders to break with discrimination, incorporating all workers of whatever nationality, colour or sex. The Haitian cane cutters are the most maltreated of the CEA workers. Their appalling conditions of life and labour are reminiscent of the days of slavery. . . . Onward, fraternal Haitian workers. We workers are one class.

What of the collective agreements drawn up between management and the individual company unions? The conditions for drawing up such agreements are specified in the Dominican Labour Code of 1951, as amended (Articles 92–118). To negotiate a collective agreement, the *sindicato* has to be registered with the Ministry of Labour, and to count on the membership of more than 61 per cent of all workers (presumably, though this is not specified, permanent workers). Registration is by no means automatic. It can be "denied or withdrawn on such grounds as having engaged in political activities, staged sympathy strikes, or otherwise transgressed permitted functions".[4] Though workers' rights are outlined in general terms in the Labour Code, the *Pacto Colectivo* gives more substance to the conditions of labour. It regulates the "salaries, the duration of the work day, rest periods and holidays, and other conditions of work" (Art. 93). Industrial action has to be approved by the Ministry of Labour, which will determine whether or not a stoppage is legal. It is legal only if the company is found to be in violation of the provisions of the negotiated agreement. Otherwise, as the Dominican Constitution abruptly declares,

> Any interruption, slowing down, paralysation of activities or deliberate reduction of output in private enterprises or those of the State, is prohibited.

Any strike, stoppage, interruption, slowing down or deliberate reduction of output which affects the Administration, the public services or those of public utility, shall be illegal. The law shall lay down the measures necessary to guarantee the observance of these rules.[5]

If illegal stoppages occur, then management is free to dismiss workers at random (for example, in the national strikes over bonus payments, the mass dismissals were justified by CEA through the illegality of the strike action). In the case of worker complaints, there are complex arbitration procedures involving government, management and worker representatives.

I examined the *Pactos Colectivos* currently in force in five separate *ingenios* (the CEA properties of Amistad, Barahona, Esperanza and Montellanos: and the private Central Romana). In conclusion — and not surprisingly — I found that existing provisions were heavily slanted towards the needs of the factory workers, and the inhabitants of the *bateyes centrales*. With regard to work hours, for example, it was stipulated in each case that the normal work period should be eight hours per day, and 44 hours per week. There should be a 30 per cent overtime payment between 44 and 56 hours, 35 per cent from 56 to 60 hours, and 100 per cent overtime rates for more than 60 hours. Only the Central Romana made specific mention of the work hours for field workers. They were 10 hours a day, 60 hours a week, with no overtime rates for anything over that amount.

With regard to social amenities — housing, recreation, medical, educational and other services — it was much the same story. In general terms, the workers might extract a commitment from management to improve conditions "wherever necessary". Thus in Barahona, CEA was to contribute to a housing plan, paying 0.02 cents for each ton of cane harvested over 150,000 tons into a general housing fund. In Esperanza, the company was to "repair and refurbish all housing whenever and wherever there was need . . . with maximum conditions of security and housing, giving baths and sanitary services to houses that require it". It also committed itself to "recondition the *bateyes*, making them fit for habitation by the workers". In Montellanos, it was to allocate 10,000 pesos per year for a housing plan, and allow workers to purchase company housing at a maximum cost of 1,000 pesos. In Amistad the company was to "agree, within the bounds of its possibilities and in agreement with the *sindicatos* covered by this *pacto*, to improve housing and speed the plans for new housing construction carried out with the corresponding state organisations".

But where concrete commitments were to be made by management, they were almost invariably for improved infrastructural facilities within the *batey central*, or limited opportunities for outside study grants (for example, dining halls, a library, a baseball pitch and the provision of an ambulance within the *batey central* of Ingenio Barahona). In Esperanza, bathrooms and toilets in the factory area; sports facilities as organised by the trade union, medicine chests in the factory and "anywhere else that CEA deems convenient", three medical dispensaries to be built and outside study grants. In Amistad, sports facilities including a softball court and children's playground, a poly-clinic and a library in the *batey central*; medicine chests in the mechanics' workshop, the laboratory and "wherever else is felt necessary". Otherwise, it was notable that all the *pactos* stressed the need for management to do everything possible to provide all-year-round employment for those people now engaged solely for the *zafra*. It has to be remembered that a vast number of Dominicans (whether the factory hands, the mechanics, the foremen, drivers, weighers or ticket-collectors) have guaranteed employment for only six months of the year. One of the major concerns of the *sindicatos* is that management should recognise the obligation to provide for this residual labour force in some way, and give them priority in out-of-season employment rather than recruit cheaper seasonal labour from outside.

It may come as no surprise that the term "Haitian worker" never once figured in any of the five collective contracts examined. The *sindicatos* were dominated first by the Dominican factory hands, accountants, mechanics or other professionals, then by the Dominican nationals with more precarious forms of employment. They could claim, with some reason, that they had enough on their hands trying to secure adequate living and working conditions for their own labour force, and more stable guarantees for the thousands of Dominican temporary workers in the sugar industry, without taking on the tens of thousands of marginal Haitians whose demands and interests might essentially be in conflict with their own. To some extent the barriers had been broken down, particularly in the Central Romana where a very large percentage of the regular labour force was of Haitian origin but had blended over time with Dominican nationals. Some analysts have noted the development of a rigid class structure within the Haitian community itself.[6] Many of the long-term *viejos* (who may have achieved a Dominican *cédula* (identity card), cohabit with a Dominican woman, have Dominican children with full rights to school education, and speak fluent Spanish) are barely distinguishable from the Dominican workers. They will experience upward social mobility, perhaps having the job of foreman or recruiter, and are likely to enjoy social security and pension rights.

The ILO's 1983 Commission of Enquiry, while making certain comments on freedom of association in the sugar industry as a whole, focused primarily on the right of Haitian workers to organise. They also noted that in recent years Dominican trade unions had been able to recruit a "growing number of Haitian workers resident on the sugar plantations, both those belonging to the State and those in private ownership". While noting the improved trade union climate since 1978 they nevertheless concluded that there were severe pragmatic constraints on the effective organisation of Haitian labourers. In the case of the imported Haitian *braceros*, the ILO's Commission members seemed to accept that trade union affiliation was well nigh impossible. First there were the practical difficulties, such as the temporary nature of their stay in the country, their isolation, lack of familiarity with trade union activities, and their very low earnings. And then,

> These obstacles are undoubtedly reinforced by the constraints to which the workers are subject, such as the restrictions on their freedom of movement and the close vigilance to which they are subject. It was also repeatedly stressed during the contacts which the Commission had in the Dominican Republic that these workers feared reprisals on their return to Haiti if they joined trade unions.[7]

With regard to the *viejos*, the ILO noted that Dominican trade unions had recently been able to recruit a growing number of Haitians resident in the sugar plantations, but mentioned the evident obstacles that were inherent in their illegal status:

> Except at La Romana, where a substantial proportion of these workers have Dominican residence papers, this category of workers is however in a very vulnerable position if they wish to become actively involved in trade union affairs, since almost all of them have the status of illegal immigrants and are therefore liable at any time to arrest and expulsion.

It also mentioned documents shown to the Commission (such as the report of an interministerial Haitian commission which had visited the Dominican Republic in 1979) which showed that the Haitian government "has been anxious to prevent political opponents in exile in the Dominican Republic from taking up grievances of Haitian plantation workers". In sum, the Commission concluded that "All these factors would tend to reinforce the obstacles to unionisation of Haitian workers in the Dominican Republic previously mentioned and explain why particularly those working only temporarily in that country should be reluctant to join a sugar union". The Commission also touched briefly on certain obstacles to full freedom of organisation for Dominican workers in the sugar industry, such as inadequate protection against anti-union discrimination by employers, and legislation which enabled the Dominican authorities to intervene in the internal affairs of trade unions by providing for the presence of Labour Ministry inspectors at certain of their meetings. In its recommendations the ILO Commission generally advocated a greater participatory role for worker organisations in the enactment of sugar policies, including worker representation on a National Advisory Committee to advise the Minister of Labour on matters within its competence.[8]

Story of a Sugar Strike, November–December 1983

In principle, the Dominican government accepted readily enough the ILO's proposals for greater participation by workers in the development of overall policies in the sugar industry. On 29 April 1983, as it later informed the ILO, a National Employment Committee was set up through Decree No. 1019 on a tripartite basis, with workers, employers and the government on an equal footing. In reality — as events during the next harvest season were to show — relations between CEA and the sugar workers' organisations remained as conflict-ridden as ever, and questions of profit sharing and worker remuneration were settled by the customary method of strikes, intimidation and repression until some concessions were made by both sides and agreement was belatedly reached.

On 23 October the National Coordinating Committee for the Struggle in the Sugar Sector, after a meeting held on the Ingenio Santa Fe, issued its five principal demands for the forthcoming harvest season. They were: (i) a bonus payment equal to 60 days' salary for both factory and field workers; (ii) the discussion and signature of collective agreements; (iii) the implementation of the plans to improve housing on the *bateyes*; (iv) enforcement of an existing Legislative Decree — Decree

No. 3180 — for the computation and payment of overtime; (v) respect for trade union freedoms. A fortnight later the Committee reported that its negotiations so far with CEA's Executive Director Eulogio Santaella had met with failure, and that it had now devised a plan of specific action to press its demands. The following day, 9 November, there would be mass demonstrations throughout CEA's twelve *ingenios*. A week later there would be a mass picket in front of CEA's main office in Santo Domingo. The Chambers of Senators and Deputies of National Congress would be asked to intervene on their behalf, and a meeting would be requested with President Salvador Jorge Blanco. If any sugar workers were laid off in the meantime, the Committee warned, there would be staggered stoppages and then an indefinite strike.

As usual, CEA first countered by pointing to its pathetic financial situation, and stating unequivocally that there would be no bonus payments that year. Its director insisted that overall losses in the past harvest had been 49 million pesos, and that the Central Bank had had to bail it out with a 45 million-peso loan in order to cover the present deficit.[9] Instead of a bonus, he later said, incentive payments would be made to workers of those *ingenios* with the best productivity records. At the same time, he revealed that 19,000 Haitian *braceros* would be brought over soon to get the 1983–84 harvest under way.

At this stage, press reaction was mixed. On 2 November *Ultima Hora* included an editorial on the threatened strike, arguing that it could lead to CEA's collapse, and three days later *El Nacional* criticised the sugar workers' approach. But on 7 November *Nuevo Diario* published a more sympathetic editorial, entitled "Tear gas and beatings against hunger", stating that it "cannot keep its silence when the National Police are using tear gas and batons in Villa Altagracia to disperse a march of sugar workers claiming compensatory salaries". Ingenio Catarey, by the town of Villa Altagracia, was at this time in the forefront of the sugar workers' protests. By 10 November, according to newspaper sources, several demonstrators had been beaten, over 300 arrested, and all commercial activity brought to a standstill after clashes between the police and the protesters.[10] A number of Congressmen from the opposition Partido Reformista now declared their support for the sugar workers, and CEA workers threatened a mass strike to paralyse all sugar activity on 20 November. Solidarity was declared by other worker unions, including the influential transport union, whose leaders claimed that their own members were directly affected because "there will be no one to pay the bus and truck fares if bonuses are not paid out to the sugar workers."[11]

By 18 November thousands of workers were reported to be on strike in Ingenio Haina, and a number of workers — as well as two local newspaper correspondents — were arrested in Barahona when the protest movement spread to the south-western plantations. CEA and the Coordinating Committee of the sugar workers' movement now came back to the negotiating table, and agreement was reached on four of the five points under negotiation. On the bonus payments, however, CEA still held out. CEA's position was nevertheless weakened when the influential Federation of Sugar Outgrowers, FEDOCA, gave its own view that the sugar workers' claims should be given consideration — although the amount of bonus payments demanded was considered by FEDOCA to be excessive.

On 21 November 200 worker delegates from 59 trade unions in the sugar industry held their third national assembly, and agreed to declare a strike on all twelve CEA *ingenios* if demands on bonus payments had not been met by the following week. Though the first stoppage was to last for only 24 hours, FENAZUCAR's General Secretary, Víctor Rufino Alvarez, warned that the strike could be of indefinite duration if "it is found there is truth in reports that CEA is planning to send the army into the *ingenios* and repress the workers". By this time CEA was becoming seriously concerned by the continuing delays in getting the 1983 harvest under way on its largest *ingenio* of Río Haina. Again, there were some moves towards a compromise settlement. On 24 November, CEA's Executive Council agreed that sugar workers should be given a loan equivalent to 20 days' wages, the amount to be paid back to CEA over two harvest seasons with CEA itself footing the interest payments. It was less than the Coordinating Committee demanded, but there was some reason to believe that this partial concession might take the bite out of the protest movement. At the beginning of the harvest the temporary workers — most of whom had been without regular pay during the six months of the *tiempo muerto* (dead season) — were penniless. With at least some cash in hand, they might be persuaded to return to work, in particular if there were further offers of incentive payments in the event of higher productivity. CEA also commenced a propaganda campaign, distributing thousands of leaflets urging sugar workers not to join the strike movement, and reportedly sending letters to wives urging them to use their influence against the stoppages.[12]

The strike went ahead on 24 November. Over 50,000 sugar workers were reported to have walked out, on all of CEA's twelve *ingenios*.[13] But while CEA put out a public statement declaring its "readiness for dialogue, and rejection of violence", the government also showed more readiness to move to repressive measures. Eight trade unionists were arrested on Ingenio Quisqueya, and police agents were said to have been stationed at strategic points on all the sugar complexes. The Coordinating Committee now instructed all CEA employees to return to work at 6 a.m. the following day, after reaching agreement with CEA that police agents should be withdrawn from all factories and all victims of arrest should be released immediately. But warnings were again given that further strike action would break out if the repression of leading trade unionists did not cease.

By 27 November, nine of the ten CEA *ingenios* which had by then commenced milling for the 1983–84 harvest were reportedly working at full capacity; only Haina was still paralysed. But the strike threats continued. After a meeting on Ingenio Consuelo, several members of the Coordinating Committee rejected CEA's offer of 20 day's salary equivalent in loans, warning that a new 48-hour strike would begin within three days if their demands were not met. An intimidatory note was now struck by the Armed Forces Secretary, Major General Ramiro Matos González, who alleged that the strikes had "conspiratorial ends" and warned that the army and police would not permit attacks on democratic institutions.[14] Around the same time CEA published its depressing balance sheet, citing debts of 354.6 million Dominican pesos by the ninth month of the year, and accumulated losses of over 57.2 million pesos. Perhaps facing the bleakness of these financial facts, the Sugar Workers' Coordinating Committee again lessened its demands, now agreeing to the

20 days' salary equivalent, though still insisting that the loans should be made against future profits, and not deducted from earnings over the next two harvest seasons as CEA had stipulated. However, as *Ultima Hora* now reported,

> The Committee says that this decision, which aims to avoid major conflicts, has been met with repression on CEA's part. They point out that the *ingenios* of Esperanza, Porvenir and Barahona have been militarised, that dozens of workers are not permitted to enter the precinct, and that many leaders and delegates of the Committee are being persecuted.[15]

At the end of November, the four *ingenios* of Barahona, Esperanza, Haina and Porvenir again went on strike. The government responded with further repression against leaders of the strike movement. As *Nuevo Diario* reported on 29 November,

> In San Pedro Macoris, the National Police is meting out persecution against the principal union leaders of Ingenio Porvenir, whose homes were "visited" in the early hours of the morning today. Police agents dressed in civilian clothing, accompanied by the assistant prosecutor, raided the residences of trade union leaders Santos Hodges, Pedro Rondón, and Asdrubal Sepulveda, among others. Sepulveda and the lawyer Juan Antonio Díaz were arrested, though released hours later.

On the last day of the month the Coordinating Committee, after denouncing the arrest and persecution of their delegates on the *ingenios* of Barahona and Quisqueya, announced yet another 48-hour strike to press for the 60 days' salary bonus. This time, the stoppages proved less effective. In Barahona and Haina the factories had to stop work, but the spokesman of the Coordinating Committee admitted that the strikes had been effective on only three of the CEA *ingenios*. He also denounced the militarisation, repression and arrest of dozens of workers in Montellanos, Barahona and Catarey where workers had responded to the calls for industrial action. On 13 December the harvest on Ingenio Haina finally got under way, signalling the end of protests for yet another season. At the end of it all, CEA may have claimed a "Pyrrhic victory". Under the eventual agreement, CEA agreed to pay out an "Easter present" of somewhere between 16 and 17 million pesos, as provided for in the collective agreements which had been in dispute, together with incentive payments on the mills which had the best productivity records. But the cost was a further worsening in CEA–worker relations, a new toll of repression and army involvement, and interminable harvest delays which would eat further into CEA's dismal productivity record.

History Repeated: The 1985–86 Sugar Harvest

During the 1985–86 harvest, the same history was largely repeated.[16] There was a similar sequence of events — the initial demands for bonuses, the bankrupt CEA's response, and the strikes followed by repression with the army moving into the *ingenios*. But there were some important differences. The workers were more willing to recognise the hopelessness of CEA's situation in the present financial circumstances, as well as the very real danger of the collapse of the sugar industry.

They thus turned to additional issues, the fight to save jobs, the fight for a diversification programme that would offer work to CEA's current employees, and the fight for a more generous quota from the US government for Dominican sugar.

On the US quota issue at least, the sugar workers were fighting together with, rather than against, CEA. With a savage reduction of its US quota from 535,000 to 302,000 tons, the Dominican government needed all the help it could muster. Thus a mass picket outside the US Embassy in Santo Domingo, organised by 16 sugar worker unions in October 1985, passed off without incident. But when a similar demonstration took place outside the National Palace a few days later — to present President Jorge Blanco with a series of demands including better housing, back payment by CEA of social security dues, better prices for national sugar production, and changes in the methods of taxing sugar exports — there was a different response. Fifteen trade union leaders were arrested, and the demonstration was swiftly broken up.

In November, the annual protests over the bonus payments commenced. When CEA's new Director, Víctor Manuel Báez, visited the *ingenio* on 28 November he was met by hundreds of workers picketing the main offices with demands for 45 days' salary equivalent, plus a further 30 days' for the *regalía pascual* (Easter present). Báez responded that CEA did not even have the funds to begin the harvest operations, as it had made no profits the previous year.

Elsewhere, sugar workers were more concerned by reports that, under a diversification plan put together by CEA, the five *ingenios* of Amistad, Esperanza, Catarey, Santa Fe and Quisqueya might shortly be closed. FENAZUCAR cited CEA reports that 20,000 *tareas* of Ingenio Santa Fe would be turned over to a private enterprise for the cultivation of African palm (a crop well known elsewhere in the world for its low level of labour intensity), and that 30,000 *tareas* of Ingenio Catarey were to be turned over to the transnational enterprise FRUDOCA for the production of pineapples, lemons, oranges, mangoes and other tropical fruits. There had been no consultation with the unions over these diversification plans, although — according to the CGT's estimates — some 30,000 sugar workers, and a further 20,000 workers in the transport, commerce and health sectors, would lose their jobs.

On 8 December 1985, 54 trade unions from the sugar industry, representing the twelve CEA *ingenios*, held a meeting at Ingenio Santa Fe in San Pedro Macoris, during which there were detailed presentations on both internal and external factors affecting the future of the Dominican sugar industry. Protectionist policies in both Western Europe and the USA, with their subsidies for domestic sugar producers and the search for non-sugar alternatives to cane production, came in for heavy criticism. While their effect on CEA's future was noted, the meeting accused the Dominican government of deliberately decapitalising CEA itself by placing a 36 per cent surcharge on sugar exports, which had deprived it of an estimated 120 million pesos per year. A seven-point set of demands was then agreed by a plenary session of the meeting: (i) that the equivalent of 30 days' salary, as compensation for all factory and field workers, should be paid from the 120 million pesos accumulated through the export surcharge; (ii) that no *ingenios* be closed, and the jobs of all workers be guaranteed; (iii) that CEA property should not be transferred to the private sector, but that a different diversification should be undertaken immediately, on the basis of bagasse and other sugar derivatives, and should be placed under state control, with the Ministry of Agriculture's involvement; (iv) that CEA pay its 22 million-peso debt to the National Institute of Social Security, so that workers might receive adequate medical attention and medicines; (v) that the housing units built under an INVI–CEA programme be handed over to the workers who really needed them; (vi) that CEA should sell its own sugar in the domestic market; (vii) that CEA should comply with Legislative Decree No. 123 and Law No. 384, producing the financial accounts required of it by law. The plenary meeting also agreed: (i) to begin mobilisation and pickets on all *ingenios* as of the present week; (ii) to request the President and CEA's Director to begin a dialogue, to search for solutions to these demands; (iii) to organise a sugar workers' march to the National Palace if there were no satisfactory response to these demands by Wednesday, 18 December.

The march on the National Palace was called off when the Interior Minister denied a permit, but spontaneous demonstrations broke out soon afterwards at Haina and Catarey (Villa Altagracia), with the workers demanding immediate payment of the 30 days' bonus. On 18 December, as the newspaper *Hoy* reported, the police broke up a sugar workers' assembly, leaving a toll of many beaten and arrested, and two minors in hospital for treatment of injuries caused by the tear gas bombs thrown by the police.[17] Early that morning, anti-riot police began to occupy the premises of Ingenio Haina. By the next day, the towns of Haina and Villa Altagracia were reported to be "wholly militarised" once again.[18] With work at a complete standstill in Ingenio Haina, and over 100 persons arrested in that mill alone, the Sugar Workers' Coordinating Committee now held a second assembly, attended by 74 separate unions. It warned that an all-out strike would soon be coming if the police and military repression did not abate.

Tension remained high throughout the Christmas and New Year period. There were the familiar disputes about CEA accounting, and the truth of the profits or losses recorded. One union group, the CGT–M, released figures claiming that CEA had actually made a profit of 31,140,000 pesos, thanks to the small rise in international sugar prices. CEA's director countered with a radically different picture, saying that the country could fulfil its existing production requirements for the US and domestic markets with the produce of only three or four of CEA's twelve *ingenios*, and that those places where further protests occurred would now be closed down.[19] On 27 December the Coordinating Committee postponed a 48-hour strike planned for that day, when the Labour Minister promised that the President of the Republic would meet with them early in the New Year. On 7 January President Jorge Blanco finally received the Coordinating Committee's representatives, apparently stating that he agreed with some of their demands, and would give them his reply within the next few days.

In the third week of January President Jorge Blanco delivered his verdict. The *zafreros*, or CEA's temporary workers, would receive a ten-day bonus payment. The 25,000 *zafreros*, he said, were the kernel of the sugar industry and were in the greatest need, as the permanent workers got "an acceptable guaranteed salary, and a *regalía* on top". The President complained in the meantime that the unions failed to understand the critical situation confronted by the sugar industry with the 40 per cent drop in the US quota as well as the fall in world sugar prices. Nothing was said about CEA payments to the Dominican Social Security Institute, the threatened closure of some *ingenios*, the plans to pass other *ingenio* lands over to the private sector, and the remaining demands which had been made earlier by the Coordinating Committee. The Committee then elected to continue its industrial action, in the meantime denouncing the continued repression and arrests of trade union leaders in the *ingenios* of Barahona, Haina, Consuelo, Porvenir and Boca Chica — all of which were said to be under military control.

The Coordinating Committee thus called for another strike, scheduled to last 48 hours at the first instance, though there were warnings that it might be extended indefinitely "because the *ingenios* of Barahona and Haina are occupied by the army, and in Barahona a number of trade union activists and militant workers are still under arrest".[20] Activity ground to a halt in Amistad, Boca Chica, Catarey, Consuelo, Haina, Montellanos, Porvenir and Santa Fe. Violent scuffles broke out between sugar workers and the police, and on 23 January they claimed their first victim. Some 40 persons were wounded after a clash in Catarey, and one sugar worker, Mario Rosa Polanco, was killed. The conservative daily paper *Listín Diario* cited eyewitness accounts that Polanco, a 24-year-old youth, had been killed by the "Casco Negro" (Black Beret) crack police unit while being led off under custody on the outskirts of Villa Altagracia.

The strike did not last. By the end of January the Coordinating Committee had reached a provisional agreement with CEA that: (i) the government would punish those persons guilty of Mario Rosa Polanco's assassination; (ii) the army would withdraw immediately from the *ingenios* and trade union precincts currently occupied by it; (iii) all detained sugar workers would be released in Boca Chica, Catarey, Consuelo, Haina and Porvenir; (iv) the repression and persecution of trade unionists would cease, with guarantees that there would be no further dismissals on account of strike activities; (v) there would be a further meeting with CEA and the Minister of Labour to deal with the bonus payments for permanent and monthly workers. But the government kept only part of its agreement. Bonus payments were eventually made at the lower rate, but months later approximately 60 union activists had still not been reinstated in their jobs at Ingenio Haina. Rumours were spread by the unions that these dismissals were only the first stage of a co-ordinated plan to weed out militant unionists from all CEA plantations. After more months of agitation, the sugar workers had little to show. The threat of *ingenio* closures and mass lay-offs still hung perilously over them, and the outlook for the future remained exceedingly bleak.

The Role of the Trade Unions: Assessment and Outlook

From the sugar workers' perspective, the strikes could hardly be termed a success. But the government had no reason to congratulate itself. After eight years in office, the PRD had done nothing to improve labour relations in the volatile sugar industry. The bonus payments demanded had been almost infinitesimal compared with the overall costs of running the monolithic sugar industry: 20 pesos a head, approximately $7 at the current rate of exchange, would have cost under $1 million for each harvest season, or under half the amount of the initial payments made to the Duvalier regime for the importation of Haitian *braceros*. The PRD's pledge to uphold trade union freedoms withered away very quickly when there were signs that the sugar workers could muster sufficient strength to press their economic and other claims. Though CEA would profess to negotiate — usually offering derisory settlement terms in the first instance — the army and police were still held in reserve in case serious protests should break out on the sugar plantations.

All of this showed the limitations of political democracy when it is not accompanied by a firm resolve to carry out structural reforms to increase the standard of living of the poorest sectors of society. The effects of the PRD's economic strategy, including the large death toll after the "food riots" of April 1984, will be examined in more detail in the next chapter. Here, suffice it to say that the increased formal opportunities to organise in trade unions were bound to lead to conflict, if the unions pressed hard for the economic claims which are generally the primary concern of any organised labour movement. The PRD's economic austerity policies — linked to increased export production and strong support for the private sector — were demanded by overseas creditors, most particularly the International Monetary Fund. They were bound to lead to clashes in the stagnant and heavily overmanned sugar industry where the prospects were bleakest and the conditions of life and labour had always been the poorest. But despite all the rhetoric concerning the Dominicanisation of the sugar industry, the PRD government never took effective measures to make cane cutting an attractive proposition for the Dominican rural labour force. For this to happen, CEA would have had to make structural investments far above the actual level. It would have needed also to give some substance to existing laws on worker participation in the sugar industry, involving the unions in long-range planning for diversification. The Dominican trade unionists were no Luddites. They accepted the need for diversification, but not for projects that turned their lands over to private companies, providing no future for the tens of thousands of sugar workers who could be laid off arbitrarily without financial compensation. The government, in its perpetual state of semi-bankruptcy, was obsessed with the immediate need to increase export earnings, whatever the social consequences. The work-force — already living at or below subsistence levels — wanted, with reason, CEA to turn its idle lands over to agricultural projects that could cater for their subsistence requirements.

The increasing recourse to imported Haitian labour, by 1985 at levels far higher than under previous governments, reflected the poor state of industrial relations. While the threat of police brutality was one way to undermine the union movement, the use of more and more *braceros* was another. While the Haitian Kongos were by no means placid — they would protest readily enough if they were not paid on time — they were less likely than the Dominican workers and the Haitian *viejos* to strike for more pay and better living conditions.

By 1986 the union movement had made some advances, and could organise synchronised protests for a brief period throughout the country. But the sugar workers' union movement was also desperately fragmented, divided into factions which were easily manipulated by one or other of the political parties. There were more than a dozen unions on Ingenio Haina alone, with each sugar workers' federation claiming to have the majority with the corresponding right to negotiate with management over the collective agreements. The PRD had organised its own union group, the UGTD, after 1978, but by the mid 1980s the UGTD had itself split into two separate factions. The CGT also split in 1983, between the CGT itself controlled by the left-wing Bloque Socialista, and the CGT–M which supported the moderately leftist PLD of former President Juan Bosch. As one analyst argued to me in June 1986, this fragmentation had weakened the union movement on the *ingenios* considerably over the past couple of years, and the divisions could easily be exploited by the incoming government of President Joaquín Balaguer.

And what of the Haitians right at the bottom of the pile? Hitherto they have had two unattractive options open to them. Until 1978, the Dominican *sindicatos* tended to ignore them altogether. An attempt to organise the Haitian *viejos* at any level would have met with severe repression, and as likely as not have prompted their immediate expulsion from the country. In some union quarters, there has now been a growing realisation that the substantial Haitian presence has been utilised to depress salaries and social benefits for Dominican and Haitian workers alike, and that any concerted nationwide pressure to improve these conditions could only succeed if the Haitian resident population were incorporated within the organised labour movement. The efforts by the CGT and FENAZUCAR to incorporate Haitians within their ranks have been tolerated to an extent by the central government. On the other hand, trade union activists who have led the recruitment of Haitian workers have regularly been dismissed from employment on the individual *ingenios*: the growing Haitian involvement on the Ingenio Haina was one factor behind the 1985–86 dismissals there. Thus the Haitians can either put up with present conditions, in exchange for the right to stay on the plantations; or they can opt for protest, knowing full well that it can easily spark off a backlash in the form of a new campaign against them terminating in arbitrary expulsion.

At the time of writing, it is a delicate balance. With existing levels of sugar production, the Haitian labour component — whether the *viejos* or the imported *braceros* — is sorely needed by CEA. But if *ingenios* are to be closed, and large land areas are to be taken out of cane production, the Haitians without legal permits of residence know they will be the first to suffer. For the immediate future the cards lie mostly with the government of Haiti, and with the international lending agencies which are meant to be bound by the provisions of the UN Charter. The Haitian government can make the realisation of future contracts conditional on guarantees that the imported Haitian *braceros* have their labour rights enforced, including the rights to freedom of organisation, in accordance with the provisions of both international law and domestic Dominican labour law. It can request a role for the Dominican trade union organisations too, in monitoring the strict enforcement of these provisions. But the Haitian government can go further, and make future agreements conditional on respect for the labour rights of *all* Haitian workers in the Dominican sugar industry. In the longer term, diversification programmes will require substantial funding from the international agencies. The UN agencies concerned specifically with the rights of refugees and migrant workers — in particular the ILO and the United Nations High Commission for Refugees — can be given a technical role in monitoring these programmes, in striving for more genuine worker participation, and in ensuring that diversification programmes do not occur at the expense of those Haitians who have borne the brunt of the bad years of the Dominican sugar industry.

Notes

1. "The World of Sugar Workers". Papers presented at the International Sugar Workers' Conference, San Fernando, Trinidad, 23–28 July 1977 (published by Caribbean Ecumenical Programme, Trinidad, 1978).

2. Carlos María Gutierrez, *The Dominican Republic: Rebellion and Repression* (Monthly Review Press, London, 1972), pp. 38–9ff.

3. *FENAZUCAR Bulletin*, CGT, Santo Domingo, May 1982.

4. Ian Bell, *The Dominican Republic* (Westview Press, Boulder, Colo., 1981), p. 229.

5. Ibid., as translated by Ian Bell.

6. See Maurice Lemoine, *Bitter Sugar*, (Zed Books, London, 1985).

7. *ILO Official Bulletin*, Vol. LXVI (Report of Commission of Enquiry), 1983, p. 137.

8. Ibid., pp. 136–9 and 161.

9. *Nuevo Diario*, 1 November 1983.

10. Ibid., 10 November 1983, and *El Sol*, 10 November 1983.

11. *El Nacional*, 13 November 1983.

12. *Ultima Hora*, 24 November 1983.

13. *El Sol*, 25 November 1983.

14. *Listín Diario*, 27 November 1983.

15. *Ultima Hora*, 29 November 1983.

16. See the account in *Cronología de la Lucha de los Trabajadores Azucareros, 1985–86* (Published jointly by CGT–FENAZUCAR, and the Centro Investigación y Apoyo Cultural (CIAC), Santo Domingo, 1986).

17. *Hoy*, 19 December 1985.

18. *El Nacional*, 20 December 1985.

19. *Ultima Hora*, 23 December 1985.

20. *Cronología de la Lucha*, op. cit., p. 42.

9 Diversification Dilemmas: The Debt Crisis and Dominican Agriculture

In 1985, CEA published an ambitious diversification plan for surplus sugar lands. It called for diversification into five major areas: other agricultural crops; energy; tourism; industrial parks; and different types of sugar. The new crops were to include pineapples, oranges, sisal, coconuts, tomatoes, mangoes and African palm trees. It was estimated that pineapple production alone could generate 3,600 permanent jobs and bring revenues of up to $75 million per year, and that African palm cultivation could generate some 700 jobs. In this plan, an extensive role was foreseen for foreign capital investment. Since then, CEA has negotiated an arrangement whereby 13,000 acres of its sugar lands will be turned over to the US-owned multinational Castle and Cooke for pineapple growing and the establishment of a juice-processing plant. Other CEA lands were to be turned over to tourism projects, in particular on its properties adjoining the Caribbean coastline, again with substantial overseas capital investment.

The trade unions, it was seen, have opposed such projects because they doubt that the multinationals will maintain the same employment levels as the existing arrangements for sugar cane cultivation. They also criticise the privatisation of the sugar industry, on the grounds that the existing work-force will be given no part in decisions about the future use of lands now owned by a nationalised industry. If unemployment is rising so steeply, and if food shortages are reaching dangerously high levels, why have successive governments proved so reluctant to turn part of the state-owned property over to subsistence crop cultivation, guaranteeing both more stable conditions of employment, and a rise in real rural incomes at a time of rapidly rising costs for imported food?

In previous chapters we have touched briefly on the historical factors which allowed for land concentration, the emphasis on export crop cultivation, and the continuing plight of both the Haitian and Dominican labour force in the sugar industry. We now have to examine the present-day structural factors, primarily at the international level, which render it so difficult to devise agrarian reform and rural development strategies which might bring the conditions of the rural population up to acceptable levels. The main argument can be simply put. Under the existing unequal terms of trade — and most particularly since the explosion of the Latin American debt crisis in the early 1980s — governments have had little alternative but to favour the export sector of agriculture, whatever the cost to domestic food production and the needs of the rural and urban poor.

In seeking remedies, one has to be realistic, and accept the very real constraints on Third World commodity producers whose economies have been linked in the past to the export market. While forced labour may not be necessary, the low wages and abysmal conditions of life and labour — features of "slavery-like" conditions — may be considered inevitable under the existing terms of trade. Such realism was accepted by the ILO's Commission of Enquiry in 1983, when it recognised that:

> The future prosperity of the Dominican sugar industry, and the pace at which the conditions of the workers employed in that industry can be improved, will to a large extent be determined by its ability to sell its product at adequate prices on world markets. The full solution of the problems which have been examined in this report will thus be dependent also on the measure of international cooperation and solidarity which developing countries such as the Dominican Republic will enjoy in matters of trade. While drawing attention to this aspect, the Commission recognises that it will call for action by bodies other than the International Labour Organisation.[1]

In its formal response to the ILO, the Dominican government evidently jumped on this point, suggesting that the ILO might become an effective ally of such countries as the Dominican Republic "in the search for fairer prices for their basic products, through coordinated action directed towards the industrialised countries and other organisations existing in the world today". The Dominican government also tried to turn the tables on the Anti Slavery Society, giving its own connotation to the emotive term "slavery":

> Furthermore, we consider that the anti-slavery associations, which took a very active part in the first meeting of the Commission of Enquiry at Geneva, could turn their efforts towards seeking fairer prices and access to the markets of the developed countries for the products on which the living and working conditions of millions of workers throughout the world depend. One of the worst forms of slavery today is practised by the developed countries when they keep down the prices of basic products by subsidising and dumping products competing with those that are vital for the countries of the Third World.[2]

The world price of sugar, as we saw in earlier chapters, plunged to new depths in the 1980s. Thus one solution — it may be argued — is to abandon this crop altogether, rather than to fight against the odds for better prices, new markets and fairer trading structures. But this is easier said than done. It is not only that a huge amount of capital is tied up in the existing industrial plant — in the factories, communications, transport and other machines. It is also that a Third World country, which depends on one or more export crops for the bulk of its foreign exchange, has little alternative at a time of severe world recession but to continue with their cultivation, if it is to meet its growing import bills. Thus the large plantations and agro–industrial enterprises tend to receive more rather than less support at a time of crisis, and the effects of financial crisis have tended to be borne by small farmers and landless rural workers. As the Sixth United Nations Report on "Progress in Land Reform" commented, for the whole of Latin America, towards the end of the 1970s:

The best agricultural lands, usually plantations or large agricultural enterprises, are used for growing export crops. The crops produced on these lands earn foreign currency and the trade and balance-of-payments position of the country depends on them. This dependence has given the landlords additional power to prevent changes, on the pretext that changes would endanger their ability to meet international trade and monetary obligations and thus weaken the whole economy. This means that in many countries the best agricultural lands are excluded from any agrarian reform programme; sometimes the Governments themselves support or protect the latifundia used for the cultivation of export crops. The problem of protecting these large enterprises becomes more acute when the owners are foreign individuals or corporations. International market fluctuations and conditions forced the national landowners to associate themselves with foreign concerns; gradually, they were absorbed into these foreign-owned commercial enterprises.

In the Dominican case, the best and largest plantations were not in the hands of *latifundistas*, but of the state itself. And yet it made no difference in this case whether the government or private landowners owned and controlled the land. The Balaguer government between 1966 and 1978 favoured commercial agriculture through its credit and fiscal policies, provided generous concessions to Gulf and Western and other foreign enterprises, and ran CEA like a huge private enterprise. The PRD's takeover in 1978 spelled little change. President Guzmán, between 1978 and 1982, himself a large landowner from the Santiago region, generally defended the interests of the larger commercial farmers against the calls for agrarian reforms that emanated at times from the left wing of his party. When Salvador Jorge Blanco took over the presidency in 1982, one of his first acts was to pledge austerity measures, together with an economic policy based on the development of agro–industry and an expansion of foreign private investment. Perhaps he had little choice. In his presidential address on assuming power, he declared his country "financially bankrupt". As the *International Herald Tribune* then reported,

> Mr. Jorge Blanco's inaugural address was a chronicle of economic devastation similar to those being heard throughout the Caribbean region as the price of imported oil rises . . . like other Caribbean countries that depend heavily on sugar for foreign exchange, the Dominican Republic is seeking relief from the restrictions that limit exports to the United States, its primary market.

Origins of the Debt Crisis

By 1982 the Dominican Republic, like almost all the Latin American nations, was hopelessly in debt. Its total debt had quadrupled from US$600 million in 1973 to $2,400 million ten years later. The collapse of sugar prices had much to do with the rapidly growing deficit. In 1981 the Dominican Republic had earned $513 million from its sugar; two years later recorded sugar production was up by 84,000 tonnes, but dividends were almost halved to $263 million.[3] The equivalent of 11 per cent of export earnings had been used for debt servicing by 1975, but this figure was up to 35.4 per cent by 1982.

By Latin American standards as a whole, the above figures may not appear too alarming. In 1982, approximately half of the total Third World debt was owed by the Latin American countries. The Brazilian and Mexican debts alone were $83 billion and $84 billion respectively. But the Dominican debt was a disturbingly high one for a small country with limited political influence. In other small states in the Central American and Caribbean region — such as El Salvador, Guatemala and Haiti — debt servicing then accounted for only 5 or 6 per cent of total export earnings, and the Dominican Republic was out on a limb. Moreover, when some two-thirds of the total Latin American debt had been loaned by private commercial banks, the larger debtors were to an extent protected by the very size of their commitments. Such states as Argentina, Brazil, Mexico and Venezuela were in a stronger bargaining position with the private banks, simply because any unilateral repudiation could have spelled imminent disaster for the world banking system. The growing fears of such repudiation were enough to make creditors temper their demands with economic realism.

The overall Latin American debt had grown so rapidly in the late 1970s and early 1980s because credit had been lent on relatively easy terms. With a glut of petro-dollars, the banks had excess liquidity, and actively sought investment opportunities in those countries which offered sufficiently favourable terms. In the more industrialised countries with the larger economies, industrial plant was built up on the basis of capital-intensive imported equipment. Large state enterprises were built up, functioning under the umbrella of government guarantees, and financing the larger proportion of investment through external borrowing. Vast public works projects were undertaken, providing some alleviation for the high unemployment levels, as agriculture was modernised and a steady flow of rural–urban migration got under way. While the emphasis of state investment was on the industrial sector, and on the agricultural export sector which earned the foreign exchange with which to service the debt, food production stagnated. The redistributive agrarian reforms, which had been undertaken in the 1960s and early 1970s to alleviate social pressures, were effectively terminated throughout the continent. With food imports available on easy terms, and sometimes on concessionary terms through the United States' PL–480 food aid programmes, there seemed to be little need to improve staple crop production. In 1970 Latin America as a region (mainly thanks to Argentine and Uruguayan production) was a net exporter of commercial cereals; by 1980 Latin America as a region was importing 10 million tons of cereals, and all countries except Argentina and Uruguay were net grain importers. Of the major states, the Brazilian food import bill was over $1.5 billion by 1979, while domestic food supplies were below 1970 levels; and in Mexico, coarse grain imports tripled between 1976 and 1981, when the Mexican food import bill from the USA alone was $2.4 billion.[4]

The growth of the middle classes, and the rapid urbanisation which accompanied it, led to changing dietary habits and patterns of food consumption which were readily exploited by US grain producers, and overseas agro–industrial and food-processing enterprises seeking a larger Latin American market for their products. The peasant diet, based on locally grown staples, was increasingly replaced by an urban diet based more on wheat bread and processed foods. In an earlier chapter it was seen how rapidly food imports to the Dominican Republic have grown over the past decade. This reflects a general pattern for the Central American and Caribbean region as a whole. As two scholars have calculated:

> In the Central American and Caribbean region as a whole, an ever-deepening reliance on food imports has increased the drain of scarce foreign exchange. Total food system imports (including imports of fertilisers, machinery etc.) for the region's principal countries, excluding Cuba, jumped from US$306 million in 1960 to about $3,434 million in 1980 in current dollars (from $260 million to $568 million in 1970 dollars) . . . the Caribbean countries which have traditionally suffered from grain dependence, imported 58% of their cereals in 1970; this rose to 69% in 1980.[5]

A lot of the food, as already noted, is provided on concessionary terms, with low interest rates and lengthy grace periods. In the Dominican Republic, for example, out of $1,500 million of food imports between 1973 and 1983, over $358 million worth were financed by the United States' PL–480 and Commodity Credit Corporation Programmes[6] (PL–480 programmes provide for dollar credits and a 20-year repayment period, with interest rates between 2 and 3 per cent). Commercial food exports have nevertheless played an ever more important role in US agriculture: the value of all US agricultural exports including processed foods was up from $6.5 billion in 1970 to just under $35 billion in 1979.[7]

Until the 1980s, at least, the Dominican Republic had enjoyed particularly favourable treatment from the United States. Under the Balaguer government investments had flowed into the country, encouraged by the generous terms offered to foreign investors. But the Central Bank had made little use of external credits, permitting the autonomous and decentralised state bodies to contract their own loans on the most favourable terms possible. In the meantime the local currency, the Dominican peso, was pegged to the US dollar at par. With widespread investment in small industry, agro–industry, textiles, food processing and tourism, a sizeable middle class developed in Santo Domingo and the provincial towns. Though unemployment and underemployment had reached high levels by the late 1970s, the Balaguer government had been able to alleviate the most immediate tensions with the help of subsidised food programmes in urban areas.

Under the first PRD government of President Guzmán (1978–82), there were signs that US confidence in the Dominican economy was waning. Following the nationalisation of one US-owned enterprise, Rosario Dominicana, in 1979, there were reports in the *Wall Street Journal* and other US newspapers that US companies were reluctant to invest in the Dominican Republic because of their doubts about its political stability and economic soundness.[8] Soon afterwards, the PRD sent a high-level team to New York, in an attempt to reassure the US business community that it still welcomed foreign investment, and no further nationalisations of significance occurred. Moreover, the PRD had pledged to take measures against unemployment, and created at least 60,000 jobs in the public sector during the first two years of office. This, on top of a wage rise of 10 per cent for public-sector employees — the first such increase for several years — disturbed the private sector. The Guzmán government also elected to consolidate the separate debts of decentralised state bodies through a single $185 million loan contracted through the Central Bank, in March 1979.

As inflation increased, it proved impossible to keep the Dominican peso at par with the US dollar. Like other Latin American countries with similar inflationary problems, the PRD resorted to a parallel exchange rate. The peso was officially still pegged to the dollar at par, but different exchange rates were to be paid to importers and exporters as the government decreed. Over the next few years the measure was to be used to subsidise certain imports, and to penalise certain exports by paying a peso rate less than could be obtained from each dollar in the semi-official exchange houses that then sprang up throughout the country.

By May 1982, the balance of payments situation was disastrous. The country was running a deficit of over $550 million, and the Central Bank had fallen some $400 million in arrears in its international payments, while overdue debt repayments were in excess of $200 million. Incoming President Salvador Jorge Blanco was compelled to go the International Monetary Fund.

The IMF and the Dominican Republic

On 21 January 1983 the Dominican government reached agreement with the IMF for an extended facility loan over a three-year period worth a total of $466 million. Of the total, $195.8 million was to be paid over in the first year, with the second tranche to be renegotiated in January 1984.

The Dominicans knew full well that stringent conditions would be applied to the IMF loan. The IMF has the role of "lender of last resort" when commercial funds are no longer forthcoming without its seal of approval; it has the "policeman's" role, demanding widespread cuts in public expenditure and other fiscal and monetary measures to reduce the deficits of debtor nations. In the case of all IMF agreements, the amount of the monetary credits may or may not be substantial, but they tend to be the criterion according to which private commercial banks, as well as official lending agencies, decide whether or not to extend further loans. Since the Latin American debt crisis first escalated in 1982, the IMF had gained notoriety for its inflexible requirements, pressing for rigorous adjustment and stabilisation programmes to be supported by stand-by or extended credits, backed up by additional credits from the private banks. The IMF has seen its role as a technical and "surgical" one, cutting out waste from government budgets, and clearing up the deficits in order to pave the way for further private investment. As its apologists have replied to critics, IMF officials did not stipulate exactly what cuts should be made or what social policies should henceforth be pursued: they insisted only that the budget should be balanced, and that sufficient savings should be made somewhere to put the economy back into shape. Officially, IMF credits were to be emergency measures, the size of the IMF's contribution being determined by the size of each member state's quota contribution to the Fund (the quota is determined for each country according to its Gross National Product, with 25 per cent of this paid in hard currency, the remainder in the country's own currency). But in real terms the role of the IMF has grown immeasurably, as the majority of debt rescheduling arrangements with official and private creditors have become anchored to its programmes. Its officials have been more or less able to dictate the measures to be followed by debtor governments which reach IMF agreements, in the areas of public expenditure, exchange controls and currency arrangements. Apart from its own contributions, the IMF has assumed the mantle of overall surveillance of debtor nations' economic performance, and has actively sought new finance as part of debt rescheduling arrangements for those countries which act in accordance with its stringent regulations. And in all cases, the nod of approval from the IMF is the avenue to funds from the private banks which follow its judgement.

In the Dominican case, the initial demands made by the IMF in the January 1983 agreement were for a phased updating of overdue payments, the observance of strict quotas for central bank reserves and credits to the public sector, the imposition of VAT on certain consumer items, and the payment of the parallel market price for almost all imports except for petroleum and petroleum products. In the first year of the agreement, a number of measures were taken by the government, including import restrictions, the reduction of public salaries, the imposition of several taxes, and the legalisation of the "parallel" market spelling an effective end to the peso's parity with the US dollar. The par rate was kept only for the import of certain key items, petrol and medicines among them.

By the end of the year, the IMF was far from satisfied. After a new round of negotiations, it insisted that Central Bank loans were still too high, that the deficit remained at an unacceptable level, and that the parallel exchange rate would now have to be eliminated altogether. The implication was that petroleum, along with all other imports, would now have to be purchased at the free market exchange rate — at a cost of approximately $800 million to the Dominican Republic. This time, President Jorge Blanco at first flatly refused, sticking to his earlier pledges that his government would not devalue the peso. On 4 January 1984, he appealed personally to US President Reagan to intervene, writing that acceptance of the IMF conditions for the second round of credit payments "could undoubtedly provoke tensions so strong that it could alter the peace and the most important functional democratic process in the Caribbean". The appeal went unheeded, and the IMF suspended its payments.

By this time, a protest movement against the IMF demands was already under way, as Dominicans took to the streets to protest against the rapid rise in food prices that had stemmed from the imposition of Value Added Tax and the rise in the real cost of imported consumer items. In early January, there were widespread demonstrations against a 10 cent increase in the cost of a litre of milk, and at the end of the month over a hundred bakeries threatened to strike over the increased cost of wheat, oil, eggs and other essential items. In February there were warnings that the cost of medicines would be doubled if the Central Bank went ahead with its threat to lift government controls from the price of medicines. On 8 February one newspaper reported that the cost of ordinary foods had increased by between 25 and 100 per cent over the past week, and that this was "only the beginning of the increases that will be seen over the next month".[10] On 20 February one politician warned that severe social unrest would ensue if the cost of seven basic items — including chicken, beans, eggs, milk and rice — was again increased.[11] And not only foodstuffs were affected. Ironmongers, construction firms, mechanics and others complained of soaring costs, warning that the price of materials was threatening the future of their industries.

In early April, when President Jorge Blanco made a brief state visit to the USA, a group of private Dominican businessmen used the occasion to express their own concerns. In a paid advertisement in the *New York Times*, presented as an open letter to President Reagan, the private sector leaders declared:

> Our economy has been hit hard by the international oil and monetary crisis, the substantial drop in revenues of our main export products, and a record of domestic economic policies adopted in the past. Today, these negative factors hinder and suffocate our country's own capacity to overcome — in a timely and reasonable way — the adverse impact caused by these negative developments. The private sector of the Dominican Republic is convinced with a deep concern that the economic crisis is characterised by a rapid increase in unemployment, run-away inflation, erosion of the purchasing power of our currency, and a sudden jump in commercial bankruptcies. But that is not all: not even the worst. We have the sad and certain prospect that other events could develop with terrible impact in our society, such as: the paralysis of basic health and food supply programs directed to our poorest people. Nationwide strikes and labour disturbances. Political unrest and civil instability. The magnitude of these current problems moves us to bring our concerns to your attention.[12]

The Reagan administration, it may be said, was adequately warned. But it gave Jorge Blanco the cold shoulder on this visit, and pressed him further to accept the IMF demands. Instead, as the *Washington Post* reported, the United States government continued to hold up about $80 million of 1984 aid funds earmarked for the Dominican Republic until the IMF demands were met, and the US Export–Import Bank and commercial banks likewise refused to make further investments until the IMF was satisfied.[13]

Against these odds, the Dominican government was forced to capitulate, accepting most of the points within the IMF package. On his return to Santo Domingo, President Jorge Blanco outlined the current state of negotiations in a speech to the nation. On petroleum he had won temporary concessions, and the price of petrol products would remain under government control for the time being. Nor would essential foods financed by foreign aid (corn, wheat and oils) be affected in the first instance. There would be no public-sector dismissals. But the price of all other imports and services — including medicines, fertilisers, pesticides and other agricultural inputs — would be freed immediately from government control; this would mean a doubling of their price. In the same speech the President announced a series of incentives to exporters, and pledged that the price of chicken, rice, pasta products, eggs and milk distributed by INESPRE (the Price Stabilisation Institute) would now be frozen.

On food products, the promises were not kept. The following day, the General Directorate of Price Controls announced a series of increases in the cost of essential food items. Wheat flour went up 15 pesos for a 100-lb bag, doubling the price of ordinary bread rolls. Milk was up from 45 cents per quart to 55 cents, and even sugar increased by 5 cents, reaching 31 cents per pound. On 23 April over 100 urban organisations called for a twelve-hour strike to demand the immediate repeal of the price increases, and a raise of the minimum salary to at least 200 pesos per month. For many of the urban poor, the latest round of price increases proved to be the final straw, and the country erupted.

On the morning of Monday, 23 April, tens of thousands of angry protestors poured on to the streets of Santo Domingo and several provincial towns. The movement began in the poorer districts of Santo Domingo, where buses were burned, main roads blocked off, and rocks hurled through the windows of the few shops that remained open. The police responded with tear gas. But when the crowds invaded supermarkets, and a group of women took over the INESPRE centre in the *barrio* of Gualey, special army troops were called in to establish control. But the riots spread rapidly throughout Santo Domingo. An electrical goods store and a local bank were burned down, as well as a PRD centre in one of the *barrios*. As the riots escalated, the army began to shoot. At the end of the first day of rioting there were six recorded deaths, and hundreds of victims of tear gas and other wounds were taken to Santo Domingo's hospitals.

Rioting broke out simultaneously in several provincial towns. From Santiago, Barahona, Jarabacoa, Cristóbal, Bani, Mao and Moca there were similar accounts of banks and commercial buildings broken into or destroyed, roads blocked by burned tyres, and INESPRE centres raided. And as in Santo Domingo, the police and army responded with force, arresting hundreds of demonstrators, and shooting into the crowds when things threatened to get out of hand.

The rioting continued for three days. By the evening of 25 April the death toll was officially given as 52 — though the government later admitted to 86 dead, and non-governmental organisations have since claimed to have the names of over 100 dead. Altogether, the government admitted to arresting over 4,300 demonstrators. As reporter Richard Meislin of the *New York Times* observed,

> The country that President Reagan, less than two weeks before, had said "shines like a beacon for freedom loving people everywhere" closed down two radio stations and a television station, and set national police to occupy union headquarters to prevent meetings that could organise further demonstrations.[14]

The government blamed the riots on leftist agitators, but the outburst was massive and apparently spontaneous. At all events the government had been expecting a mass reaction, and President Jorge Blanco later commented that the riots were "predictable and anticipated". As one trade union leader later commented, of the 64 people identified in hospitals and morgues, 31 had been shot through the eyes, "an apparent indication that the troops called out to stop the rioting were shooting to kill rather than to wound".[15] Clearly, the army had been instructed to give no quarter in crushing the revolts. It was a belligerent overreaction by a government nervous about the extent of the unrest that its unpopular measures would trigger off. A few days later, police occupied the five trade union offices in Santo Domingo, to prevent a further demonstration against the price rises, while the most prominent union leaders remained behind bars for several weeks. Thousands of troops remained on guard for days in Santo Domingo and the major provincial towns.

For a few days after the April riots, the Dominican Republic was in the headlines of the world press. The Dominican upheavals led to renewed debate concerning IMF methods, and the need for more flexible approaches to countries with the severest short-term problems. On 1 May, an editorial in the *New York Times* strongly criticised the IMF, noting that,

> At least 60 are dead after the bloodiest riots since the Dominican Republic's civil war a generation ago. The proximate cause: a sharp increase in food prices decreed by a democratic Government seeking an International Monetary Fund loan. The real culprit: a lending system that lacks a storm cellar for conscientious politicians. . . . Better ways need to be found to reward a society for accepting austerity, to match the punishments for squanderers. The Dominican Republic, meanwhile, is left with the least desirable outcome: it risks further turmoil whether or not it yields to demands for cheaper food. A world monetary policy that produces this choice nourishes neither capitalism nor democracy.[16]

There was less criticism overseas of the PRD government itself, even though widespread repression was now unleashed against trade union leaders and other social activists who threatened to organise further protests. In May, eight unionists were arrested when they tried to organise a demonstration against further rises in food prices. CGT leader Julio de Peña Valdez was arrested three times altogether between late April and early July. And every time new price increases or IMF negotiations were announced, the government carried out preventive arrests of key political and union figures. The staggered arrests continued until late August, when the government finally capitulated to further IMF demands. On 30 August, as negotiations came to a climax, some 20 political and labour leaders were arrested in Santo Domingo, Santiago and San Pedro Macoris, in a series of pre-dawn round-ups. Surveillance was also increased around the homes of other political and labour leaders, including former President Juan Bosch. In the meantime the Interior Minister, Major General Ramiro Matos González, warned that any further disturbances would again be met with force. The April massacre, still fresh in people's minds, was enough to keep the Dominicans in their homes. But it was a pathetic reflection on the state of Dominican democracy, if every negotiation with the International Monetary Fund had to be preceded by this kind of repression.

Though the April violence had shocked international public opinion, the IMF pressed ahead with its demands for more stringent austerity measures. Immediately after the April riots, Dominican Congress approved a minimum salary rise to 175 pesos per month, less than the 200 pesos the unions were demanding, but enough to stretch the budget yet further. But when negotiations with the IMF were resumed, the point at issue was once again the petroleum price. The IMF relaxed its earlier demand for removing price controls on petroleum, but nevertheless insisted on a 75-cent premium in the short term which would raise the real petroleum price by 50 per cent. On this point the Dominicans were adamant. On 24 May negotiations with the IMF were suspended, although the Dominican government now stood to lose millions of dollars of US aid funds which had been tied to acceptance of the IMF's latest conditions. Government ministers warned that acceptance of the latest batch of conditions would have led to "full-scale civil strife" in the current economic and social conditions. As Economy Minister Orlando Haza then commented to foreign press reporters, the quest for better terms with the IMF did not mean "that we are unwilling to put our house in order. It means that we want to keep our house and not let it go up in flames."[17]

Soon afterwards, negotiations were once again resumed. When the IMF cut off its next credit tranche, and other lenders followed in its tracks, the Dominican government still appeared to have no alternative. As the *Washington Post* reported in June 1984,

> As a result of Jorge Blanco's refusal to cut the government subsidy on petroleum, thus increasing its price, the IMF withheld the second installment of a three-year 430 million dollar loan. Lender governments of the Paris Club and commercial creditors, which had made negotiation of their loans contingent on agreement with the IMF, cut off still more credit. The United States held up about 24 million dollars in 1984 aid for the same reason.[18]

And so, despite a brief flurry of bravado on the Dominican side, the IMF could still call the tune. On 30 August President Jorge Blanco announced that petroleum prices would be increased by 20 cents per gallon, and that after seven months of protected negotiations an agreement had been reached with the IMF which would now provide approximately $200 million in credits.

For the urban poor, the effects of austerity have been felt since then in the continuing price rises for food items. In January 1985, two Dominican authors made a careful calculation of such increases over the previous year. On average, the increases had been between 50 and 100 per cent, though bread was up almost 200 per cent, and soya oil by 163 per cent.[19] There has been no repeat of the countrywide April 1984 food riots, but every significant increase has led to further protests, violence and occasional backtracking by the government. In January 1985, for example, the next round of negotiations with the IMF led to a new austerity package, bringing additional price rises of up to 50 per cent for certain food items. When the unions threatened strike action, the government responded in much the same way as the previous year. Approximately 100 leftist leaders were arrested in the week beginning 5 February, but a strike called for 11 February still paralysed three-quarters of all economic activity in Santo Domingo. On this occasion, President Jorge Blanco agreed to rescind some price increases, announcing an 18–20 per cent reduction for bread, pasta, cooking oil and milk on 13 February.[20]

Thus the IMF recipe spelled a cycle of stringent demands, tentative price increases, reluctant governmental concessions, popular and trade union protests, slender wage rises, an inflationary spiral, and further IMF demands as a result. The cycle may be repeated again. Either that, or the incoming government of President Balaguer will prove less flexible to the Dominican populace, making no concessions in the form of compensatory wage increases to meet the rising cost of living. But that will spell an end to the tenuous consensus that has survived up till now, and herald another era of severe repression for the Dominican Republic.

The export sector stands to benefit, in particular those who diversify into new export crops for which there is current world demand. Converting their dollars at the free market rate, they should be able to withstand the higher import costs — in particular if the new government follows the PRD policy of providing incentives for the export of new crops. But with imported food subsidies effectively eliminated, at the behest of the international financial institutions, Dominican governments can no longer afford to buttress the export sector alone, at the expense of the subsistence peasantry. The way in which the new government responds to the growing demands for redistributive land reform will be a test of its commitment to the alleviation of social tensions. And it will also be a test of the lending agencies' commitment to longer-term solutions for the country. The food subsidies, and the consequent balance of payment deficits, may not be to the liking of overseas creditors. But they arose in the first place because no one wanted to invest in staple foods, when there were greater profits to be realised elsewhere.

Notes

1. *ILO Official Bulletin*, Vol. LXVI (Report of Commission of Enquiry), 1983.
2. ILO Governing Body, 224th Session, GB 224/21/4/ 15–18 November 1983 (reply of the Dominican government).
3. "Causas y Manejo de le Crisis Económica Dominicana, 1974–84", *FORUM*, Santo Domingo, 1986, p. 93.
4. Miguel Teubal, "Internacionalización del Capital y Complejos Agro-industriales: Impactos sobre la Agricultura Latinoamericana" (unpublished manuscript, presented to Eleventh Congress of the Latin American Studies Association, Mexico, 1983).
5. Peter Marchetti and Solon Barraclough, "Agrarian Transformation and Food Security in the Caribbean Basin" (The Hague, Netherlands, June 1983 (unpublished conference document)).
6. *FORUM*, op. cit., p. 143.
7. Teubal, op. cit.
8. Latin America Regional Reports, RC 79–01, 23 November 1979.
9. *New York Times*, 29 April 1984.
10. *El Caribe*, 8 February 1984.
11. *Ultima Hora*, 20 February 1984.
12. *New York Times*, 9 April 1984.
13. *Washington Post*, 30 April 1984.
14. *New York Times*, 29 April 1984.
15. *Washington Post*, 1 May 1984.
16. *New York Times*, 1 May 1984.
17. Ibid., 31 May 1984.
18. *Washington Post*, 16 June 1984.
19. José Serulle Ramia and Jacqueline Boin, *Hacia Donde Va el País* (Ediciones Gramil, Santo Domingo, 1985), pp. 72–4.
20. *Latin America Monitor*, London, March 1985.

10 Searching for Remedies: National and International Dimensions

This has been a harrowing account of forced labour, traffic in persons, secret monetary transactions for the effective sale of workers, brutality against Haitian workers, and sub-human living conditions on the sugar plantations of the Dominican Republic. It has also been a story of an apparently absurd paradox, where one poor country that cannot provide employment for its own urban and rural poor nevertheless feels obliged to import tens of thousands of cane cutters from a neighbouring country — an even poorer one — because its own nationals, with some reason, equate the life and work of cane cutters in the sugar industry with slavery. Thirdly, it has served as a case study of the total mess in which a country which has traditionally relied on agricultural exports for its foreign exchange earnings finds itself today. It depicts the crisis facing a country which has allowed its domestic food-growing industry to suffer, as it relied more and more on both commercial and concessionary food imports to meet the needs of its national — and increasingly urban — population. Once caught in the trap of the export model, a country like the Dominican Republic finds it almost impossible to extricate itself. The model is bound to mean a deficit economy when the price of the country's exports collapses at a time of world recession. The international financial institutions and the banks turn on the heat, demanding more exports and fewer imports, austerity measures and enforced domestic savings, leaving few available resources to create employment, stimulate production, and invest in national needs including the need for increased food production. Finally, it has shown that such a model easily lends itself to repression. The analysis has looked behind the formal façade of Dominican democracy over the past two decades. Though formal democracy has existed since 1966, and democratic institutions have apparently been strengthened between 1978 and 1986, the limitations of this formal democracy became very apparent whenever the least privileged groups, both in the sugar industry and in the marginal urban sector, demanded a fairer share of an ever smaller cake. Repression in the sugar industry, and repression of the entire population when it protests against rising food prices, is likely to be part and parcel of Dominican life for many years to come. The recent return to power of a government whose previous term in office spelled widespread repression and frozen wages reflects the failure of the social democratic governments between 1978 and 1986 to find a viable solution to the country's problems. The immediate outlook is certainly bleak.

In Haiti, at the time of writing, there is perhaps some cause for optimism. Haiti is now at the crossroads. Whereas food riots and popular protest in the Dominican Republic were quelled by twin policies of partial concessions and outright repression, in Haiti the protest movement after 1985 grew rapidly among the urban poor and the youth movement, until it spelled the sudden demise of the Duvalier regime in February 1986. But little has been done as yet to revive the economy, to reform the agrarian structure, and to provide real hope for a country where 80 per cent of the total population still lives on or off the land — by far the highest percentage in the whole of Latin America and the Caribbean. The Haitian church, which played such a prominent role in bringing about Duvalier's fall, has made urgent appeals for agrarian reform, for the distribution of state lands to small peasants and landless rural labourers, for an agrarian census and the redistribution of farms illegally appropriated by the Tontons Macoutes, for reform of the taxation system, and for a reduction of the cost of basic foods and other essential consumer items.[1]

But a revival of Haitian agriculture will require huge overseas investment on highly generous terms, and there are few signs that such aid will be forthcoming in the current international financial climate. As the Economist Intelligence Unit noted in March 1986, there were still a number of constraints on the long-term development of the Haitian agricultural sector, including: soil erosion due to the reduction of forest land and inadequate land cultivation; the small size of farms; the lack of security of land tenure; the inability of peasant farmers to invest in new technologies; and inadequate irrigation, storage and transport facilities. To overcome these problems, it noted, and to allow Haiti to achieve and maintain self-sufficiency and export capacity before the end of the decade, would require the mobilisation of hundreds of millions of dollars of resources "which is not within the reach of the Port-au-Prince government nor on the agenda of the aid donors".[2] It predicted that imports would stay in the range of US$300–400 million, with food and oil continuing to account for around 40 per cent of the total, as in the 1980–85 period. And it also noted that an agro-investment code was under review, which "should attract foreign investors willing to take advantage of CBI (Caribbean Basin Initiative) duty free entry into the USA to produce goods such as fruits out of season, exotic fruits and vegetables".[3] Private foreign investment would inevitably be directed towards the export sector of agriculture.

In early 1986, the effects of the recent unrest in Haiti had still not reached the rural areas. Life there continued in the same way, below adequate subsistence levels, and there was every reason to believe that the impetus to migrate to the Dominican Republic would continue. And of the several hundreds of thousands of Haitians already in the Dominican Republic only a small number — primarily the middle classes and the political exiles — were returning home. Thus the large Haitian presence in the Dominican Republic promised to be a volatile issue for the years to come.

The Haitians have reason to feel uneasy. In recent years the overtly racist campaign against Haitians and Dominicans of Haitian origin has not abated, but rather has gathered momentum as the Dominican economy falls on hard times. The Haitians as a group cannot have welcomed the return of Joaquín Balaguer to power. In 1984, Balaguer published a book giving his personal views on the Haitian question. Haiti, he said, continued to constitute a threat of almost immeasurable proportions. The clandestine penetration threatened to disintegrate the "moral and ethnic values" of the Dominican family, whereas the Haitian labour force constituted "unfair competition for the Dominican working class". He thus speculated that "this danger, if it is not stemmed in time, will in the end facilitate the absorption of the Dominican Republic by Haiti." Reverting to a familiar theme Balaguer warned that "The old ideal of the political indivisibility of the island may ultimately be realised through these factors which are fundamentally harmful, if not for territorial security, at least for the social and spiritual security of the Dominican Republic."[4]

At least Balaguer, then out of power, was willing to recognise that the plight of the Haitian *braceros* was intolerable, and that the two governments were largely responsible. To quote the penultimate paragraph of his book:

> The iniquitous exploitation to which the Haitian *braceros* are subjected today, victims of an illicit commerce in which the governments of both parts of the island participate with an equal degree of corruption should be substituted, within a regime of national and international collaboration as described, by another more humane one, alien to this new form of denigrating slavery which is practised at the present time in the Dominican sugar *ingenios*.[5]

The onus is now on Balaguer himself. Can he keep his pledges, or was this yet another empty promise from a politician out of office? And what can be done internationally to humanise conditions? How to find a suitable blend of the carrot and the stick?

One temptation is to seek sanctions. One Washington-based human rights group has, in the past, considered petitioning the US government to seek the banning of the Dominican sugar crop from the US market on the grounds that it is produced under forced labour conditions. A US law enacted in 1976 had in theory barred the importation of all commodities produced "wholly or in part . . . by convict labour and/or forced labour and/or indentured labour under penal sanction".[6] Forced labour, for the purposes of this law, was defined as "all work or service which is exacted from any person under the menace of any penalty for its nonperformance and for which the worker does not offer himself voluntarily". Under US customs regulations, any person could file a petition asking the US Commissioner of Customs to bar from entry into the country any good produced by convict, forced or indentured labour, as defined in Section 1307 of the Act. The onus was on the petitioning group to provide evidence that the sugar had in fact been harvested by methods in violation of US law, before the consignment entered the country and was therefore beyond the jurisdiction of the Commissioner of Customs. An alternative was to seek the barring of shipments from a particular sugar mill, if the petitioner could establish a practice of continuing forced labour over a period of time on any one enterprise.

The above-mentioned petition considered by the Washington-based human rights group was not produced, primarily because of the difficulties in gathering specific evidence before the export of cane in each harvest year. But in 1984, when the US government's Caribbean Basin Initiative went into effect, eliminating tariffs for certain products exported from the Caribbean region to the United States, officials from the US Department of Labour attempted to insert a labour clause in the Caribbean Basin Economic Recovery Act, designed to link favourable treatment on the US market to adequate labour conditions in the industries where the export commodities were produced. Of the 18 criteria mentioned in the Act, some were overtly political — such as whether or not the country was Communist — others were less so. Seven of the criteria were considered to be mandatory, thus prohibiting the US President from naming a country for CBI preferential treatment unless they were met. Others were discretionary, thus only recommending the President to take them into account in his designation decisions. The labour provision was discretionary, requiring the President to consider the degree to which workers in each country were afforded "reasonable workplace conditions" and enjoyed the "right to bargain collectively". As one official of the US Department of Labour has written on the background to these CBI-linked proposals:

> The primary reason for the labour criterion is a concern that labour laws and conditions in some countries would prevent the benefits of the Caribbean Basin Initiative from reaching the workers. By promoting free trade unions, the United States intended not only to contribute to democratic pluralism, but also to provide foreign workers the institutional base needed to earn their rightful share of the income generated by the Initiative. A second reason for the labour criterion is to safeguard American workers from unfair foreign competition. By using the statutory labour criterion, the United States would have leverage against a participating country that exported to the American market products made under "sweatshop style" working conditions.
>
> Aside from the narrow provision in US trade law that prohibits the importation of products made by convict or forced labour, the Caribbean Basin Initiative is the only US law that makes foreign labour conditions a specific consideration in providing trade benefits to other countries. While international fair labour standards have been a longtime goal of organised labour in the United States, the Initiative is the first time this concept has been incorporated into US tariff legislation.[7]

Both Haiti and the Dominican Republic were eligible for designation under the Caribbean Basin Economic Recovery Act, and designation letters were sent to each country urging certain changes. Haiti's designation letter contained several recommendations on the situation of *braceros* in the Dominican Republic, including: (a) a statement that Haitian sugar workers going to the Dominican Republic be allowed to keep their travel documents and contracts; (b) instructions to the Haitian Embassy in Santo Domingo regarding improved inspections of sugar plantation conditions; (c) a request to the ILO to provide technical assistance with regard to the problems of the sugar workers. For the Dominican Republic, the US government's designation letter was based largely on the findings and recommendations of the ILO's 1983 Commission of Enquiry. Specifically, the designation letter included the following recommendations: (i) an agreement to allow workers to choose the plantation they work on; (ii) an agreement that the national police will make sure that plantation security forces do not prevent workers from giving up their jobs and leaving the plantation; (iii) a statement that further improvements in working conditions would be made in 1984; (iv) a statement that sugar workers must be given a break during the day and one day off per week in accordance with the contract; (v) a statement that workers receive at least the minimum wage; (vi) a commitment to provide government inspectors to oversee the weighing of cane.

Such measures, with possible sanctions or benefits, could undoubtedly begin to bite, and prove the most effective form of overseas pressure for the improvement of conditions. But there are two major problems. First, all bilateral agreements can be used selectively, to seek improved conditions for political allies and sanctions against others; this is particularly the case where the labour provisions are only part of a broader set of conditions that may have nothing to do with technical and labour aspects. At that time, the US, for overtly political motives, withdrew its sugar quota from Nicaragua, where the conditions of sugar workers had evidently improved since the overthrow of the Somoza regime in 1979. Secondly, such bilateral pressures can have protectionist motives, and may in reality be utilised as a pretext for reducing quota arrangements, rather than for seeking genuine improvements in labour and marketing conditions for the traditional commodity exporting-countries.

On the first point, some comparative assessment is required. Are the conditions of the Haitian *braceros* uniquely bad, if compared with the plight of sugar workers worldwide? Are these forced labour conditions exceptional, or can similar cases be found elsewhere in the world? Does sugar, more than any other commodity, lend itself to slavery-like conditions in the modern world?

Over the past few years — either on behalf of the Anti Slavery Society, or for other human rights and development organisations — I have investigated the conditions of sugar workers in such diverse countries as Colombia, Ecuador, Guatemala, Guyana, Nicaragua and the Philippines. Certain aspects are common to the industry worldwide. Because of the nature of sugar production, cane cutting and milling takes place for only half the year (except in Colombia where, for climatic and geographical reasons, it continues throughout the year). In some cases, cane cutters stay on the plantations throughout the year, but live a miserable existence during the "dead season" when there is generally no fixed salary. And payment rates during the harvest are generally based on piece-work. During the harvest, large numbers of cane cutters are brought in. In Ecuador and Guatemala, they are indigenous small farmers and landless peasants, recruited by independent labour contracts under conditions that will be described in more detail below. A similar recruitment system is to be found in the Philippines, where the *braceros* (known there as *sacadas*) are brought in from the surrounding small islands to the major sugar-producing island of Negros. Though trade unions tend to exist in sugar industries throughout the world, and have a long history of labour militancy and an equally long history of bitter repression, the migrant workers are rarely able to enjoy the benefits of collective labour contracts, health care, social security, education and so on. The labour movement in the sugar industry is often split between the moderate and more privileged company unions (dominated by the factory workers and the skilled labour force) and the industrywide field-worker unions, which are often debilitated by the regular influx of unorganised migrant workers. Moreover, attempts to organise the cane cutters themselves have, as in the

Dominican case, frequently met with the most bitter repression at the hands of local and national authorities.

Two countries where living and working conditions differed little from those in the Dominican sugar industry were Guatemala and the Philippines. In the former country, Guatemala, the cane industry is relatively small, and the major export crop is coffee. In the coffee, cotton and sugar sectors alike, the seasonal migrant labour is performed by the impoverished Mayan Indians, who occupy small plots in the highlands of the country, and are trucked down in their hundreds of thousands to the coffee, cotton and sugar plantations for the months of the harvest season. The large farmers employ their own recruiting agents — known variously as the *contratista* or *habilitador* — who scour the highland villages at the times of greatest food scarcity, and make advance payments to sign up the recruits, known as the *cuadrilleros* in the Guatemalan sugar industry. The *contratista* is often himself responsible for transporting the migrant workers to the plantations, and may then double up as *capataz* or brigade leader when the harvest gets under way. The Guatemalan Labour Code contains sufficient guarantees for the protection of migrant workers, but they have rarely been enforced. In 1970, the ILO criticised the "low wages out of proportion to the sacrifices that the workers had to endure", the "sub-human conditions in the transport from the place of origin to the workplace, and back", and "lodging and living conditions of the migrant workers and their families which were totally unacceptable with regard to hygiene, health, education and morality".[8] And when I carried out my own investigations in rural Guatemala at the end of that decade, I could find no improvements. The daily wage in the sugar industry remained as low as US\$1.12 until 1980, when all the *ingenios* were paralysed by an unprecedented strike involving permanent and seasonal workers alike. The strike was technically illegal, under laws that banned any strike action during harvest time, but the military government of the time capitulated quickly under nationwide pressure, almost tripling the legal minimum salary on the plantations. Reprisals, Guatemala-style, followed quickly upon the strike, and many of the strike leaders were murdered by paramilitary groups in the aftermath. Reportedly, many of the labour contractors in the Indian highlands were part of the paramilitary bands. They were said to use their homes as private gaols, to retain all personal documents of recruits in order to control anyone attempting to break his contract, and also to charge exorbitant interest rates which then had to be worked off on the coastal plantations.

In the Philippines, I visited the sugar island of Negros in 1980, 1983 and 1984, and saw conditions go from bad to worse as the sugar industry moved into its present crisis period. As in Guatemala, the migrant labourers were recruited through the *contratista*, who received a lump payment from the plantation owner, and was also reputed to take a large cut from the wages of the contracted *sacadas*. The *anticipo*, advance payment, was also utilised widely here in order to garner the labour force from the other islands. As the National Federation of Sugar Workers once described the system:

> Because of *anticipos* and fear that they will run away, contractors and/or *hacenderos* pay only at the end of the milling season. The practice (which is

illegal under Minimum Wage Law) spawns so many other kinds of problems like: the overpricing in *cantinas* (company stores): cheating in the amount of tonnage cut and loaded: forced borrowing at usurious rates: and forced labour. Since the "sacadas" are not paid for the whole of the milling season, they do not even have enough money to attend union meetings in town. Paid on the last day, they do not have the opportunity to examine the payrolls. They either accept the *sumada* (total) as presented by the contractors (who cheat them all the time) or they are abandoned.[9]

In Negros, however, the *sacada* contingent is now a small percentage of the total labour force. Most of the cane cutters live all the year round on the island, in poor thatched huts on the fringes of the plantations, earning regular wages only for the six months of the harvest season. In the dreaded *tiempo muerto* they survive thanks to a "rice loan" made by the planters with government support, the payment deducted from the earnings of the next harvest season. When I last visited Negros in August 1984, planters were complaining that they could no longer make the rice loan, because their earnings had dipped so catastrophically over the past year. At the same time, government officials told me of plans for the closure of several *ingenios*, that would lead to the lay-off of an estimated 200,000 workers. In fact, sugar production was then declining dramatically, partly because of problems over the Philippine sugar quota in the USA, and partly because the pricing arrangements under a sugar trading monopoly introduced by the Marcos government had cut deeply into the sugar planters' profits. Though the Philippines had an estimated milling capacity of some 3.5 million tonnes, production was down from 2.3 million tonnes in 1983, to 1.6 million in 1984, and there was a further drop to 1.1 million tonnes for the next harvest season. In May 1985 the magazine *Asia Week* reported that an estimated 200,000 workers had already been laid off, and that more dismissals were expected.[10] In the same month a Philippine magazine published accounts of near starvation throughout Negros, as "This year, however, the meaning of 'dead season' takes on a frightening new dimension as most of the 350,000 or so sugar workers and their families are reduced to eating sweet potatoes and bananas once or sometimes twice a day."[11] As tensions increased the island became the largest growth point for the NPA guerrillas, and the government brought Negros under heavy military control. Accounts filtered to the outside world only after the most brutal killings, such as the massacre of over 20 people in the small sugar town of Escalante in September 1985.

Doubtless, many other examples could be given. The current crisis of the sugar industry in the Philippines in particular suggests that — at least in so far as wages and living conditions are concerned — the Dominican experience is not altogether unique. But in both Guatemala and the Philippines the underlying social tensions have now escalated into major civil insurrections, with guerrilla movements deriving much of their support from the peasantry and the landless rural labour force. In these cases a repressive agro–export development model — based on land concentration, declining food production, eviction of the peasantry from subsistence lands, militarisation and effective denial of the right to organise — is now taking its toll.

We now turn to the other side of the coin. The drastic effects of austerity policies imposed by the International Monetary Fund since 1982 have already been analysed. But the finger of responsibility cannot be pointed at the IMF alone. The IMF is in some ways a scapegoat. It is the international agency called in when financial deficits have already become so great that the private banks refuse to make further loans. IMF policies are in urgent need of reform. The Fund must be persuaded that balance of payments deficits can only be reduced over a long period of time, when trading arrangements themselves work more to the advantage of the producers of those agricultural commodities which — as often as not — are now exported at a net loss. International financial institutions, as well as bilateral donors, have to be pressed to analyse more seriously the social effects of their financial demands, in fuller consultation with other United Nations agencies and with all the social partners in the countries affected. Rather than sanctions and surgical cuts, the obvious need is for more concessionary financial assistance during the crisis period. The technical questions, as to where the money should be put, are beyond the scope of this book. There are arguments for increasing productivity in the sugar industry, and arguments for placing the emphasis on diversification projects. The most important thing is that, whatever options are chosen, the investors and donors must be made to consider the social as well as the technical component. In the early 1980s, for example, when the Dominican government approached the World Bank for a US$35 million loan to finance the rehabilitation of its sugar industry, the bulk of the funds was to be spent on the renovation of CEA factories, the construction of new railway tracks, irrigation and drainage studies, and other technical programmes. The Bank's feasibility study, while noting that the severe shortage of cane cutters had been one of the greatest obstacles to increased productivity in recent years, had no recommendations on measures to improve living conditions. In contrast, other studies in the Dominican Republic — in particular the assessments conducted by the National Planning Office — have argued that the greatest obstacles to higher productivity lie precisely in the workers' living and working conditions. It would help if the workers who were meant to be represented on CEA's governing council had as much say as the technicians in determining where overseas assistance should be directed.

But concessionary aid is of far less importance than the price of cane sugar itself, and the outlet for the crop in the major consumer countries. Of all the agricultural commodities produced in the Third World, sugar cane is the only one to have a direct competitor in the temperate countries of the advanced industrial world. First there is sugar beet, which at least until recently had far higher production costs than sugar cane. Then there are the countless sugar substitutes, such as iso-glucose or HFCS (high fructose corn syrup) which are rapidly replacing sugar itself as artificial sweeteners in soft drinks and processed foods.

The subsidies given to sugar growers in the advanced industrialised countries, in particular the beet farmers of Western Europe, make no economic sense and, from the humanitarian point of view, are scandalous. It was seen earlier that, when global sugar production increased by some 25 per cent during the 1970s, at a time of declining per capita sugar consumption in the wealthier countries, much of the growth took place in Western Europe as the result of an expansionary production policy adopted during the enlargement of the European Economic Community (EEC). Production, heavily subsidised under the Common Agricultural Policy (CAP), tripled in the five years between 1975 and 1979. Britain's acreage under sugar beet cultivation at least doubled during that period.

The situation has not changed by the mid 1980s. The basic facts have been presented in a recent publication by the London-based Catholic Institute for International Relations (CIIR), which criticised the short-sightedness of the European Community's Common Agricultural Policy. The EEC's sugar regime provides guaranteed prices for 11.8 million tonnes of European beet sugar, and now allows 1.3 million tonnes of imports at the privileged EEC price under the terms of the Lomé Convention. But since EEC consumption is around 9.3 million tonnes per year only, there is an annual surplus of almost four million tonnes, to which must be added a variable amount which cannot be sold in the EEC and does not receive guaranteed prices or export subsidies. CIIR calculates that the EEC currently supplies around 20 per cent of the world sugar market, becoming the world's second largest producer after Cuba, with its sugar export subsidy costing the Community's taxpayers around US$3 million per day. Furthermore, the EEC's belligerent production policies have destroyed the international price-setting mechanisms, established under the International Sugar Agreement (ISA), which should in theory act as a lifeline for Third World cane producers at a time of collapsing world prices. As CIIR comments:

> Although partial recompense is made to some Third World sugar exports through the Lomé Convention's Sugar Protocol, over-production in the EEC has destabilised the world sugar market, with profound consequences for non-ACP sugar exporters like Brazil, Thailand and the Philippines. Despite this, the EEC has refused to accept the export limitations of the ISA, a body set up by the main sugar trading nations to regulate world trade and stabilise world prices. The last round of ISA negotiations broke up in 1984, in part because the EEC demanded an unacceptably high export quota as a condition of its joining. Although the Community has since joined the ISA, the agreement now operates solely as an administrative arrangement with no controls over exports of member countries.[12]

The Dominican Republic, like Brazil, the Philippines and Thailand, is not an ACP member, and relies on the US market for its privileged export quota price. But the outlook is similarly bleak in that direction. When the Dominican quota for the US market was slashed by over 40 per cent early in 1986, with the Reagan administration under pressure from domestic beet and cane producers to impose yet further cuts on imported sugar, the outlook became desperate. A few optimists predict that the worst is over, that the market will lift in the coming years from its lowest ever free market price of 3 cents per pound. But realists know full well that the days when sugar was "king" are over.

These adverse factors at the international level are no justification for the slavery-like conditions of the Haitian workers in the Dominican Republic. Nothing can justify the forced labour, the raids, the military abuse and the corruption that goes along with it. Sugar is in crisis worldwide, and the plight of sugar workers is likewise desperate throughout the modern world. But in many countries, abuses occur because private landowners — admittedly helped by the security forces — evade their obligations under labour law, resorting to widespread human rights violations in order to extract whatever profits they can as the cake becomes smaller. In the Haitian and Dominican case, governments are directly responsible. In the Dominican Republic the government, the army and officials of the State Sugar Board have acted together, with an apparently cynical disregard for the findings and recommendations of international human rights groups that came to investigate. Events of the 1985–86 sugar harvest demonstrate this fully enough.

For the years to come, human rights groups, trade unionists and governmental and inter-governmental lending agencies should pay close attention to the conditions of Haitian and Dominican sugar workers. There should be regular on-the-spot enquiries. As the new Haitian government has apparently now requested, an agency such as the ILO should be asked to monitor more fully the provisions and implementation of any future bilateral agreement. And international trade union federations should play a more active role, giving public and logistical support to attempts by the Dominican trade union groups to organise cane cutters, including the Haitian migrant workers within their ranks. The private non-governmental aid organisations, which have played such an important role in grassroots development work throughout the Third World, should increase their food production and nutritional projects within the sugar plantations. They should give active support to the sugar workers' calls for diversification projects that meet their own immediate needs, rather than the grandiose export projects from which they stand to benefit very little.

And sanctions? The most effective pressure, one feels, is for a larger role by international organisations — perhaps even the International Sugar Organisation itself — in monitoring conditions in the major producer countries. When the next round of negotiations for an International Sugar Agreement gets under way, human rights groups should press for the introduction of a social clause, which — among other things — would directly penalise countries that continue to produce the sugar crop under conditions of forced labour. Pressure for sanctions through the US government's Caribbean Basin Initiative or the EEC's Lomé Convention will prove more controversial, as the Third World producer nations sniff protectionist motives behind such humanitarian initiatives. It was, after all, investment and intervention from the United States and Europe which changed the face of the Haitian and Dominican economies, and made them dependent on a sugar industry that Western European and North American interests are now well on the way to destroying. From Jean-Claude Duvalier and his friends who have pocketed the fruits of the Haitian *braceros'* labour, to the Dominican civil and military officials who have signed the secret contracts or sanctioned the capture of Haitian peasants, from the Washington politicians who have made or broken the sugar quotas of Third World sugar producers, to the EEC technocrats who have subsidised European sugar exporters to the detriment of traditional cane producers, all have had a measure of complicity in this tale of modern slavery.

Notes

1. *Message Pastorale des Évêques d'Haïti: Priorités et Changements* (Imp. La Phalange, Port-au-Prince, 1986).

2. *The New Caribbean Deal; the Next Five Years*, Economist Intelligence Unit special report (London, March 1986).

3. Ibid.

4. Dr Joaquín Balaguer, *La Isla al Revés: Haiti y el Destino Dominicano* (Librería Dominicana, Santo Domingo, 1984), p. 156.

5. Ibid., p. 231.

6. 19 U.S.C. 1307, 1976.

7. Foreign Labour Developments, *Monthly Labour Review*, November 1984.

8. ILO, *Informe al Gobierno de Guatemala sobre Colonización, Transformación Agraria, Desarrollo Rural y Trabajo Agrícola* (Geneva, 1970).

9. National Federation of Sugar Workers, *There's Blood in Your Sugar* (Negros, Philippines, n.d.).

10. *Asia Week*, 31 May 1985.

11. *Mr and Ms*, Manila, Philippines, 10–16 May 1985.

12. *The Common Agricultural Policy* (comment published by the Catholic Institute for International Relations, London, 1986).

Contract between the Dominican State Sugar Board and the Government of Haiti for the Importation of Haitian Cane Cutters

CONTRACT (translation)

In accordance with the Agreement on the recruitment in Haiti and entry into the Dominican Republic of labourers, concluded on 14 November 1966 between the Governments of the two countries, and in order to establish financial clauses for the execution of the said Agreement concerning the recruitment of Haitian agricultural workers to be brought to the Dominican Republic for the sugar cane harvests 1982–83 and 1983–84.

Between:

His Excellency Theodore E. Achille, Secretary of State for Social Affairs of the Republic of Haiti, by virtue of the Act of 28 August 1967, of the one part; and

The State Sugar Board (CEA), an autonomous body of the Dominican State established under Act No. 7 of 19 August 1966, duly represented by Dr Manuel E. Ledesma Pérez, Industrial Relations Manager of CEA, Mr Ramón Antonio Jiménez Rojas, Financial and Programme Manager of CEA, and Dr Roberto S. Mejía García, Deputy Legal Adviser of CEA, acting by virtue of the special power of attorney conferred upon them for the purpose, dated 29 October 1982, which forms an integral part of this contract, of the other part,

IT HAS BEEN AGREED AS FOLLOWS:

Article 1

The State Sugar Board (CEA) makes the request to the Haitian Government, which the latter accepts, to hire, for each of the sugar cane harvests 1982–83 and 1983–84, up to 19,000 Haitian agricultural workers for the needs of the Dominican sugar estates.

Article 2

The CEA undertakes:

(a) to hire in accordance with existing Haitian legislation the 19,000 agricultural workers which it needs for the Dominican sugar estates. The hiring shall be carried out in Haiti by representatives of the CEA at recruitment centres established for the purpose by the appropriate services of the Haitian Government. The duration of the hiring operations shall not exceed 30 working days;

(b) to cover whatever costs it may be necessary to incur for the work of epidemiological control established by the Secretariat of State for Public Health and Social Welfare of the Dominican Republic for all the Haitian agricultural workers hired;

(c) to provide for the transport of the Haitian agricultural workers from Malpasse (Republic of Haiti) — Jimaní (Dominican Republic) to the work centres in the Dominican Republic by coaches duly equipped for comfort and safety. The cost of transport from the recruitment centre to Malpasse in Haiti shall be borne by the Haitian Government;

(d) to cover the costs of food and lodging during travel time from the recruitment centres to Malpasse in Haiti and from there to the work centres in the Dominican Republic;

(e) to pay the Haitian agricultural workers wages equal to those paid to Dominican nationals for work of the same kind;

(f) to make available to the Haitian agricultural workers during their stay at the various work centres and until they leave the Dominican Republic housing units or common lodgings equipped with the statutory hygienic and sanitary facilities, including drinking water, as well as furniture (table, chairs, bed). These dwellings shall be covered by a roof to protect the workers from bad weather;

(g) to enable the supervisors and inspectors of the Haitian Embassy in Santo Domingo to visit the places where the Haitian agricultural workers are to live, prior to their arrival in the Dominican Republic. The housing units shall also be provided with metal beds with mattresses, drinking water, suitable places for regular baths and other amenities for the workers. Adequate and hygienic rooms shall be installed so that workers shall have suitable places for their daily meals;

(h) to extend to the Haitian agricultural workers during their stay in the Dominican Republic the benefit of Dominican legislation on social security, compulsory sickness insurance, social assistance, employment accident insurance, weekly rest, maternity insurance, annual bonus, etc. An injured worker who has not been given medical discharge at the time of his repatriation shall be entitled to coverage of all subsequent costs of treatment and to all the benefits provided for by law;

(i) to pay the Dominican immigration tax and the fees for registration at the Haitian consulate;

(j) to repatriate the workers at the end of the harvest for which they were recruited, with travel expenses (meals and daily allowance) paid, from the workplace to Malpasse, with 15 days' notice to the Haitian Embassy prior to repatriation.

Article 3

The CEA undertakes to require the carrier transporting the Haitian agricultural workers to take out an insurance policy for at least US$1,000 against transport accidents for each and all of the Haitian agricultural workers during the journey from Jimaní to the work centres, as well as during their repatriation from the work centre to Jimaní, without prejudice to hospital expenses, medical fees and other compensation provided for by the relevant legislation. These provisions shall also extend to the supervisors and inspectors of the Embassy who accompany the Haitian agricultural workers in the coaches.

Article 4

The CEA undertakes to pay each Haitian agricultural worker the amount of one Dominican peso daily from the day of his arrival in the Dominican Republic to the day on which the work for which he has been hired begins, which amount shall be paid to him wholly in cash.

Article 5

Within the ten days following completion of the hiring operations the CEA shall communicate to the Haitian Embassy in Santo Domingo a list of all the Haitian agricultural workers hired for each Dominican sugar estate together with the travel documents. The travel documents shall be returned to the workers concerned at the time of their repatriation.

Article 6

The CEA undertakes to report to the Haitian Embassy in Santo Domingo, as well as to the Social Security Institute of the Dominican Republic, any accident in its work centre or in the performance of the work. In the event of an employment accident causing the death of a Haitian agricultural worker, the CEA formally undertakes to pay all the expenses and indemnities provided for by law and to assist the Haitian Embassy in Santo Domingo, in its relations with the Dominican Social Security Institute, to ensure that those entitled receive the benefits provided for in Act No. 385 of 11 November 1932 concerning employment accidents, subject to submission of the documents proving their status. The death of any agricultural worker shall be reported to the Haitian Embassy the same day on which the CEA learns of it, and information shall be supplied to the Dominican civil and military authorities indicating the circumstances in which the death occurred.

Article 7

In the event of an accident sustained by a Haitian agricultural worker outside the work centre for which he was hired, the CEA undertakes to report it to the Haitian Embassy in the Dominican Republic within five days from the date on which it had due knowledge of the accident, in order to be exempt from liability.

Article 8

Each Haitian agricultural worker hired by the CEA shall work exclusively on the sugar estate to which he is assigned. The CEA shall be entitled to authorise the transfer of one or more workers from one of its sugar estates to another when production needs so require.

Article 9

Each agricultural worker hired by the CEA shall enjoy generally all the other benefits provided for by the Agreement of 14 November 1966.

Article 10

The CEA undertakes to cover the expenses involved in hiring the 19,000 Haitian agricultural workers (passports, identity cards, X-rays, general medical examination, overtime for the employees of the Ministry of Social Affairs, etc.) and their transport from the recruitment centres to Malpasse.

Article 11

The supervisors and inspectors of the Haitian Embassy assigned the special task of protecting and defending the Haitian agricultural workers shall be remunerated by the CEA.

Article 12

Fifteen days prior to the expiry of the period for which the Haitian agricultural workers were hired, the CEA shall notify the Haitian Embassy, by letter, of the date of repatriation. The CEA undertakes to repatriate at the end of the sugar cane harvest the 19,000 Haitian agricultural workers, who shall be the same persons as those who were hired at the various centres established in Haiti for the recruitment of the said workers. The Haitian Embassy shall immediately inform the Haitian Government. The Haitian agricultural workers shall be repatriated at the expense of the CEA. They shall be transported in coaches duly equipped for comfort and safety.

Article 13

The Secretary of State for Social Affairs of the Republic of Haiti shall be authorised to designate not more than five officials to carry out inquiries on the conditions of labour relations in accordance with this Contract.

Article 14

It is agreed that the Haitian Embassy in the Dominican Republic shall be empowered to designate 106 inspectors and 24 supervisors for the purpose of representing before the CEA the Haitian agricultural workers hired, assisting them in any claims and advising them on the fulfilment of their duties.

Article 15

The supervisors and inspectors, together with the officials and employees of the CEA, shall be present at the Malpasse-Jimaní frontier from the beginning to the end of the arrival of the Haitian agricultural workers in the Dominican Republic and at the various work centres and shall see that the workers are not transferred to a work centre other than that to which they have been assigned.

Article 16

The supervisors and inspectors shall visit the housing units where the Haitian agricultural workers are to live prior to the latter's arrival in the Dominican Republic and shall be entitled to apply to any civil, military or para-military official or employee in the area of the sugar estates for the purpose of solving any problem that may affect the Haitian agricultural workers.

Article 17

The supervisors and inspectors shall visit without hindrance and with full freedom of action the sugar cane plantations where the Haitian agricultural workers are working, the places where the cane is weighed and the places where the wages are paid, and may, whenever necessary, approach any employees, regardless of their rank, for the purpose of defending the interests of the Haitian agricultural workers. This shall in no case be construed to mean that they may prompt the workers to take decisions prejudicial to the work for which they have been hired.

Article 18

In order to facilitate the work of the supervisors and inspectors, the CEA undertakes to provide them with suitable lodging at the compound or sector to which they are assigned.

Article 19

The normal salary of each supervisor shall be RD$400 monthly and the normal salary of each inspector shall be RD$230 monthly, during the sugar cane harvest. The total amount of the salaries shall be remitted each month by the CEA directly to the Haitian Embassy, according to the Haitian Government's instructions on the matter, for payment to the beneficiaries.

Article 20

As soon as the Haitian agricultural workers begin to arrive in the Dominican Republic, the CEA shall place at the disposal of the supervisors and inspectors, in order to facilitate their work, four vehicles in good running order, with their respective drivers. The CEA shall cover the costs of lubricants and maintenance of the vehicles and shall deliver to the Haitian Embassy in Santo Domingo each month, for the travel of the supervisors and inspectors, 1,425 gallons of diesel oil, with a sufficient number of toll tickets.

Article 21

The CEA undertakes to instruct the sugar estates to allow the Haitian agricultural workers a lunch break from 12 noon to 1.30 p.m. Sundays shall be non-working days. The CEA shall also make available to the Haitian agricultural workers recreational centres which shall be organised by its Department of Social Affairs.

Article 22

The CEA shall notify the Haitian Embassy, by letter, of the date on which harvesting will begin at each sugar estate.

Article 23

In the event of an accident to a Haitian agricultural worker, the CEA undertakes to provide him free transport from the place of the accident to the health centre where he is to receive medical care.

Article 24

The CEA undertakes to pay each Haitian agricultural worker for each metric ton of sugar cane cut the amount of RD$1.83 in Dominican currency. In the event of an increase in the wage of Dominican workers of the same category as the Haitian agricultural workers, the latter shall receive an equal wage in accordance with the statutory provisions on the matter, and the Haitian Embassy in Santo Domingo shall be notified accordingly. Each Haitian agricultural worker shall also receive, like Dominican agricultural workers, a bonus or incentive pay for each metric ton of sugar cane cut and loaded in the 1982–83 and 1983–84 harvests, the amount of which shall be withheld and accumulated for payment at the end of the harvest at the time of repatriation. Appropriate supervision shall be established for this purpose.

Article 25

In no case shall the amount deducted for social security from the earnings of each Haitian agricultural worker exceed the strict limits set by the relevant legislation.

Article 26

The CEA undertakes to pay each Haitian agricultural worker hired the amount of the annual bonus to which he is entitled in accordance with existing Dominican legislation on the matter.

Article 27

The CEA undertakes to ensure convertibility to United States dollars of the savings made by the Haitian agricultural workers in the Dominican Republic from payments for sugar cane cutting, at the time of their repatriation.

In Witness Whereof, the respective authorised officials have signed the present Contract, in two originals, one in French and the other in Spanish, both of which are equally authentic.

Done and signed in Port-au-Prince, Haiti, on 30 October 1982.

For the Ministry of Social
Affairs of the Republic of
Haiti:

Theodore E. Achille,
Secretary of State for
Social Affairs

For the State Sugar Board:

Dr Manuel E. Ledesma Pérez,
Industrial Relations Manager

Ramón Antonio Jiménez Rojas,
Financial and Programme Manager

Dr Roberto S. Mejía García
Deputy Legal Adviser

ADDENDUM

Between:

His Excellency Theodore E. Achille, Secretary of State for Social Affairs of the Republic of Haiti, by virtue of the Act of 28 August 1967, of the one part; and

The state Sugar Board (CEA), an autonomous body of the Dominican State established under Act No. 7 of 19 August 1966, duly represented by Dr Manuel E. Ledesma Pérez, Industrial Relations Manager of CEA, Mr Ramón Antonio Jiménez Rojas, Financial and Programme Manager of CEA, and Dr Roberto S. Mejía García, Deputy Legal Adviser of CEA, acting by virtue of the special power of attorney conferred upon them for the purpose, dated 29 October 1982, which forms an integral part of this contract, of the other part,

IT HAS BEEN AGREED AS FOLLOWS:

1. The costs of recruiting the 19,000 Haitian agricultural workers and transporting them from the recruitment centres to Malpasse are fixed at the amount of US$2,250,000 for each sugar harvest, and are to be met by the CEA by separate payments. For the 1982–83 harvest, payment of the said amount shall be made on or before 8 November 1982. For the 1983–84 harvest, payment of the said amount shall be made on the date stated in the request for recruitment of Haitian agricultural workers, when made by the CEA.

The operations for sending the Haitian agricultural workers shall begin not more than ten days after the date on which, for each harvest, the above-mentioned amount is paid, except in cases of *force majeure*.

2. The cost of registration at the Haitian Consulate in the Dominican Republic is fixed at the amount of US$3 for each Haitian agricultural worker registered at that Consulate.

3. The CEA undertakes to pay each Haitian agricultural worker at the time of his return or repatriation to the Republic of Haiti the amount of US$25 as travel

expenses (meals and daily allowance) from his respective workplace to Malpasse.

4. The CEA shall pay to the Haitian Government, for each repatriation, the amount of US$129,010 to cover the costs of transporting the 19,000 Haitian agricultural workers from Malpasse to the centres where they were hired, once they have been repatriated.

5. Each Haitian agricultural worker shall also receive a bonus or incentive pay of RD$0.50 for each metric ton of sugar cane cut and loaded, in the 1982–83 and 1983–84 harvests, the amount of which shall be withheld and accumulated for payment at the end of the harvest at the time of repatriation. Appropriate supervision shall be established for this purpose.

6. Since Article 26 of the primary Contract, referring to bonuses payable to the Haitian agricultural workers, is worded in general terms and since the said workers must be repatriated before the date on which the financial transactions of the CEA are closed, it is agreed to fix at US$30 the amount which each Haitian agricultural worker shall receive by way of such bonuses for the 1982–83 and 1983–84 harvests, which amount shall be paid to him at the time of his repatriation following the end of the harvest, thus complying with the provisions of the said article.

7. In pursuance of this agreement, the Haitian Government may, at the request of the CEA, authorise the engagement of an additional number of Haitian agricultural workers needed for the 1982–83 and 1983–84 harvests, for an additional proportional amount in accordance with the provisions of paragraph 1 of this text; their recruitment shall take place within the normal operations or at a subsequent date.

Done and signed in Port-au-Prince, Haiti, on 30 October 1982.

For the Ministry of Social
Affairs of the Republic of
Haiti:

Theodore E. Achille,
Secretary of State for
Social Affairs

For the State Sugar Board:

Dr Manuel E. Ledesma Pérez
Industrial Relations Manager

Ramón Antonio Jiménez Rojas
Financial and Programme Manager

Dr Roberto S. Mejía García
Deputy Legal Adviser

Annotated Bibliography: Suggestions for Further Reading

This bibliography does not aim to indicate all sources used in the research and writing of this book. It lists certain books and other sources of interest to the reader who may wish to investigate in more detail the issues covered by the book.

General Reading: Haiti and the Dominican Republic

On the Dominican Republic, there are very few general works in English. The most thorough is *The Dominican Republic* by Ian Bell (Westview Press, Boulder, Colo., 1981) which contains a detailed account of Dominican historical developments from the conquest up to the end of the Balaguer government in 1978, as well as lengthy sections on social conditions and the economy. A new work is *Politics, Foreign Trade and Economic Development: a Study of the Dominican Republic* by Claudio Vedovato (Croom Helm, London and Sydney, 1986), a serious academic work that focuses on the historical and structural obstacles to equitable development. *The Dominican Republic: Nation in Transition* by Howard Wiarda (Frederick A. Praeger Inc. and Pall Mall Press, 1969) has some useful facts. More up to date is *The Dominican Republic: a Caribbean Crucible* by Howard Wiarda and Michael J. Kryzanek (Westview Press, Boulder, Colo., 1982). *The Dominican Republic: Rebellion and Repression* by Carlos María Gutiérrez (Monthly Review Press, New York and London, 1972) is a journalistic account that pictures the highly repressive atmosphere of the early 1970s.

In Spanish, a highly readable historical survey is *Manual de Historia Dominicana* by Frank Moya Pons (Universidad Católica Madre y Maestra, Santo Domingo, 1981). A useful social survey is *Composición Social Dominicana: Historia e Interpretación* by Juan Bosch (Alfa y Omega, Santo Domingo, 1981). A sober history up to the early 1960s is *La República Dominicana* by Ricardo Pattee (Ediciones Cultura Hispánica, Santo Domingo, 1967). There are several recent scholarly works in the Marxist tradition, the most thorough being the historical books by Dominican professor Roberto Cassá, *Historie Social y Económica de la República Dominicana* (2 vols, Ediciones Alfa y Omega, Santo Domingo, 1979) and *Modos de Producción, Clases Sociales y Luchas Políticas* (Punto y Aparte, Santo Domingo, 1984).

On Haiti, a useful brief introduction in English is *Haiti: Family Business* (Latin America Bureau, London, 1985). An immensely detailed general work is *Written in Blood: The Story of the Haitian People, 1492–1971* by R.D. and N.G. Heinl (Houghton Mifflin Company, Boston, 1978). Two scholarly studies by Mats

Lundahl, more specifically concerned with economic and rural conditions, are *Peasants and Poverty: a Study of Haiti* (Croom Helm, London, 1979) and *The Haitian Economy: Man, Land and Markets* (Croom Helm, London, 1983). An older work well worth reading, for a comparison of conditions almost 50 years ago is *The Haitian People* by James G. Leyburn (Yale University Press, New Haven, 1941). The classic work in French on Haitian rural conditions is *Le Paysan Haïtien* by Paul Moral (new edition by Editions Fardin, Port-au-Prince, 1978).

Slavery in Haiti and the Dominican Republic

Negro Slavery in Latin America by R. Mellafe (University of California Press, Berkeley, 1975) covers slavery in the entire continent. *The Negro in the French West Indies* by S.T. McCloy (University of Kentucky Press, 1966) describes slavery institutions in the French colony of Saint-Domingue. *The Black Jacobins* by C.L.R. James (London, 1938) provides one of the best accounts of the Haitian slave rebellions. *Los Negros y la Esclavitud en Santo Domingo* by Carlos Larrazabal Blanco (Colección Pensamiento Dominicano, Santo Domingo, 1975) is the best Spanish account of colonial slavery in the eastern part of Hispaniola.

Growth of the Sugar Industry and Dominican Economic History

A good book in English is *The Dominican People, 1850–1900* by H. Hoetink (Johns Hopkins University Press, Baltimore, 1982). *Between Slavery and Free Labour in the Spanish-speaking Caribbean in the Nineteenth Century* (ed. Manuel Moreno Fraginals, Johns Hopkins University Press, Baltimore and London, 1985) has articles by Dominican authors on labour relations in the early sugar industry. *The Americans in Santo Domingo* by Melvin M. Knight (Vanguard Press, New York, 1928) is a lucid and critical account of the US occupation in Santo Domingo, with much data on the early sugar industry and the accumulation of Dominican lands by overseas entrepreneurs).

In Spanish, *La Caña en Santo Domingo* by Juan J. Sánchez (first edition, 1893, reproduced by Ediciones Taller, Santo Domingo, 1972), is a contemporary account of the adverse effects of the growth of the sugar industry on the living conditions of Dominican peasants, as well as a description of technical developments in the industry. There are various recent books on the Dominican social formation in the late 19th and early 20th centuries, again focusing on the adverse social effects of the development of export agriculture. One of the most detailed is *El Proceso de Desarrollo del Capitalismo en la República Dominicana, 1844–1930* by Jacqueline Boin and José Serulle Ramia (2 vols, Ediciones Gramil, Santo Domingo, 1979). A shorter book is *Proletarización y Campesinado en el Capitalismo Agroexportador* by Wilfredo Lozano (Ediciones INTEC, Santo Domingo, 1985). On the breakdown of communal lands a useful article is "De la Propiedad Comunera a la Propiedad Privada Moderna" by Guillermo Moreno (in *Estudios Dominicanos*, vol. IX, No. 51, 1980). *Estudios Dominicanos* also contains a series of articles on "Economía y Sociedad en la República Dominicana, 1844–1930" in its January–April 1984 edition. Dominican sociologist José del Castillo has written widely on labour relations in the early 20th-century Dominican sugar industry, with a focus on the role of the Caribbean *Cocolos*. Two of his articles are "La Inmigración de Braceros

Azucareros en la República Dominicana, 1900–1930" (Cuadernos del CENDIA, Universidad Autónoma de Santo Domingo, Vol. 162), and, with Walter Cordero, "La Economía Dominicana durante el Primer Cuarto del Siglo XX" (Fundación García Arévalo, Santo Domingo, 1980). A good book on the rise and growth of the Dominican sugar industry from the late 19th century onwards is *Azúcar y Dependencia en la República Dominicana* by Franc Báez Evertsz (Editora de la Universidad Autónoma de Santo Domingo, 1978).

The Trujillo Era

Of several books available, a very readable one is *Life and Times of a Caribbean Dictator* by Robert Crassweller (McMillan, New York, 1966). In Spanish there is a hugely detailed economic history of the Trujillo era, *Capitalismo y Dictadura* by Roberto Cassé (Editorial Universidad Autónoma de Santo Domingo, 1982). The terrible massacre of the Haitian immigrants in 1937 has been portrayed in the novel *El Masacre se Pasa a Pie* by Freddy Prestol Castillo (Ediciones Taller, Santo Domingo, 1972 and other editions).

Sugar and the Social Structure: the Dominican Republic after Trujillo

There are several works by American authors on the events surrounding the US invasion of 1965. One interesting account of the years between Trujillo's death and the invasion is *Overtaken by Events: the Dominican Crisis from the Fall of Trujillo to the Civil War* by John Bartlow Martin, US Ambassador of the period (Doubleday & Company, New York, 1966). Juan Bosch has given his own account of the aims of his brief government in *The Unfinished Experiment* (Pall Mall Press, London, 1968). Two books by US academics about the invasion are *The Dominican Intervention* by Abraham Lowenthal (Harvard University Press, Cambridge, Mass., 1971) and *The Dominican Crisis: the 1965 Constitutionalist Revolt and the American Intervention* (Johns Hopkins University Press, Baltimore, 1978).

A useful study of Dominican militarisation under Balaguer is *Arms and Politics in the Dominican Republic* by G. Pope Atkins (Westview Special Studies, Boulder, Colo., 1981). An academic account of agrarian policy under Balaguer in English is *Peasant Politics: Struggle in a Dominican Village* by Kenneth Evan Sharpe (Johns Hopkins University Press, Baltimore, 1977).

A number of books in Spanish have criticised the inadequacy of agrarian reform measures under the Balaguer and PRD governments, and have stressed the need for redistributive land reform measures. Among others can be mentioned: *Problemas de la Estructura Agraria Dominicana* by Carlos Doré y Cabral (Ediciones Taller, Santo Domingo, 1979), *Reforma Agraria y Luchas Sociales en la República Dominicana* by Carlos Doré y Cabral (Ediciones Taller, Santo Domingo, 1981), *Resistencia Campesina, Imperialismo y Reforma Agraria en la República Dominicana, 1899–1978* by Pablo Marinez (Ediciones CEPAE, 1984), and *El Impacto Económico de la Reforma Agraria, 1977–1982* by Francisco T. Rodríguez (Friedrich Ebert Stiftung, Department of Investigations, Editora Nuevas Rutas, Santo Domingo 1982). The *Revista Estudios Dominicanos* of the Instituto de Estudios Dominicanos has an important series of articles on the "Problemática

Agraria Nacional" in its Year 1, no. 2 edition, May–August 1984. And the FORUM series of books published by the Friedrich Ebert Stiftung includes a book on *Presente y Futuro de las Reforma Agraria en la República Dominicana* (Santo Domingo, 1985). On the trade union situation, CGT leader Julio de Peña Valdez has written a book on *El Movimiento Sindical Dominicano, 1961–1983* (Santo Domingo, 1984).

Haitians in the Dominican Republic

The Dominican government's National Planning Office (ONAPLAN) has published two reports on the role performed by Haitian labour in the Dominican economy. One of these, "Participación de la Mano de Obra Haitiana en el Mercado Laboral: los Casos de la Caña y el Café" (Santo Domingo, 1981), shows how there has been an increasing dependence on Haitian labour in all sectors of the rural economy. The other, "Empleo en la Zafra Azucarera Dominicana" (Santo Domingo, April 1981), describes the growing dependency on Haitian labour in the sugar industry, and investigates possible alternatives. There are a number of further studies on the role played by Haitian labour in the sugar industry in particular. *Azúcar y Política en la República Dominicana* by André Corten and other authors (Ediciones Taller, Santo Domingo, 1973 and other editions) contains historical surveys on Haitian migration. *Azúcar y Haitianos en la República Dominicana* by José Manuel Madruga (Ediciones MSC, Santo Domingo, 1986) analyses Haitian migration to the Dominican Republic within the framework of overall Caribbean migration. Estudios Sociales, Año XVIII, No. 59, Jan–March 1985, contains a series of essays on the theme *Haitianos en la República Dominicana.*

Then there are two books of a very different kind, denigrating the Haitian presence in the Dominican Republic and drawing attention to the "Haitian threat". *Proceso Histórico Dominico–Haitiano* by Carlos Cornielle (Publicaciones América, Santo Domingo, 1980) is, despite its title, a crude and basically racist diatribe against the Haitians. More scholarly, but equally hostile to the Haitian presence, is *La Isla al Revés: Haiti y el Destino Dominicano* by Dr Joaquín Balaguer (Librería Dominicana S.A., Santo Domingo, 1984).

Haitian Forced Labour in the Dominican Republic

The Anti Slavery Society has prepared two reports on Haitian Migrant Labour in the Dominican Republic, which stress their slavery-like conditions. The first was presented to the United Nations Working Group on Slavery in 1979, the second in 1982. The International Labour Organisation published in 1983 its comprehensive "Report of the Commission of Enquiry appointed under Article 26 of the Constitution of the International Labour Organisation to examine the Observance of certain International Labour Conventions by the Dominican Republic and Haiti with respect to the Employment of Haitian Workers on the Sugar Plantations of the Dominican Republic" (ILO Official Bulletin, Special Supplement, Vol. LXVI 1983, Series B). Apart from giving a detailed account of the proceedings and results of its on-the-spot investigations, the report also contains the proceedings of earlier hearings at which independent witnesses gave evidence.

The World Council of Churches migration department has prepared two reports, "Migrant Workers in the Dominican Republic" (1978) and "Sold like Cattle:

Haitian Workers in the Dominican Republic" (1982), which contain several translated Dominican press articles on forcible recruitment and forced labour conditions.

Dominican lawyer Ramón Antonio Veras has published much of his own evidence in his book *Inmigración, Haitianos, Esclavitud* (Ediciones Taller, Santo Domingo, 1983). A forthcoming book which focuses on both historical factors and abusive present-day conditions is *El Bracero Haitiano: Estudio de la Migración de Trabajadores Haitianos a la República Dominicana* by Franc Báez Evertsz (Friedrich Ebert Stiftung, Santo Domingo, forthcoming).

The Dominican Debt Crisis and the April 1984 Food Riots

Some economic background to the crisis is given in the Forum Publication No. 18, *Causas y Manejo de la Crisis Económica Dominicana, 1974–1984* (Santo Domingo, 1986). A hard-hitting critique of IMF policies in the Dominican Republic is *Hacia Donde va el País?* by José Serulle Ramia and Jacqueline Boin (Ediciones Gramil, Santo Domingo, 1985). The social effects of IMF policies have been analysed in several editions of CEPAE magazine (Apartado No. 252–2, Santo Domingo). A day-by-day account of the April 1984 food riots, based on a series of press cuttings, is *Revuelta Popular* in *Actualidad Popular* (publication of IPECP, Apartado postal 20329, Santo Domingo).

Further Haitian Reading

On the US occupation of Haiti, a highly critical assessment is *Occupied Haiti* by Emily Greene Balch and others (The Writers Publishing Company Inc., New York, 1927). A more academic account is *The US Occupation of Haiti, 1915–1934* by Hans Schmidt (New Brunswick, 1971).

A well-documented survey on Haitian agricultural conditions is *Agricultural Development in Haiti* (An Assessment of Sector Problems, Policies and Prospects under Conditions of Severe Soil Erosion) by Clarence Zuvekas (USAID, Washington, DC, 1978). And an excellent recent book on the Haitian rural economy is *El Comercio del Café en Haiti* by Christian Girault (Spanish edition published by Ediciones Taller, Santo Domingo, 1985 — original in French, 1983).

On recent Haitian events are the weekly newspaper *Haïti-Observateur* (50 Court Street, New York, NY 11201), the weekly newspaper *Haïti Progrès* (1280 Flatbush Ave, New York, NY 11226) and the Port-au-Prince weekly *Petit Samedi Soir* (B.P. 2035, Port-au-Prince).

Index

THE ANTI-SLAVERY

SOCIETY FOR THE PROTECTION OF HUMAN RIGHTS

180 BRIXTON ROAD LONDON SW9 6AT TELEPHONE 01-582 4040

AS the methods of oppression have changed over the last two centuries, so the face of slavery has changed too. But the inability to withdraw one's labour is still the fundamental factor characterising the abuse of many millions of men, women and children particularly, but not exclusively, those in the Third World.

The Anti-Slavery Society arose in 1839 out of the ashes of previous bodies opposed to enslavement. It is the world's oldest human rights organization and the only one devoted exclusively to combating modern forms of slavery.

These forms were codified by the United Nations in the 1956 Supplementary Convention on the Abolition of Slavery, the Slave Trade and Institutions and Practices Similar to Slavery. The Society is proud of its primary role in shaping the definitions of this international instrument.

The Society's main work today is concentrated on the remnants of traditional chattel slavery; bonded labour; and exploitative child labour. It is also concerned with the plight of indigenous peoples, having merged in 1909 with the Aborigines' Protection Society, which was founded in 1837.

The number of slaves in the world today can only be an estimate: an informed guess would be about 200,000,000.

The Society welcomes members. Annual membership: £10. Associate annual membership: £3. Life membership: £125.